The author graduated in law with a bachelor of law degree in 1963 at the University of Adelaide, and was admitted to the bar in South Australia in the same year. He worked in law firms in mostly civil work until appointed a stipendiary magistrate in South Australia in 1970, then the youngest such appointment. He moved to the Northern Territory of Australia as a stipendiary magistrate for three years before returning to SA in 1975. He worked as a barrister from 1980 to 1986 before taking up an appointment as a stipendiary magistrate in Canberra. He remained there for thirteen years and then practised as a barrister in SA for three years, then back to the NT as a stipendiary until 2005. He worked back in SA as an auxiliary magistrate for the next seven years until retirement in 2012. He was the inaugural secretary of the South Australian Magistrates Association, then its president. He became the inaugural secretary of the Australian Capital Territory Magistrates Association, and the editor of the Australian Association of Magistrates' journal. He is the author of the several legal texts. Always interested in sport, he played Australian rules football, lacrosse, cricket, basketball, and tennis.

Dedication

Cheers to the producers, writers and actors of 'Downton Abbey'. They illustrate perfectly the point I am trying to make about the gap between the rich and the poor. I never saw anyone from 'upstairs' do an honest day's work.

Michael Ward

HOW JUSTICES OF THE PEACE RULED ENGLAND

Copyright © Michael Ward (2016)

The right of Michael Ward to be identified as author of this work has been asserted by him in accordance with section 77 and 78 of the Copyright, Designs and Patents Act 1988.

All rights reserved. No part of this publication may be reproduced, stored in a retrieval system, or transmitted in any form or by any means, electronic, mechanical, photocopying, recording, or otherwise, without the prior permission of the publishers.

Any person who commits any unauthorized act in relation to this publication may be liable to criminal prosecution and civil claims for damages.

A CIP catalogue record for this title is available from the British Library.

ISBN 9781786128645 (Paperback)
ISBN 9781786128652 (Hardback)
ISBN 9781786128669 (E-Book)
www.austinmacauley.com

First Published (2016)
Austin Macauley Publishers Ltd.
25 Canada Square
Canary Wharf
London
E14 5LQ

Acknowledgments

To my wife Liz, for putting up with me and this book. To the inspiration from all the authors listed in the bibliography. To all my fellow magistrates in South Australia, the Northern Territory of Australia and the Australian Capital Territory, and to all our customers and the victims thereof.

Chapter 1

The beginning

Pre-Conquest-1361 (The Justices of the Peace Act)

In 1027, when Robert of Normandy bonked Arlette, the tanner's daughter, he probably gave little thought to the long-term consequences. One of these was Guillaume le Bâtard. Le Bâtard's succession as the Duke of Normandy was beset by two major problems. He was illegitimate and he was only twelve years old at the time. He had to be tough in order to survive. He was. He did.

When he conquered England in 1066, he was not about to tolerate any nonsense, and he and the 1,500 or so followers who settled in England placed the majority of its two million inhabitants into varying degrees of slavery. Those inhabitants and their descendants remained in that condition for the next 800 years. The institution of justices of the peace evolved to assist with and eventually to lead this subjection.

Guillaume himself didn't like England, and spent much of the rest of his life back in France, but not before re-distributing the land in England among himself and his followers.

They numbered about 1,500: 12 greater barons, 140 lesser barons and about 1,300 others, mostly Knights with the first name of 'Sir' the landed gentry.

Over the next 800 years, it was the descendants of these Knights and the landed gentry who were appointed justices of the peace, and came to rule England.

Together with the King's Council (variously called the 'Witan,' 'Curia Regis', 'King's Court', 'King's Council', 'Privy Council', and 'the Cabinet'), and parliament, the gentry held the majority of England in various forms of subjection until the mid-19th, and in the case of women, until well into the 20th century.

Overview

The immutable motto for justices of the peace is 'Fiat justititia ruat Caelum', loosely translated as 'Let justice be done though the heavens fall in', but often mischievously mistranslated: 'If justice is done, the heavens will fall in.'

There is some debate about the quality of criminal justice delivered in the past by the magistrates of England. But justices of the peace were responsible for far more than the administration of the criminal law. For about 350 years, they actually ruled England.

The factors which propelled the gentry forward were: the role played by the gentry in maintaining law and order over the centuries both before and after the conquest; the infliction of full feudalism on England by the Conqueror; the redistribution of land and power by the Conqueror; the prolonged absences of the post-conquest kings and their nobility fighting in France or on crusades, leaving their sheriffs in control of England; the power and corruption of the sheriffs and their occasional ineffectiveness in maintaining law and order.

From well before the conquest, free men[1] made the decisions in the shire, hundred, village, manor and burrough courts presided over by the 'lord': the Ealdorman (Earl) or his deputy, the sheriff, in the case of the shire; the hundredman, or occasionally the sheriff, in the case of the hundred; the Lord of the manor, in the case of the village or manor courts; and the mayor in the case of the burrough.[2] It seems that up to, and to a dwindling extent after, the conquest, the consensus of the freemen ('the gentry') overrode any views held by the presiding official. As time went by these courts were presided over more and more by the sheriffs. Sheriffs began to treat the consensus view as advice only which the sheriff was free to accept or reject. Yet, from time to time the role that the gentry had played in the courts was remembered, and various tasks connected with the courts were assigned to them. Ultimately, and in association with the other factors mentioned, this process resulted in the system of Quarter Sessions run by justices of the peace.

The full feudalism imposed by the Conqueror [3] ensured that the same system prevailed over the whole of England, binding all subjects. Its main effect was that it forced prolonged absences not only of the monarch but, because of feudal obligations, of the nobility as well. These absences were no longer confined to putting out spot fires of rebellion within England or at the borders with Scotland and Wales, but in France and Ireland as well. These prolonged absences left big gaps in law enforcement in England. True, there were times before the conquest when rebellion or severe unrest broke out within England, particularly at its borders, but internal travel within England was relatively quick and easy compared with trying to get back from France or Ireland in a hurry to extinguish uprisings. That situation had never existed before the conquest.

William dispossessed nearly all the Earls of England of their land and redistributed it amongst his Barons. The Earls were reduced to the status of villeins. The English sheriffs were replaced by members of the Norman nobility. This caused great resentment and turmoil within England for centuries.

The sheriffs were left at home during the absences of the King and the nobility, their task being to control any unrest. Often they were able to do this by the ruthless exercise of power. Their power led to the "Crown's incurable fear of the

---

[1] Landholders who held their land by free tenure, as opposed to villeins who held by unfree tenure: see pp. 8, 9.
[2] Professor Baker: *An Introduction to Legal History*, 4th edition, pp. 6, 7.
[3] See heading 'Feudalism', p 6.

sheriffs."[4] Paradoxically, there were times when the sheriffs were unable to bring turmoil or insurrection under control. The authorities in the form of the King or his Justiciar and council were forced to look elsewhere for assistance. They found it in the gentry.

Justices of the peace became the fighting arm of the nobility and gentry of England, to retain control of the country for their own use and enjoyment, to the exclusion of the hoi polloi. Most of them lived off the rent monies they received from their tenants, and did no active work. Their preoccupation was to maintain the status quo, and ensuring there could never be any large-scale intrusion into their ranks by 'the lower classes'. To ensure that, the 'lower classes' would have to be kept in subjection.[5]

This book examines the rise and fall of the justices, explores the claim that they ruled England and puts the quality of their endeavours under the microscope. For the purposes of this work, 'magistrate' and 'justice of the peace' are interchangeable, as are 'shire' and 'county.'

The 350 years during which it is asserted that justices of the peace ruled England spans the entire 16th, 17th, 18th and the first half of the 19th century.

The magistracy still exists in much reduced form today. It reached its heights with the Tudors, and remained at that level throughout the Stuart regime, weathered a dip during the Commonwealth, and recovered for the remainder of the Stuart and the bulk of the Hanover dynasties, before being trimmed back from about 1850 to responsibility only for minor crime and liquor licensing.

Magistrates' actions need to be considered against the historical background in which they took place. This book briefly examines the history of the following subjects.

- The politics and economy of the various eras.
- Legalised punishment, torture, whipping and disfigurement.
- The feudal system, its rise and fall.
- Court systems.
- The development of imprisonment as a punishment.
- Slaves.
- Enclosures of land by the gentry, to the exclusion of ancient rights by labourers and field-workers and their families.
- The poor.

---

[4] Professor Baker, op. cit, citing Plunknett's *Concise History of the Common Law* 5th edition, 1956.

[5] The reader will have to make up her or his mind about the truth of this assertion. Evidence in support is scattered throughout this book. The way the gentry viewed 'the poor' is set out at pp. 59-61.

- The Poor Laws: the idle rich versus the idle poor; vagrants and the like.
- Local Government.
- The rise of the gentry to power.
- Corruption within the magistracy.
- Stipendiary magistrates.
- The export of the magistracy.
- The treatment of children.

Particularly during the Tudor era, justices of the peace sucked up more and more power, to the point where they controlled the Kings' advisory body, the Privy Council; they dominated the legislature, parliament; they conducted all local government functions in both the cities and the country; they were in charge of the constabulary; they were responsible for raising and training the militia in times of crisis. They dominated the administration of the criminal law.

Although the magistrates in England have now lost their administrative and police functions, they still deal with 97% of all the crime committed in England, so they are still important in that sense.

Since the institution was exported to each of England's former colonies, it has significance for the history in those countries as well. These include the United States, India, Pakistan, Bangladesh, Sri Lanka, Malaysia, Singapore, Hong Kong, Canada, Australia, New Zealand and various African and Pacific Island countries. South America and Antarctica seem to be the only continents free of justices of the peace.[6] In those other places, for a number of reasons, justices of the peace have been reduced to the task of document witnesses, but the offshoots of the magistracy in the forms of Quarter Sessions, Intermediate or District courts, stipendiary magistrates and other primary court judges handle the bulk of both civil and criminal cases in those countries. So, the history of justices of the peace is important in those countries as well.

Commentators such as FW Maitland[7] point to the uniqueness of the system of justices of the peace. It was unique to Britain and its offshoots for three supposed reasons. One is that the justices were amateurs, the unqualified gentry undertaking the task. They had no legal qualifications. This aspect of the magistracy must be qualified because in its early days, insistence was laid upon at least one member of the bench having legal qualifications. This rule was later relaxed. The second reason was that the task was part-time. This assertion is at least partly true. The third aspect of uniqueness is based upon a fallacy, namely

---

[6] Although the author and six others were appointed magistrates for the Australian Antarctic Territories, no justice of the peace or magistrate has ever actually held court there.

[7] *The Shallows and Silences of Real Life*, Collected Papers, HAL Fisher editor, Cambridge University Press II, 1911, p. 470.

that the justices were unpaid. They were in fact rewarded by the state for their work[8] and many of them profited from the position in less orthodox ways.

As to the assertion that they ruled England during the period in question (from about 1500 to about 1850), justices of the peace then dominated the monarchs' advisory council (later the Privy council and later still, the Cabinet), dominated both the House of Lords and the Commons, and were responsible throughout the length and breadth of England for carrying out the laws of the land, laws which they themselves had promulgated. They administered every aspect of local government, from money to bridges; from weights and measures to the construction and maintenance of roads; from the most important task of supervision of the manufacture of malt (for beer, whisky and gin), to regulation of the cloth trade; from raising the militia to running the police; from the regulation of wages to the fixing of prices of commodities; from the supervision of gaols, lunatic asylums, dosshouses, poorhouses, houses of correction, workhouses and Bridewells, to the suppression of vagrancy and the poor. They were responsible for sniffing out and suppressing heresies and heretics and ensuring attendance at church. On top of all that, through Quarter Sessions, General Sessions, Special Sessions and Petty Sessions, they were responsible for the administration of criminal justice. It is true that, in administering justice, they were subordinate to the Royal Courts and in particular the Assizes Courts (the travelling arm of the Kings Bench), and for a while, the Star Chamber. But the Star Chamber was abolished in 1641, and the Assizes courts only sat twice each year for a limited time in each county. In their absence, the justices of the peace cleaned up the vast bulk of criminal cases in England, including felonies, and imposed the death penalty and sentences of transportation. F W Maitland said:

> "A history of the 18th century which does not place the justices of the peace in the very foreground of the picture will be known for what it is- a caricature."[9]

Sir Thomas Skyrme said:

> "They were the effective rulers of the land."[10]

Justices of the peace were drawn from the gentry and the nobility, although the latter rarely participated in the work of the justices – they were content to leave these various tasks to the gentry.

The nobility were those people whose first name was 'Archbishop,' 'Bishop,' 'Lord', and (possibly) 'Sheriff.' The gentry were the upper strata of society immediately below the nobility and consisted of Knights (first name 'Sir'), Burgesses and wealthy freeholders of land. For the most part, they did no productive work, and let their land to others to work, receiving a proportion of crops, labour or rent monies (scutage) in return. It was only in their ample spare

---

[8] See pp 53-54
[9] Fisher, ibid, p. 468.
[10] *History of Justices of the Peace*, Barry Rose Publishers, volume 2, p. 37.

time that they held court as justices of the peace. They were 'the idle rich.' The rest of the population were 'the poor.'

The rise of the gentry to power did not happen overnight. It was gradual and surreptitious. This is that story.

Goodbye Romans

The decline of Roman Rule and the *Pax Romana* in Britain from the 5th century AD resulted in a power vacuum. Internal warfare amongst the various tribes of England was followed by successive waves of foreign invaders: the Picts, assorted German tribes, Scandinavians and the Normans. The rule of law was severely shaken. The centuries following are known as the Dark Ages for good reason. They resulted in the feudal system, incomplete before the Norman Conquest, complete shortly thereafter. The feudal system remained in force until the late 14th century when it collapsed through a combination of circumstances.

This is relevant to the story of Justices of the Peace, because the collapse of feudalism exactly coincides with the rise to power of the gentry in the guise of Keepers and Justices of the Peace: 'the magistracy,' as the institution became known. The collapse of feudalism is remarkable for more than its coincidence with the creation of justices of the peace. The causes of the collapse of feudalism actually contributed to the creation of the magistracy. Further, the dying embers of feudalism, in the form of free tenure of land, were the benchmark for those eligible to become justices of the peace. Conversely, unfree tenure (villeinage), or no land tenure at all, was the mark of ineligibility to become a justice, but rather to become a target for the wrath of the justices. Feudalism and land tenure are fundamental to the creation of the magistracy.

The collapse of feudalism also coincided with the decline of the power of the sheriffs. The sheriffs had previously been responsible for law and order. Whether the decline of the sheriffs was caused by the demise of feudalism, or by their own excesses, remains a matter of speculation.

Feudalism

It is necessary to bear in mind that England was a rural society before and after the Romans withdrew, and remained so for centuries after the Norman Conquest. It relied almost wholly upon agriculture to survive.

Professor Hargreaves[11] suggests that, in the absence of any proper system of enforcement of law and order, land holders clumped together for mutual protection in this period. Law and order were absent for centuries. Over the course of time, the weaker became the vassal of the stronger. Smaller landholders transferred ownership of their land to the stronger, who became the overlord, in return for the right of the tenant to remain in possession of the land and to keep its profits. A proportion of the produce would be given to the landlord. The arrangement involved the mutual obligation of protection, and the vassal

---

[11] *Land law of New South Wales*, Hargeaves and Helmore, 1963 Law Book Company, pp 8-14

providing labour to work the overlord's land. That is as good a guess as any as to how the system developed. It took hundreds of years to develop, and even by the time of the conquest, it had not developed universally. There were still tracts of land not yet incorporated into the feudal tenure system. These tracts were held by strong individuals who chose neither to dominate lesser individuals, nor seek protection from the stronger. For present purposes, these individuals held their land by freehold tenure, although 'freehold' came to have a different meaning after the Norman Conquest: see next section headed 'Feudal Land Tenure.'

Monarchs relied upon the feudal system. In order to raise an army, they would let portion of their lands to their vassals in return for the provision, when needed, of Knights on horseback and other fighting men. In turn, the Royal vassals ('tenants-in-chief') would sub-let the land, or portions of it, in return for goods and services. These sub-tenants might in turn further sub-let the land, or some of it, in return for goods and services. This process, called 'sub-infeudination' could carry down to the 5th, 6th or even further levels, with six or seven levels of 'mesne lords' interposed between the King and tenant in actual possession. It became difficult for the King to control the remote tenants in possession. Ultimately it was necessary for something to be done to prevent further fragmentation of authority by banning further sub-infeudination. This was done by the passage of an act of parliament, the statute '*Quia Emptores*'.[12] With the conquest in 1066 came the end of freehold tenure, and feudal tenure became the sole form of land holding in England.[13] Hargreaves also states that England was the only country to be completely feudalised.[14] The nature of post-conquest feudal land tenure is considered in the next section.

There is some uncertainty about the number of tenants-in-chief[15] under the Conqueror. Hargreaves and Helmore[16] state that the whole of England was divided by the Conqueror amongst 1,500 tenants-in-chief, apparently from a study of the Domesday Book. On the other hand, apparently from the same source, the Encyclopaedia Britannica[17] concludes:

> "Fewer than 180 great tenants-in-chief were given large parcels of land distributed about the country."

The discrepancy may or may not hinge upon the use of the adjective "great". The "fewer than 180" figure more or less equates with the number of Barons in England at that time, twelve of them being called 'greater Barons', and the rest of them 'lesser Barons'. 'Greater Barons are those that are best worth placating.' [18] In other words, they were closer to the King, great fighting men, and more aggressive and thuggish. These twelve are said to have held one quarter of all the

---

[12] 1290 (18 Edw I)
[13] Hargreaves op cit p 11
[14] ibid
[15] Those who held land directly from the King.
[16] ibid
[17] 15th edition, volume 29, p.33.
[18] JEA Joliffe, *The Constitutional History of Modern England* 3rd edition p. 203

land in England. It could well be that William also made a large number of land grants to his other followers, without elevating them to the nobility. P. Ackroyd[19] has the number of Barons at the time of Magna Carta (1215) at 197. Trevelyan[20] has the numbers of the nobility at a mere 53 at the outbreak of the War of the Roses (1455). He says the numbers had fallen to only 29 at its conclusion (1485). There was undoubtedly a process of natural attrition in the ranks of the nobility, with the death of a Lord without any heir to inherit. This was not a rare occurrence in the middle ages, with its high infant mortality rate, and quite a number of peerages came to an end in wars. The numbers of the nobility fluctuated wildly. There would be a severe diminution of their ranks during a war, a frequently occurring event. Their numbers might be temporarily pumped up by the monarch. There are several instances of monarchs selling rank to the highest bidder. Their numbers were considerably reduced by the Black Death and, as indicated, by the War of the Roses (1455-1485).

The precise number of the nobility or tenants-in-chief is not strictly relevant to the history of justices of the peace. However, the nature of feudalism is relevant.

Theoretically, the King was always supreme. In practice, one of the great dangers to the King was that feudalism involved giving power to the nobility, obliging each of them to keep what was, in effect, a standing army of Knights and other soldiers. The King had to work hard to keep them on his side. Some Kings were not very successful at this.

Another danger lay in the power given to sheriffs (see the later heading 'sheriffs'). They too had the right to raise armed forces. Sometimes the sheriffs (and the Barons) got out of control.

Feudal Land Tenure

There were two types of feudal land tenure: free and unfree. The differences between them are that, although free tenure obliged the tenant to work for the Lord, his obligations were limited and always pre-determined. The obligation typically would be to perform so many days each year ploughing the Lord's land. Later, but not too long after the conquest, the service became redeemable by the payment of a fixed sum of money called 'scutage,' which we now call rent. The free tenant had rights to his land which were recognised and enforceable by law. On his death, his interest in the land went to his heirs (sons). They were obliged to pay a sum of money to the Lord, appropriately called 'escheat,' to perfect the transfer. If the tenant died without heirs, the land reverted to the Lord. This type of tenure came to be called 'freehold', although because of the obligations that went with it, it was not as free as the 'freehold' that existed before the conquest.

With unfree tenure, the tenant never knew when he would be required to work for the Lord, or what duties he would be required to perform. He held his land at the whim of the Lord. In the 12th century the Royal Courts (Common Pleas) began to

---

[19] 'The History of England Volume 1, p. 170
[20] *History of England* 3rd edition, Longmans

recognise some rights of the unfree tenant to the land, to the extent he could not be ejected in breach of existing customs, but few could afford such adjudication.

An unfree tenant could not leave the area without the permission of his Lord. Unfree tenure was called villeinage, and the tenant a villein or cottager. The difference seems to be that the area tilled by a villein was larger than that tilled by a cottager, which was merely a subsistence level plot. Unfree tenure was referred to as a form of servitude, a polite term for slavery. Indeed, it is probable that the villeins and cottagers were the descendants of slaves left over from Roman times. Slavery was still practised pre-conquest, and it seems likely it was carried on after the conquest under a different name.

There were several categories of free tenure in England, for example: grand serjeantry, Knight service, the spiritual tenure of bishops and monasteries, and the most common form, socage. Grand serjeantry was the service rendered to the Lord of a personal nature: the legendary arse-wipes, wardrobe organisers, bottle counters and fart-catchers. There was even a Grand Serjeantry for holding the King's head while he was chundering[21] crossing the channel. Spiritual tenure bound the Bishop or Abbott to say prayers for the Lord or his family, a much needed service in most cases, and to supply fighting men when called upon to do so. Knight service was the requirement that the Knight was at the beck and call of the Lord to supply himself on horseback, appropriately armoured, and with a certain number of other soldiers. Socage obliged the tenant to perform pre-determined agricultural services for the Lord.

By the end of the 14th century, even with unfree tenure (villeinage), the tenant became personally free and able to pay a fixed rent (scutage) in lieu of services, thanks to the intervention of the Royal Courts, the Black Death and the collapse of the feudal system. Professor J H Baker[22] states:

> "By the 15th century at the very latest, there was no socially identifiable villein class."

The lasting legacy of the feudal system was the class system, the 'them' versus 'us' mentality grafted onto the English persona.

Feudal Political Power

In theory, all political power resided in the King. But it was a big country, and too big for one person to administer. So the King was obliged to consult and to delegate. On a nationwide basis, this was done by the King's Court, the 'Curia Regis'. In the King's absence, it was presided over by the 'Justiciar.' Further, from time to time, the King liked to seek advice from his nobility. From time to time, the nobility felt constrained to give their advice to the King, whether he sought it or not. From such meetings, the institution of parliament evolved.

Local power in the shires was delegated to the Earls or Barons. However, as was the case with the King, they were often absent fighting the King's wars, as they

---

[21] Australian slang for mal de mer.
[22] *An Introduction to Legal History*, 4th edition, p. 411

were obliged to do under the feudal system. The Kings appointed shire reeves or 'sheriffs' for the counties (shires) to be responsible for local government in the absence of the Earl or Baron. The sheriff was a stay-at-home official, and as time went by he accumulated much power. He became responsible for raising revenue, for the construction and upkeep of castles, the detection and arrest of criminals, presiding in the shire courts, and occasionally, twice each year, in the hundred courts. Bishops and Abbots were responsible for administration, which included law and order, in the areas controlled by the church, and also had responsibility for naughty priests and nuns. In the villages, administration was controlled by the Knight of the manor. From the 13th century, with the advent and development of parliament, the nobility and gentry combined together to assert more and more authority.

That the Kings, Barons and Earls were absent for much of the time is apparent from a few examples. The Conqueror was away from England for 16 years of his 22 year reign. His son William II was absent for most of his 13 year reign, fighting in Scotland, Wales and Normandy. Henry I, although regarded as a good ruler, was away for much of his reign, fighting his brother Robert in Normandy and then the King of France in France. Richard I was in England for only six months of his life, let alone his 10 year reign. Who, then, ran the country during these absences? The central rule was conducted by the Curia Regis (King's Court) led by the Justiciar. Locally, in the absence of the Barons and Earls, each county or shire was run by its sheriff. Ultimately the sheriffs became too powerful to the point where they posed a threat to the Crown and the nobility.

The towns had slightly different arrangements. They were usually run by their leading citizens called 'Burgesses,' or 'aldermen.'

Justice was always in the hands of the Kings, Earls, Barons, Sheriffs, Bishops and Abbots until the King's judges began to assert their authority. The court (justice) system is dealt with more fully later. It is important to the story of justices of the peace, because it is that system into which the gentry were thrust, or perhaps more accurately, into which they thrust themselves, as well as becoming responsible for local administration and a host of other matters.

Sheriffs

Sheriffs were in existence before the conquest, probably originating as deputies to the Ealdorman (heads of shire) under Alfred (849-899). They assisted the Ealdorman in his administrative duties, and survived the conquest as an institution. However, the existing sheriffs were replaced by Norman appointees from the Norman nobility.

The plain fact of the matter is that the Kings often chose to go to war, particularly after the conquest, to subdue Wales, Scotland or Ireland, and to maintain or attempt to regain estates in France. There was no particular need for any of these wars, except that the Kings wanted more and more land over which to hold sway. The Kings and the people of England could have lived happily and peacefully within the boundaries of England once things settled down after the conquest. But to the ruination of the ordinary people, who stood to gain nothing at all from such extra-territorial conquests, the various Kings insisted upon expanding their empire. This required fighting men. That required large sums of money and the insistence upon feudal dues. The feudal dues meant that each Earl or Baron had to present themselves together with Knights, pikemen and other foot soldiers to assist the Kings' latest whim. This left the home front ungoverned, and so a stay-at-home official, the sheriff was necessary.

The story of the sheriffs is an example of the maxim 'power corrupts.'

The sheriffs earned a bad reputation well before the legendary sheriff of Nottingham, and the almost mythical Richard the Lionheart. No doubt they were selected for their tax-gathering capacity and ability to maintain a semblance of law and order. Under Stephen (1135-1154), they were bribed to give Stephen support during the anarchy, by being appointed 'in fee and inheritance', in other words, the office became hereditary. Before, it had been granted at the King's whim. A hereditary office is always a sure route to misuse of power and corruption. Stephen even increased the areas over which some of the sheriffs presided. For example, Geoffrey de Mandeville became the sheriff for Essex, Hertfordshire, Middlesex and London, and was elevated to the rank of Earl.

Professor J H Baker[23] says:

> "Although there was no policy of attacking the ancient assemblies, there was a continuing policy under the Normans and their successors of harnessing the power of sheriffs. The Crown's 'incurable fear of the sheriff'[24] was no doubt well founded, for the potential power of the sheriff- as continental experience of analogous officials showed- was such as to challenge the King's own authority."

Not surprisingly, Stephen's successor and erstwhile foe, Henry II, set about Stephen's arrangements with the medieval equivalent of a baseball bat. In 1170, he instituted the 'Inquest into Sheriffs.' He sacked all 23 of them, and then reinstated only six of those 23. He countermanded the 'in fee and inheritance' aspect of the sheriffs' office, and once more it became an office held during the King's pleasure, and moreover one that was closely examined each year.

It became obvious during the reign of Richard the Absent (1189-1199), that not only were the sheriffs corrupt, but they were ineffectual. A possible reason for their ineffectiveness is that they were spread too thinly on the ground. By this time, there was a maximum of one sheriff for each shire. To rectify this situation, and to put down Prince John's insurrection, Hubert Walter, Richard's Justiciar, created the office of coroner in 1194, one for each county. One of the coroners' main functions was to keep an eye on and report upon the sheriff. The coroner also had to step in and preside at the shire court if the sheriff had a personal interest in the outcome of any litigation. He was, in effect, the deputy sheriff. He

---

23   *An Introduction to Legal History*, 4th edition, Oxford University Press, p. 23
24   Quoting from Plunknett's *Concise History of the Common Law* 5th edition, p.105

also had another function, which remains with the office to this day, to enquire into and report upon any sudden or suspicious death.

Hubert Walter followed on the appointment of coroners the very next year, in 1195, by appointing Custos Paces (keepers, guardians or custodians of the peace) in each shire. This was necessary because of the turmoil created by the King's brother John's insurrection in his attempt to usurp the throne. The keepers of the peace were chosen from the Knights of the various counties, or Burgesses in the towns. This was the first crisis which lead to the institution of the magistracy. The chart, beginning at page 27, shows that freeholders played a vital part in the court system, even before the conquest. Given the deficiencies in, and the Crown's distrust of the sheriffs, Hubert Walter turned again to the freeholders for help.

It was logical to appoint these Knights as guardians because of the roles they or their ancestors, as freeholders, had in making decisions in the hundred and shire courts, both before and after the conquest. Initially, the appointment of the guardians was only to deal with the particular situation which had arisen, and was for a limited time. Their role was to assist the sheriffs, to whom they were subordinate. They performed their tasks by taking oaths of allegiance to the King, and recognisances (promises) to keep the peace, on pain of fines and imprisonment. Over the next 200 years, they morphed into justices of the peace. They had power of arrest and detention over strangers.

Towns were run by their leading citizens, called Burgesses. Often towns were given a Royal Charter, allowing them to be more or less self-governing, in exchange for an annual fee paid by the town to the royal coffers. Later, the rulers of towns came to be called 'aldermen', a name derived from the word 'Ealdorman,' the head sherang of a shire ('Earl' also comes from the same source. 'Burgess' was derived from 'burrhs', the name given to the fortified buildings erected by Alfred the Great in his campaign to recover England from the Vikings). If any official such as a constable, or later, a justice of the peace was to be appointed for a chartered town, the town council had the right to nominate the official. Outside the chartered towns, justices were appointed by the monarch on the advice of the Chancellor at first, but later on the advice of the Lord Lieutenant of the county.

In 1215, Magna Carta contained a provision preventing sheriffs from hearing pleas of the Crown (accusations of treason or felony). According to Magna Carta, pleas of the Crown were henceforth to be dealt with by itinerant justices sitting with 4 Knights of the county. This provision was not always observed. It was necessary over the next 100 years or so to reinforce this provision with edicts and Acts of parliament, outlined below.

If it became necessary to appoint keepers for an emergency, four of them were usually appointed for the particular shire where the emergency occurred.

During the reign of Henry III (1216-1272), Henry was forced to sign the Provisions of Oxford in 1258. Amongst other things, these provisions decreed that four Knights in each county be appointed to hear complaints of wrongdoing by the sheriffs and their bailiffs. Henry later renounced the Provisions of Oxford.

This led to a revolt by the Barons, led by Simon de Montford. During the ensuing civil war, both the King and de Montford summoned Knights to their assistance, and de Montford actually appointed four Knights from each county to maintain law and order. This would suggest that by this time, both sides, de Montford and his barons on the one hand, and the King and his forces on the other, had little faith in the ability of the sheriffs.

After the King had defeated the rebel forces, he continued to appoint keepers or guardians of the peace. They were also directed to elect from amongst themselves, Knights and Burgesses for parliament.[25]

Under Edward I (1272-1307), writs were directed to sheriffs to appoint keepers of the peace to assist them in arresting malefactors. Thus, at the beginning of his reign, sheriffs were still in charge of the keepers. By the end of his reign, this batting order was reversed, and

> "Writs were directed to the sheriffs to issue summonses to jurors of presentment to appear before the keepers."[26]

Sheriffs never had the same power again.

This change of status was later confirmed by statutes, taking power off the sheriffs and giving it to the keepers of the peace to 'punish offenders according to their guilt'[27]; giving a name change to keepers and confirming their power to hear and determine felonies[28], and which provided that all indictments should be taken before the justices of the peace at their sessions.[29]

Joliffe sums up the fall from grace of the sheriffs:

> "Already the principal vices which were to bring the medieval order to ruin are present, Lordship unlawfully exercised, the corruption of juries, sheriffs who use the letter of the law to deny fair trial and justices whose decision is pre-arranged.
>
> Much of the blame was laid upon the sheriffs. Not only the community, but several counties individually complained that their people were being undone by 'false juries, chosen by the sheriffs'."[30]

Parliament

When the King called his Barons together for their advice, he was unwittingly setting the scene for the later institution of parliament. One occasion when the King was forced to listen to advice from his Barons was in 1215 at Runnymede,

---

[25] Rymer O. *Select Charters* p. 792
[26] Skyrme *The History of Justices of the Peace* volume 1, p. 12
[27] 1344, 18 Edw. III st. 2, c.2
[28] The Justices of the Peace Act of 1361, 34 Edw. III, cc.1-11
[29] 1461, 1 Edw. IV, c.2
[30] *The Constitutional History of Medieval England* 3rd edition, pp. 410, 411

when he was obliged to accept Magna Carta. (King John later repudiated Magna Carta, but that is irrelevant to this history).

It was John's unsuccessful French adventures that led to his confrontation with his Barons. Such adventures were costly, and John's constant demands for the supply and provisioning of his army with both manpower and money were too much for his Barons. His importuning came hot on the heels of his brother Richard's importuning for the same commodity in order to fund his disastrous crusade and the inevitable ransom for his rescue. It was all too much for the Barons.

Much of Magna Carta addressed local issues, but part of it set out the framework for the future development of the justice system. It laid the foundation of two institutions which exist today, parliament and the jury.

Magna Carta was forced on John at Runnymede by his Bishops, Earls and Barons. They were motivated by concern with protection of their own interests and not the interests of the whole population, with one exception. Magna Carta extended protection to those with the status of Knight. It provided nothing for the general population of England.

The major significance of the charter was that for the first time others (here, the Barons, Earls and Bishops) were able to challenge the hitherto unchallengeable royal powers. Trevelyan says that later generations misinterpreted its clauses to the point where:

> "…it became the symbol for the spirit of our whole constitution. Pittites boasted of the free and glorious constitution which had issued from the tents at Runnymede, now attacked by base Jacobins and levellers; radicals appealed to the letter and the spirit of Magna Carta against gagging acts, packed juries and restrictions of the franchise. America revolted in its name and seeks spiritual fellowship with us in its memory. It has been left to our own disillusioned age to study it as an historical document, always remembering that its historical importance lay not only in what the men of 1215 meant by its clauses, but on the effect which it has had on the imagination of their descendants."[31]

Magna Carta specifically forbade sheriffs, constables and bailiffs from conducting courts. Thenceforth, courts were to be conducted exclusively by the itinerant justices sitting with four Knights of the county where the offence occurred. According to Stubbes:[32] "We may question whether these regulations were strictly observed." However, subsequent edicts, writs and legislation reinforced Magna Carta's provisions, shedding sheriffs and substituting justices of the peace and the Assizes Courts.[33]

---

[31] *History of England* 3rd edition, Longmans p.172
[32] *The Constitutional History of England* 6th edition, p.607
[33] Footnotes 27, 28 and 29.

The gathering at Runnymede in 1215 was, in effect, the first meeting of parliament, with the House of Lords (Barons, Earls and Bishops) telling the King what to do.

Early Parliaments

The institution of parliament was consolidated under the reigns of the next two Kings, Henry III (1216-1272) and Edward I (1272-1307).

John had resisted the consolidation or recurrence of any assembly resembling that at Runnymede which produced Magna Carta. His successors, however, came to believe that such convocations were a convenient means of "smoothing out differences and adjusting common action between powers who respected one another – King, Church, Barons and certain classes of the common people such as the Burgesses and Knights." [34] "No one respected the villeins and they had no part in parliament."[35] Apart from allowing the Barons etc. to let off steam, parliament became useful for raising taxes, enacting laws and finding out what was going on out there (so the King and his curia could do something about it).

The House of Lords was the original parliament, consisting of Earls, Barons, Bishops and Priors.

The Burgesses were selected residents from the towns. The Knights were in charge of villages. It was customary for Knights to accompany their Lord on journeys to meet with the King to add their muscle power. The cavalcade was the medieval equivalent of an offer that could not be refused. It is presumed that this is how the Knights managed to worm their way in to the rights supposedly granted by Magna Carta. They were there, en masse, at Runnymede.

The House of Commons evolved informally over the centuries when representatives of the Burgesses and Knights met together behind closed doors to formulate their policy or stance to particular issues. During the reign of Henry III (1216-1272) writs were issued to the keepers of the peace directing them to arrange for appointment to parliament of Knights and Burgesses.[36]

At these meetings over the next 150 years, the Commons lobbied for increased powers to be given to the gentry by building upon the powers given to the custodians of the peace. After initial opposition, it appeared as if the Lords were content to let the Knights and Burgesses take over the running of the country from them. The nobility probably believed that they could rein the gentry in if they got out of control, and they thought their willingness (to give the Commons the lead) meant less work and more leisure for the Lords.

Apart from their meetings held simultaneously with the meetings of the Lords, the Knights and Burgesses went home and resumed their roles as local governors in their villages and towns. For those of them who were custodians of the peace, their powers gradually increased as the powers of the sheriffs declined. In earlier

---

[34] Trevelyan op cit p. 192
[35] ibid
[36] Rymer O. *Select Charters* p.792

days the gentry were under the control of the sheriff. Later, during the reign of Edward Longshanks (1272-1307), the sheriff came under the control of the meetings of the gentry.

At a national level, there were two institutions governing the country: the parliament and the Curia Regis. The name of the curia changed under Henry VII to the Privy Council. All its councillors were justices of the peace. The Council advised the King and published his edicts. It was usually run by the Chancellor of the Exchequer. It was the justices of the peace who carried out the orders of the parliaments and the King's council.

Courts in feudal times

In ancient times, a court was simply a meeting of concerned people to thrash out problems. Kings held court. Villages held court. Hundreds held court. Shires held court. Courts might discuss such diverse issues as what type of grain to plant in what paddock; what country we should invade today; who owed who what money or service; who occupied what land; and whether any offences had been committed by which person. Initially decisions were made by consensus of the more important land holders. By the time of the conquest, there were a confusing multitude of courts.

Perhaps the oldest and longest lasting of the courts was the shire court, later called the county court, in the beginning usually presided over by a bishop and sheriff jointly, who were supposed to accept the consensus decision of the important persons of the shire (freeholders of land)- a forerunner of the jury. These courts faded in importance as time went by and the King's Courts took over.

The shire was divided into hundreds (called wapentakes in the north). The hundred consisted of 100 hides, a hide being the area required to support one family, its size varying in different parts of the country according to its ability to produce food. Hundreds had courts where decisions were made by 'hundredmen,' leading citizens in the hundred. Twice each year, these courts were presided over by the sheriff, for the purpose of taking oaths of loyalty to the King called 'frankpledge'.

Then there were the manor or village courts, presided over by the Lord of the manor, usually a person of the status of Lord or Knight. These courts were important for recording who had rights over land in a village, but also decided all manner of things of interest to the villagers.

In the towns that developed during the medieval period, if they had royal recognition (a 'charter') as a borough, they had borough courts presided over by the mayor sitting with his aldermen. These towns were responsible for appointing their own officials, but in practice this did not amount to a democracy. The mayor and his aldermen simply nominated their friends and relatives to the council.

Then there were the specialty courts: the courts of Pie Poudre (dealing with disputes arising from fairs and markets); Honours Courts; Courts of Chivalry; Courts of Wards; Courts of Danelaw; Courts of Sewers; Forest Eyres; University

Courts; Trailbaston Courts (courts specially convened to put down disturbances); the Court of the Lord High Constable and Earl Marshall (from late feudal times, dealing with treason and prisoners of war); Admiralty Courts (from very late feudal times), and the Ecclesiastical Courts.

Finally, superimposed on the above were the King's courts, offshoots of the Curia Regis. These developed over time into the courts of Eyre, the Assizes courts, the King's Bench, the Common Pleas, the Chancery Court and the Exchequer.

The courts of Eyre were held in each shire every seven years or so. Their main purpose was to throw their weight about and ensure that the shire had been paying its (un)fair share of tax, as well as maintaining proper roads, bridges etc. They also dealt with crimes. They took the opportunity to take oaths of loyalty to the monarch. These courts were exceedingly unpopular and reasonably short lived. They were replaced with the Assizes courts, which visited each shire twice a year. These assizes courts became the travelling arm of the King's Bench which eventually anchored itself in London. The King's Bench heard both civil suits and criminal matters. After it became anchored in London, its criminal work was confined to crimes occurring in London, and crimes occurring in the country were dealt with by the Assizes courts or, from the early 14th century, justices of the peace sitting in Quarter or General Sessions. The Common Pleas court was a civil court only, and there was a deal of competition between it and the Kings Bench for custom. The Exchequer was more administrative, dealing with revenue-raising in the form of taxation, but was a civil court as well dealing with matters arising incidentally from taxation. The Chancery, although of ancient origin, was not really a feudal court, but evolved in the 16th century to fill in the gaps of the common law courts, dealing with civil suits on an evolving equitable basis.

The earlier Kings allowed the shire, hundred, manor and specialty courts to remain in existence, and at first many elected to remain with the local courts, but as time went by, more and more came to realise that the Kings' courts were more efficient and cheaper and resort was made more frequently to them, and the importance of the other courts began to fade.

Right at the end of the feudal society, in the early 14th century, the courts of the Justices of the Peace evolved and over time came to dominate the criminal law and all aspects of local government. In so far as the criminal law is concerned, these courts were always subject to the King's Bench/Assizes courts, but the Assizes courts only sat in each area twice each year, whereas the justices' sessions were more or less permanently sitting, in one form or another (Quarter, General, Special or Petty Sessions). They did by far the greater bulk of criminal prosecutions and all the local government work, as well as their constabulary functions, the administration of the poor laws, weights and measures, the supervision of the currency and regulation of wages and prices.

Village Life and the Beginning of Enclosures

A typical medieval village might have 200 people living in 2 or 3 dozen houses. The main house situated on maybe 5 acres (2 hectares), was the manor house wherein dwelt the Lord of the manor. His actual status was probably that of

Knight, holding his land of the Earl or Baron who lived in the main town of the shire. The Knight probably held much more land around the village, but others worked it for him, according to the customs of feudalism. Next door to his manor house was the church with a detached dwelling for the priest. There might be a dozen houses on quarter acre blocks for the freeholders and another dozen on smaller lots for the villeins and cottagers. There would be a mill and miller's house situated on a stream. Surrounding these buildings was the business end of the village, its arable lands, fields, crofts, commons, waste lands and woodlands. The commons were pastures where the villagers kept their horses, pigs, sheep and cattle. The arable fields consisted of many strips of land which were distributed amongst the villagers to work, sown with wheat, rye, barley, oats or beans. The arable strips would not be evenly distributed between the inhabitants. A villein usually held strips totalling maybe 10 acres (4 hectares), a cottager maybe half that, and the freeholders more than that. It varied.

> "It befits him (the cotter) to have 5 acres, more, if it be the custom of the estate, and if it be less, it is too little."[37]

Generally speaking, the Norman Conquest did not interfere with such arrangements.

All villagers would be required to work the Lord's fields for him, and to contribute a proportion of the yield from their lands to the Lord. The freeholders only owed a limited and pre-set number of hours to the Lord. The villein existed at the landlord's whim, and could be called upon at any time to work the Lord's fields for him, or perform other services as his slaves. There might be some changes in the arrangements, in that a freeholder might fall into debt, and be forced to sell his land or portion of it. Particularly after the statute Quia Emptores (1290), cashed-up villeins might be able to purchase the freeholder's interest, and become a freeholder, *but only in respect of that land.* The purchaser, however, would remain a villein (unfree tenant or slave) in respect of his original land. In other words, he still owed slave-like obligations in respect of the original holding. Only the collapse of feudalism was to relieve him of this obligation. After Quia Emptores, the purchaser of land owed no feudal obligations to the local Lord or Knight, in respect of that land, but held the land directly 'of' the monarch.

There was a bad downside for those who remained only as villeins into the 15th century: more often than not they found themselves evicted by the bailiffs at the behest of the Lords of the manor, hell-bent on reclaiming and enclosing as much land as they could for sheep-raising.[38]

With the rise in the price of raw wool, and the ability of English wool mills to process it, wool became the engine to drive the English economy. This spelt doom to many supposedly idyllic English villages and their

---

[37] From a document published in about the year 1,000 AD entitled 'Rectitudines Singularum Personarum' ('Right and duties of all persons'), reprinted in Bland, Brown and Tawney's work *English Economic History*, Bell 1914.

[38] Enclosures, important to the story of vagrants and jsp alike, are considered at pp. 39-40, 64-66, 68, 71-72, 82-83, 95-96, 117-118, 134-136, 139-140.

inhabitants. The Lords of the manor reclaimed and enclosed whatever land they could and used it for rearing sheep. The sudden increase in the value of sheep, together with the shortage of labour caused by the Black Death beginning in 1348, and the rise in inflation following that plague, conspired to destroy village life and the lives of those remaining after the plague.

> "...the modern destruction of villages which brings dearth to the Commonwealth. The root of this evil is greed. As Christ wept over Jerusalem, so do we weep over the destruction of our own times."[39]

According to P. Ackroyd:

> "In his own county [he was here referring to Rous' county, Warwickshire] there are more than 100 deserted villages, the vast majority of them cleared in the 15th century. The rights of freeholders [...] were in principle protected, but those who dwelled in the land by custom [referring to the unfree tenure of villeins] could be evicted with impunity. Much of the population moved a few miles perhaps, and continued working the land. A few were not so fortunate. The rootless phenomenon known as 'the sturdy beggar' is first mentioned in the 1470s. [...] many people suffered from the pace of economic change, but others benefited from it. The successful small farmer was now paying rent for his land as a tenant, rather than performing labour duties. The small freeholder, known as the yeoman, is also more in evidence. The class of villein or serf gave way to a labourer working for a wage."[40]

Ackroyd also instances the village of Thorpe in Norfolk where:

> "100 people left their houses weeping and becoming unemployed and finally, as we suppose, died in poverty and so ended their days."[41]

It was the 'sturdy beggar' who was to take up much of the time of the justices of the peace.

The Rise of the Gentry and Burgesses; Tough Times; Keepers and Justices of the Peace

To say that England was turbulent in the centuries after the conquest would be to understate the case. Set out hereunder is a compaction of history to the end of the 14th century. By then, justices of the peace had been well and truly launched, and the sheriffs sidelined. One theme that recurs during those 300 years is the greed and obstinacy of the monarchs. They refused to give up on their French possessions, or, if they had already been lost, they stopped at nothing to try to retrieve them or to enlarge them. Ultimately, it was all wasted endeavour and

---

[39] John Rous, *Historia Regum Angliae*, written in the 15th century
[40] *The History of England* Volume 1, p.358
[41] Op cit p.151

wasted money. Their greed cost the people of England dearly in life, time, money and resources. It beggared the country. The usual law enforcers were often absent from the country, and disorder became chronic. The Kings did this without regard to the hardships that their constant demands for more and more money caused the ordinary people of England. Natural phenomena like failed harvests, drought and the Black Death caused hardship, but the hardship was often compounded by the King simultaneously demanding the enforcement of a tax so that he could hang on to some far off place like Anjou or Gascony. The anguish built up over the years to the point where it was beyond the capacity of the sheriffs to enforce law and order.

The turbulence began with the conquest itself. William the Bastard laid waste to the area around London and devastated the north of England. When the English retaliated by forming guerrilla groups, William accelerated the dispossession of English Lords, Sheriffs, Bishops and Abbotts, and substituting Normans. Former landowners found themselves mere tenants, with villein status, of land they had previously owned.

In 1086, the harvest failed simultaneously with the infliction upon the inhabitants of a malignant fever upon 50% of the population.

> "The wretched victims had nearly perished from the fever. Then came the sharp hunger and destroyed them outright."[42]

Before, during and beyond William's reign, the procedure of Tolt was used to get a dispute before the shire courts. This involved the applicant demonstrating to four Knights that there had been a breach of her or his rights. The Knights would then refer the matter to the court. The procedure of Essoin also involved four Knights visiting a person who claimed to be too ill to attend court to verify or reject that claim. If they were satisfied that he or she was too ill, they could excuse her or his appearance.

Under William II (Rufus), his Norman magnates rebelled against him, preferring to have his older brother Robert of Normandy on the throne. Once that was sorted, Scotland invaded England in 1091. William II invaded Wales. Constant battles took place between the English and Wales, Scotland, Northumberland and Normandy.

Under Rufus' brother, Henry I (1100-1135), Normandy was invaded, necessitating bulk taxation on the English, who were beggared by an extraordinary series of bad harvests.

Under Stephen (1135-1154), England was invaded by the Scots in 1138. Repelling the Scots sucked up all the money left in the treasury. Then the 'anarchy' began, with Henry's daughter Matilda invading England from France. The subsequent war lasted for 16 years. During the anarchy, in order to gain support, Stephen appointed his sheriffs 'in perpetuity.' This gave them the right to

---

[42] From 'The Anglo-Saxon Chronicles' cited at page 136 in Ackroyd's *The History of England* volume 1.

hand over the office to their sons. He also increased the areas over which they held sway. Geoffrey de Mandeville, for example, became sheriff of Essex, Hertfordshire, Middlesex and London. The sheriffs became too powerful and ran amok.

When Matilda's son Henry II (1154-1184) ascended the throne, he set about evening up the score with the Barons and sheriffs who had supported Stephen. Much of Henry's reign was spent in France. However, he reversed Stephen's edicts with regard to the sheriffs and dismissed the lot of them. Of the 23 sheriffs, only 6 were re-appointed. In 1174, Henry had to beat off invaders from Scotland and Flanders. Following the assassination of Thomas Beckett, Henry's penance included the passing of an edict that henceforth, churchmen could only be tried in church courts. 'Benefit of clergy' thus came into being.[43]

Henry successfully resisted a rebellion by his two sons in France. They must have been forgiven, because they went on to become the next two Kings of England.

Under Henry's reign, juries of freeholders (Knights and other important landholders) were given power to determine cases where it was alleged a person entitled to possession of land had been unlawfully ejected (the procedure of novel Disseisen), and cases where a dispute arose as to inheritance upon death (the procedure of Mort D'Ancestor).

Richard I (1189-1199). Richard Coeur de Lion (or more accurately, Richard the absent) bankrupted England by heading off on a crusade and allowing himself to be captured and held to ransom. He spent virtually no part of his reign (or indeed, of his life) in England, and his Justiciar, Hubert Walter, was obliged to take drastic steps to avoid a coup by Richard's brother John. He appointed Knights as coroners (in 1194) and guardians or keepers of the peace (in 1195). Both these groups of officials were supposed to assist the sheriffs in the maintenance of law and order. One of the functions of the coroner was to keep an eye upon the sheriff, and report any misdeeds to the Justiciar.

The keepers of the peace were the forerunners of the justices of the peace. Initially they were only appointed on an ad hoc basis, to tackle a particular crisis. The first such crisis was the attempted coup by the King's brother John. Over time many other crises necessitated the appointment of keepers, until they began to be appointed on a permanent basis from early in the 14th century. The keepers assisted by taking oaths of loyalty from various subjects, and 'binding over' others to either keep the peace or be of good behaviour. 'Binding over' involved the person bound over promising to forfeit a specified sum of money if he or she

---

[43] The only way to test the validity of a claim by an accused to be a churchman was to see if the claimant could read. It was assumed that only clergy could read. So if someone 'claimed the book', he or she was given a passage to read from the bible. If they could successfully read it (or had previously memorised it), they were discharged from the courts of the realm. Of course, they were liable to be tried by the church courts, but the church courts were forbidden by Cannon Law from imposing the death penalty. Often the church courts were not interested in pursuing the offender. The farcical procedure of benefit of clergy (see also pp. 98, 107-108, 154) was not abolished until 1827.

breached the peace, or misbehaved (as the case may be). Failure to pay the money on breach resulted in incarceration until the money was paid.

From time to time under Hubert Walter and subsequent monarchs, writs were issued to selected Knights to conduct gaol delivery, the basic criminal court hearings, and sentencing those found guilty. (Persons accused of crime were kept in gaol and the gaols had to be periodically emptied. There was no power to grant bail until 1483.[44]

If there was a competition for the most evil King of England, the vote would probably be awarded jointly to Richard's brother John (1199-1216) and Richard III (1483-1485) (There are plenty of other entrants for the title). John also attempted to milk the English cash-cow dry. His greed to retain and expand his French possessions, his taxations, and his incompetent leadership all led directly to a Barons' revolt in 1215, resulting in his forced agreement to Magna Carta. John lost all the French possessions except the Channel Islands. War also had to be waged with Wales, Ireland and Scotland. All of these difficulties were compounded by a period of great inflation, and ended in civil war when John repudiated Magna Carta. Greater reliance had to be placed on the keepers of the peace to maintain some semblance of order.

Henry III (1216-1272) This inept, obstinate and unfortunately long-lived King was only 8 years old when he came to the throne. His regents quarrelled. Some Barons refused to pay tax. He was weak, credulous, ineffectual and impulsive. He, too, wasted money on fruitless invasions of France. This was against the wishes of his Barons, who considered it pointless and wasteful, and doomed to failure. He surrounded himself with French advisors. He attempted to have his son installed as King of Sicily, forking out large sums of English taxpayers' money to the Pope to try to do so. The harvest of 1257 failed. Wheat more than doubled in price. There were:

> "...an innumerable multitude of poor people, swollen and rotting, lying by fives and sixes in pig sties, on dunghills and in the dirt of the streets."[45]

Sixty per cent of the population were classified as 'too poor to pay tax.' This figure remained reasonably constant over the centuries. There was yet another Barons' revolt led by Simon de Montford. The King was forced to agree to the Provisions of Oxford in 1258, which included a complete shake-up of the way England was to be governed. The King agreed to these provisions, but like his father before him with Magna Carta, he subsequently repudiated the provisions, and civil war broke out. Both sides gave every indication that they were relying upon the gentry and the Knights in particular, to support them and to assist in maintaining law and order. After de Montford's defeat in 1265, the King engaged in a wholesale purge of the Barons who had opposed him.

---

[44] By 1 Rich III, c.3, and see Baker, op. cit, p. 24.
[45] Matthew Paris, reported in Ackroyd op cit at p.193.

Edward I (1272-1307). 'Longshanks' reign was not without incident or trouble. He was absent from England when his father died, and in no hurry to get back. It was two years before he materialised for his coronation. That two year period was marked by disorder and private feuds between the nobility, presumably between the supporters of de Montford and the previous King. The parliament called for 1275 had 800 representatives summoned, 100 Lords and 700 gentry. Clearly the latter outnumbered the former. The gentry were from the ranks of the Knights and Burgesses, but included other prominent citizens. The task of raising taxation was given to the gentry. They met together to plan this in the chapter house at Westminster. Thus began the House of Commons.

The King replaced most of the sheriffs with men he knew and trusted. The implication from this is that he did not trust the existing sheriffs.

He invaded and conquered Wales. In 1285, parliament passed the Statute of Winchester. This was necessary, as its preamble makes clear, because law and order had broken down. Marauding hordes of ex-soldiers were running amok. The gentry were warring amongst themselves, hiring gangs of thugs to pursue their interests. The Statute of Winchester set up the policing system that was to operate for the next 544 years, until repealed and replaced by the Police Act of 1829. It attached responsibility for crime to the neighbourhood where the crime took place. If the residents were unable to deliver the perpetrator to the authorities, they themselves were held liable to the victim in damages and were fined. No doubt this had an effect upon the reporting of crime, because the victim's lot would be difficult if all his or her friends and neighbours had to fork out because of his or her complaint. But what a great way to drop the incidence of reported crime! The act also established hue and cry, watch and ward, arming of households and clearing vegetation from roads, vegetation wherein might lurk a highway robber.

During a three year absence of the King in Gascony, France (1286-1289), widespread fraud was discovered within his administration, including by the Chief Justice of the Common Pleas, who was forced into a humiliating public abjuring of the realm (leaving England forever) by walking barefoot from London to Dover.

Further troubles:

- In 1295, the King invaded Scotland.
- In 1297, the King invaded France.
- In 1297, Scotland invaded England.

All these wars required much money and the necessary taxes were referred to as 'extortions.' A domestic rebellion was brewing. At one point, Edward seized the entire output of wool from England to support his wars in Wales and France. War with Scotland continued throughout the rest of his reign. Ackroyd op. cit. at page 224 refers to "a strident and often violent society".

It was also during this reign that the keepers of the peace ceased to be subordinate to the sheriff. Sheriffs became subordinate to keepers of the peace.

Edward II (1307-1327). This was a reign "of almost unmitigated disaster."[46] A series of failed harvests resulted in starvation and galloping inflation. The price of bread and other essential commodities rose eightfold. The people were laid low with starvation and enteric fever. Many died.

War with Scotland continued. There were many raids by marauding gangs from Scotland in the north of England.

There were disputes between the King and his Barons over the quality of the advice he was receiving from his advisors. Another civil war resulted with the King's forces triumphant. He had 26 Lords executed.

Elsewhere in England, gangs of vagabonds engaged in robberies and assaults. Keepers of the peace were appointed on a permanent basis. They were also entrusted with responsibility for weights and measures and the coinage of the realm. Edward II was deposed by a coup orchestrated by his ever-loving wife Isabella, and his 14-year-old son ascended the throne.

Edward III (1327-1377): The Emergence of Justices of the Peace

Edward's reign was marred in that at the outset it was achieved by a coup d'état. The Statute of Westminster (1327) specifically provided for keepers of the peace to be appointed to guard against any backlash. The war against Scotland was eventually won with victory at Halidon Hill in 1333. The Hundred Years' War with France began. The country was yet again taxed to beggary. The tax impositions resulted in hostility and violence throughout the country. The Scots were again defeated in 1346.

The Black Death descended on England in 1348. This was the beginning of the end of the feudal system and of domination by the sheriffs, and the beginning of a long ascendency of the gentry. The Black Death, probably a combination of bubonic and pneumonic plagues, cut the population of England by one third (some say by one half). The workforce was so diminished that almost half of England's cultivatable land fell into disuse. The value of land fell dramatically. Cashed-up villeins and even cottagers were able to seize the chance and buy land.

Feudalism died with the plague, but it took a further 50 years and a peasant's revolt to bury it.

Of course, the plague and subsequent drop in land values were not the only causes of the death of feudalism. The shortage of labour certainly contributed. A major, perhaps the main, factor was inflation.

Scutage (rent) paid to landlords had remained fixed for centuries. There had been massive occurrences of inflation over the years, particularly under John, Henry III and Edward II. Further inflation accompanying the Black Death was the final straw that broke the camel's back. Scutage became worthless. There was no point

---

[46] *Encyclopaedia Britannica*, 15th edition, volume 29, page 40.

keeping a villein if he was only paying what had become a nominal and virtually worthless rent. About the same time, courts began recognising that villeins and cottagers had rights. The Statute Quia Emptores (1290) ensured that any transfer of an interest in land could not be blocked by a landlord higher up the chain, and ensured that the transfer would be recognised by the manor courts. The statute also ensured that no feudal dues attached to the land sold, and that the purchaser henceforth held the land directly of the King.

As for the decline of the sheriffs, they were renowned for ineffectiveness, unreliability, corruption, bullying and self-promotion long before the 14th century. During the anarchy, sheriffs often changed allegiance. Henry II felt constrained to dismiss all bar 6 of them. This significantly weakened the sheriffs. Keepers of the peace had to be appointed in 1195, and at various times thereafter because the sheriffs were inept. Under John, greater reliance was placed on the keepers than the sheriffs to try to keep a semblance of order. Magna Carta (1215) forbade sheriffs from hearing pleas of the Crown. Under Henry III and de Montford, both sides in the civil war looked to the gentry rather than the sheriffs to maintain order. Under Edward I, the first big parliament was stuffed with gentry, 700 of them. Longshanks replaced his sheriffs because he didn't trust them. At the beginning of Edward's reign, keepers were subject to the sheriffs. By the end of the reign, sheriffs were subject to the keepers.[47] Writs were issued to the sheriffs to issue summonses to jurors of presentment (the forerunner of committal proceedings) to appear before the keepers. Other authors also refer to the corruption of the sheriffs of this period.

For centuries, Knights had played a part in the administration of justice. They were the decision makers in the old hundred and shire courts. They made decisions as to whether there be a hearing into a breach of a person's rights: the procedure of Tolt. They made decisions about whether a person could be exempt from attending court: the procedure of Essoin. They were occasionally appointed to do gaol delivery. They were responsible for the issue of writs of Novel Disseisen and Mort D'Ancestor. They then moved up a gear to become guardians of the peace.

In 1344 an act of parliament[48] took power off the sheriffs and gave it to the keepers of the peace "to punish offenders according to their guilt". From this time on, they became known unofficially as 'justices of the peace.'

The Ordinance of Labourers (1349) and the Statute of Labourers (1351) gave power to the keepers of the peace to peg wages and restrict the movement of labourers, following the Black Death in 1348.

The Justices of the Peace Act of 1361 gave the official stamp of approval to the keepers' name change; gave them the power to hear and determine felonies, and confirmed some of their existing powers (for example, over weights and measures). The power to hear and determine felonies was strongly opposed by the

---

[47] Skyrme *The History of Justices of the Peace* volume 1 p.12.
[48] 18 Edw. III st.2, c.2

nobility, judges, lawyers and the clergy. The power was briefly rescinded in 1362, but permanently restored in 1369. A compromise of sorts was offered to the legal fraternity, in that each bench of justices of the peace had to have at least one member of the quorum on it.

The quorum was a list of magistrates who were thought to be a cut above the rest. If there was no justice of the quorum present at any sessions, the sessions could not take place. Usually and certainly at the beginning, the justices of the quorum were lawyers or people who had some legal training. By the 17th century, most justices were appointed to the quorum whether they had legal training or not. By that time few lawyers sat as justices. By an act of 1732, [49] solicitors were specifically forbidden from being justices of the peace. Appointments to the quorum and to the office of justice of the peace were always made by the King or Queen on the recommendation of the Chancellor, who in turn got his recommendation initially from the local Baron or Earl. In the early Tudor period, there came into existence for each county an official called the Lord Lieutenant, usually the counties' principal Earl or Baron, who was responsible for the militia of the county and also the head person for the county of the justices of the peace. It was upon his recommendation that appointments came to be made to both the justices and to the quorum (in the towns operating under Royal Charter, the town council had the right to nominate its justices).

As far as the nobility were concerned, their opposition was overcome by all of them being appointed to the office of Justice of the peace. This was probably calling their bluff: in reality, few of the nobility were interested in the office, and they very rarely exercised their right to sit as justices until the time of the French Revolution.

The government fixed a qualification to be a justice of the peace: he had to be a landholder whose rents from the land amounted to at least $10 per annum. This may not sound much, but was a fortune in medieval times. The amount fixed as the benchmark was increased from time to time in accordance with inflation.

Summary

The rise and rise of the gentry coincided with the collapse of feudalism and the collapse of the power of the sheriffs. It began with the appointment of guardians of the peace in 1195. The pivotal points were Prince John's uprising beginning in 1193; the Statute of Westminster of 1327; the act of 1344 giving justices power to determine felonies; and the Justices of the Peace Act of 1361.

The upshot of these centuries of embuggerance was that the baton of law and order was finally handed to the last in the queue, the gentry, in the guise of justices of the peace. The turmoil of the reigns of the first three Edwards was the last straw. It is not as if the gentry were perfect. Others had been tried and found wanting. The gentry were simply the best of a bad lot.

---

[49]   5 Geo. 2, c.18

Chart of gradual assumption of power by the gentry

Time	Disturbance	Government Action	Comment
William I, 1066-1085	Resistance to his reign. Consolidating the conquest. The harrying of the north. Legal disputes.	New system imposed in the form of the Curia Regis, but with retention of the old customary courts. Disputes heard and determined by Curia Regis or itinerant justices or local courts (shire, hundred or specialty).	Jurors were sometimes summoned to give a verdict. As per custom, shire and hundred courts usually gave verdict by those in attendance. Juries came into common usage under the Normans. The attention of the shire court could be invoked by a complaint demonstrating to four Knights that there had been a breach of rights (the procedure of tolt). A person who claimed to be unable to travel to court through illness would be visited by four Knights. If they were satisfied that the person was indeed too ill to attend court, they could adjourn his appearance (the procedure of essoin).
William I, William II, Henry I and Stephen 1066-1154	Absent fighting in Wales, Scotland and Normandy; the Anarchy	Greater and greater reliance on the sheriffs	Sheriffs unable to control widespread unrest or insurrection. Sheriffs becoming unpopular with the people and the King. Instances of false imprisonment and extortion by the sheriffs were becoming frequent. All this resulted in the 1170 inquest into sheriffs.

Richard I 1189-1199	Insurrection by Richard's brother John. Out-of-control and ineffectual sheriffs.	Ad hoc commissions issued to guardians of the peace from 1195 onwards, issued to Knights. From time to time, guardians were issued with commissions, not only to keep the peace, but for gaol delivery, which involved criminal court hearings and sentencing.	Those appointed were usually Knights in the country or Burgesses (leading citizens) in the townships. This distinguished England from other European countries, who looked to a paid bureaucracy (J R Strayer in the introduction to 'The English Government at work, 1327-1336).
John 1198-1216	Barons' revolt, culminating in 1215 with Magna Carta.	Magna Carta specifically provided that courts were to be conducted by itinerant justices sitting with 4 Knights of the county.	
Henry III 1216-1272	Baron's revolt led by Simon De Montford. King's unpopular demands for excessive taxes, firstly to pay the Pope for Henry's son to be the King of Sicily and secondly to pay for the King's incompetent wars in Gascony.	The Provisions of Oxford 1258 During the De Montford led rebellion, both the King and De Montford ordered three Knights from each county to assemble at Windsor (King) and St Albans (De Montford). Most Knights sensibly ignored these summonses. De Montford then appointed four Knights from each county to be keepers of the peace to maintain law and order. At first, the King adhered to the support of his sheriffs, but then he, too, began appointing his own keepers. After De Montford's defeat, the King continued to rely upon his gentry as custos paces. They were, however, only appointed in response to particular crises in the areas of the crises. They had power to raise forces, to	The provisions of Oxford provided firstly for a 24 man law reform commission, 12 members nominated by the Barons and 12 by the King. This commission was to select and supervise ministerial appointments. Sheriffs were to be replaced by Knights, four of them in each county, to hear complaints of wrongdoing by the sheriffs and their bailiffs. Parliament was to meet 3 times each year. The country was to be run by a 15 man council and the King jointly. It was the King's subsequent refusal to follow the provisions that led to the Baron's revolt. During the period when De Montford ruled England, he continued to appoint keepers of the peace. Their other duties included

			direct the militia so raised, and collect taxes. Their authority, at least temporarily, overrode that of the sheriffs.	arresting wrongdoers and keeping them in custody, in effect to await further instructions. They were also to arrange for the election of Knights and Burgesses to parliament: Rymer, O, i, 792 'Select Charters'.
				'Novel disseisen' was the writ issued to remedy the situation where a person in possession of land was illegally dispossessed.
			From time to time, Knights from particular shires might be appointed to carry out the judicial functions of novel disseisen and mort d'ancestor.	'Mort d'ancestor' was the writ issued to determine settlement of a deceased estate where there was any dispute.
				It will be seen that the gentry is gradually being shoehorned into judicial work, through the procedures of tolt, and essoin, occasional gaol delivery, the taking of oaths of allegiance, the powers of arrest and the writs of novel disseisen and mort d'ancestor. This was in addition to military and constabulary duties. Further, they were being appointed to parliament and it was during this period they actually outnumbered the Lords.
Edward I 1272-1307		War in Wales (1277-1282)	In 1277, writs were issued directing sheriffs to appoint keepers of the peace and to assist them in arresting malefactors.	In 1278, the class of persons who could be appointed as keepers (or guardians, or custos paces or even justices of the peace as they were sometimes being called) was extended beyond Knights to freeholders with an annual income of at

			least £20.
1285	Unacceptable increase in homicides, robberies, arson and the failure of juries to convict.	The Statute of Winchester 1285	The increase of robberies etc, and the failure of juries to convict are specifically mentioned in the preamble to the statute. The act laid the foundations for the policing of England for the next 540 years, until the Police Act of 1829. It made the following provisions. Firstly, the whole community where the robbery etc. was committed was made responsible for any felony committed in its area. If the offender was not brought to justice, the whole community was fined and made to pay damages. The act also consolidated the practice of 'hue and cry' whereby a suspect was to be pursued. The act also set up a system of watch and ward to police towns and villages, particularly at night. Each family was required to supply a guard in rotation. All strangers encountered were to be kept in custody overnight. If nothing suspicious was found on them, they were to be released in the morning. If something suspicious was found, they were to be handed over to the sheriff to be dealt with according to law. Roads were to be cleared of vegetation to

			a width of 60 metres 'to prevent malefactors hiding with evil intent.' All householders were to arm themselves with swords, bows and arrows and the like. This was to be enforced by inspections of arms twice each year by the itinerant assizes judges. (In 1287, this responsibility was taken from the assizes judges and given to the keepers of the peace).
			According to Skyrme *The History of Justices of the Peace*, vol 1, p.12, at the beginning of the reign of Edward I, keepers were subject to the sheriff. Towards the end of the reign, the position was reversed: writs were directed to the sheriffs to assist and obey the keepers, and to issue summonses to jurors of presentment to appear before the keepers.
			Professor Harding in *The Origin and Early History of the Keepers of the Peace* (Transactions of the Royal Historical Society) 5th series,

1300	Alleged breaches of the Royal charters by Royal officials and others.	An article 'Super Cardas' was issued by parliament to give power to 3 Knights or other suitable persons in each county to hear and determine these allegations of breaches of the Royal charters.	volume 10, 1960, p.100) asserts that these appointees were the first of the primarily judicial keepers and the first justices of the peace, although that phrase would not come into general use for another half century. This is open to question, depending upon the view you take of the earlier bestowal of powers to hear writs of novel disseisen, mort d'ancestor, and to conduct gaol delivery.
1301	Opposition encountered by the King in raising men and money to carry on the war in France against Phillip the Fair.	Firstly, commissions were issued to a lawyer and a Knight in each county to hear allegations of wrong done in the King's name because of the war. Secondly, Edward I was forced to negotiate a peace with France.	

Edward II 1307-1327	According to the *Encyclopaedia Britannica*, 15th edition, vol. 29, page 40, his whole reign was an "almost unmitigated disaster."	More reliance was placed on the gentry. Knights and Burgesses increased their say in parliament, and were appointed more and more to public office, including that of keeper of the peace, which came to be established on a permanent basis. Keepers were given power over coinage, ensuring the standards thereof. They were given supervision over weights and measures. They were given supervision over prices, ensuring they did not rise above those of Edward I's reign. Keepers were given power to arrest on suspicion of crime and to lodge those arrested in custody to await the King's orders (this meant until gaol delivery could take place, initially by the Assize judges). In 1316, the keepers were given power to inquire into the commission of felonies and trespasses. A commission was issued to the keepers of Kent authorising them to conduct gaol delivery, which gave them power to try and sentence those whom they	During this period, keepers were required to make monthly returns to the Curia Regis of their proceedings and to give them the names of offenders.

		had arrested.	
Edward III 1327-1377	Edward III became King at the age of 14 when his mother and Roger Mortimer overthrew Edward II. The crisis was therefore fear of unrest.	The second Statute of Westminster 1327 (1 Edw.III, st. 2, c.6) specifically provided for the appointment of keepers of the peace. All previous appointments had been made under the authority of a King's edict.	The House of Commons (the gentry's house) had strongly petitioned the King or his regent to use them, the gentry, to keep the peace. The move was strongly opposed by the Chief Justice of the King's Bench, Geoffrey Scrope, who urged that the peace be kept by professional itinerant judges. The gentry's petition prevailed. However, the statute did not provide the keepers with the power of arrest, which they had previously on occasion under their commissions. There followed years of lobbying in a contest between the lawyers and judges on the one hand, and the gentry on the other. The former argued for more commissions for lawyers as itinerant judges.
1330-1370	There was a serious increase in lawlessness due to soldiers returning from the wars in France. The unattached soldiers became predators in their own land. Soldiers raised by the nobility pursuant to the feudal order, with the blessing of the King, on their return to England	In 1329, keepers were authorised to hear and determine felonies and trespasses: 2 Edw III cc 1-7. One year later, this authorisation was rescinded, and keepers obliged to remit all indictments to the Assizes.	Fluctuations of this nature continued over the next 30 years.

	were used by the nobility to wage war on one another, as well as on the rest of the community.		
	It became obvious that the sheriffs were corrupt and showing signs of undue independence.		
1330-1360		A statute was passed in 1344 (18 Edw III, st.2, c.2) taking power off the sheriffs and giving it to the keepers of the peace to punish offenders "according to their guilt."	This act required the keepers to sit with a person learned in the law. The gentry accepted this limitation.

This requirement that one of the justices of the peace had to be of the quorum remained for centuries, but its practical effect was negated in time. To be of the quorum initially meant that one of the justices had to be learned in the law. Gradually however, justices came to be appointed to the quorum who were not learned in the law, and by the 17th century, almost all justices of the peace were of the quorum. |
| 1348 | The Black Death and its consequences, specifically the dramatic decline in the population, resulting in scarcity of labour, inflation and ultimately to the dismantling of the feudal system.

Continuing lawlessness, labour | The Ordinance of Labourers 1349 (23 Edw III and the Statute of Labourers 1351 25 Edw III) st.2. | By this ordinance and act, Keepers were given the power to peg wages and restrict the movement of labourers. Under these provisions, employers could be fined for paying more for labour than the fixed wage, and labourers fined, imprisoned and branded for receiving more than the fixed |

	shortages, inflation and high taxes.		wage or for straying from their parish.
1361		The Justices of the Peace Act 1361, 34 Edw III, cc1-11.	Despite opposition from the nobility, lawyers and judges, and the clergy, the gentry prevailed. Over the next 8 years from 1361 to 1369, the power given by the act to hear and determine felonies was removed and replaced, but permanently restored in 1369. Over the next 200 years, the justices of the peace acquired control of parliament; all local government responsibilities; charge of the militia and constabulary, and determined the vast bulk of the criminal work. They ruled England.

Chapter 2

The Shambles: 1361-1485

The Ineffectiveness of the Early Justices

It is a pity that the reign of Stephen has purloined the phrase 'the anarchy', because it neatly fits the 124 years following the Justices of the Peace Act of 1361, and indeed, the whole period between the conquest and the Tudors. However, 'the shambles,' being a slaughterhouse, will fit the metaphorical bill nicely. That period before the reign of Henry VII varied in its shambolic quality, but it was always a shambles to a greater or lesser degree.

The shambles was led from the top.

- William the conqueror caused the death of King Harold at the battle of Hastings in 1066.
- King Henry I probably either killed or caused to be killed his brother, King William II.
- Henry II had his chancellor, Thomas Beckett, killed.
- Richard I, Coeur de Lion, murdered 3000 prisoners of war at Acre during the 3rd crusade.
- John murdered his nephew Arthur in 1202.
- Queen Isabella orchestrated the murder of her husband, Edward II in 1327.
- Richard II murdered his uncle, Thomas of Gloucester.
- Henry IV murdered Richard II in 1399.
- Edward IV murdered his brother Clarence and Henry VI in 1471.
- Richard III murdered his two nephews, one of them a 14-year-old boy, King Edward V.
- Henry VII had Richard III killed in battle.

Encouraged by the example set by their monarchs, the nobility, the gentry and the justices of the peace, joined in the fray. The middle ages were a free-for-all brawl. Here are some examples.

After the renunciation by Henry III of the Provisions of Oxford in 1258, civil war broke out in which the Barons were constantly changing sides.[50] "Claims (over disputed lands) were decided by force, and the great Lords were only too eager to step in to their own advantage."[51]

The Earl of Lancaster built up his estates from the confiscated estates of the de Montfords after the battle of Eversham in 1265. (One of the main causes of long-lasting feuds amongst the nobility and the gentry was the forfeiture of estates, caused in turn by the fact that in every battle, insurrection and revolt, one had to take sides, and the consequence of being on the losing side was forfeiture of the loser's estates. Over the years, resentment built up, and the person or his heirs continued the feud to try to get the estates back).

In 1348, the Black Death struck, cutting the population of England from about 4 million to about 2.5 million.

The peasants' revolt of 1381 involved justices of the peace at a number of levels. In the first place, they were a substantial cause of the revolt. The justices were exceedingly unpopular with the peasants and labourers because of their heavy-handed pegging of labourers' wages, and restriction of movement of the peasants after the labour shortage caused by the Black Death. Surprisingly, some of the justices joined in the revolt. However, a number of justices became the target of the peasants and were put to death.

> "Members of the Gentry class were not slow to try to further their own interests. This also applied to the leading Burgesses. The readiness of some of the justices to take advantage of the lawlessness which followed the 1381 rebellion was a manifestation of the violent nature of society in general which characterised the middle ages [...] At all levels, from the royal family downwards, feuds could erupt into open warfare, and it was only natural that similar situations should arise amongst the justices themselves. As the number of justices in each county increased, they sometimes became divided into rival groups which on occasion resorted to physical violence." [52]

Sessions of the peace were often interrupted when other justices or members of the nobility arrived fully armed and accompanied by a rabble of retainers, hell-bent on disrupting the sessions. This was usually so if a retainer of the nobility was due before the sessions charged with some offence, and especially so if a member of the nobility was charged.

The 1351 Oxfordshire records relate: "Like madmen possessed by an evil spirit, (they) came in large numbers to the town in manner of war and assaulted (Thomas de Langele) keeper and justice of the peace and chased him into the Abbey of Eynesham, besieged him therein and threatened to burn him if he did

---

[50] *The Middle Ages* by John Gillingham and Peter Earle, p.25
[51] Ibid p.24
[52] Skyrme op cit pp. 43,44

not deliver to them all the indictments and accusations against them [...] and prevented him and his fellows from holding their sessions."

Many of those who perpetrated these offences came from the same social background as the gentry who served as justices. A sitting of Oyer and Terminer (your basic criminal sitting), was broken up by the appearance of a Knight with sword drawn taking one of the justices by the throat.[53]

In 1428, the Duke of Norfolk and the Earl of Huntingdon engaged in a violent feud and both were dismissed as justices of the peace.

The Paston family letters are filled with accounts of wrongdoing that went unpunished and of nobles who exercised justice (if that was what it could be called) for their own advantage. Endless stories are told of armed gangs threatening tenants, besieging manors and invading courts of justice.

John Paston wrote to the Archbishop of York, complaining of 'a great multitude of riotous people, to the number of a thousand or more, who broke, despoiled and drew down his manor house at Gresham, drove out my wife and servants and took and bore away all the goods and chattels." The gang then fortified the manor and kept out Paston as well as the King's justices of the peace.

In 1461, Edward IV usurped the estates of his former enemies, 113 of them in all, and granted them to his supporters. He created 7 new Barons.

Edward was obliged to intervene in a feud between the Greys and the Vernons of Derbyshire.

The senior Knights of Herefordshire petitioned the King: "That they dare not (summons, charge or arrest) malefactors for dread of murdering, and to be mischiefed in their own houses, considering the great numbers of the said misdoers."[54]

Edward IV regularly intervened in court processes to ensure favourable outcomes for his supporters.

In 1454, Sir John Falstaff bribed a jury to favour his case. "Juries of the period were, on a routine basis, bribed or intimidated. In practice, the law was rotten and worm-eaten. We may say the same of parliament and the court."[55]

One consequence of the Black Death (1348) took years to gather momentum and it took a number of other causes to trigger this particular result. The shortage of labour and diminution of the population meant a sudden collapse in the value of land. Many cashed up citizens, as well as rich landowners were able to profit from this situation by buying up what appeared then to be relatively valueless land. Then entrepreneurs began turning wool into a valuable commodity by making and exporting cloth at good profits. Landowners seized upon this to graze sheep instead of growing crops. Sheep did not require nearly as much labour as

---

[53] Select Cases before the King's Council, 1390, p. 79.
[54] Ackroyd, op cit, p.381
[55] Ackroyd, op cit, p. 342.

crops. So successful and profitable was this new industry that many landowners began seizing common pastures and enclosing them with fences or hedges.[56] Landlords ejected tenants. The dispossessed began to move elsewhere seeking jobs. This was undesirable from the point of view of the nobility and gentry, who still required some labour on tap when it suited them, and so it became an offence to be one of those ejected from premises and wandering to and fro seeking employment. They were labelled vagrants or vagabonds and mercilessly persecuted for the next 500 years.[57]

By the end of the War of the Roses, the nobility had all but destroyed itself, with only 29 of them left. Those that remained or were appointed in their stead never again enjoyed their previously unchecked power. They did raise their ugly heads again from time to time, but never got away with the sustained ferocity and unpunished crime of the middle ages. Henry VII only appointed 5 Lords during his reign. Cardinal Wolsey brought the nobility to heel during Henry VIII's reign to a large extent.[58]

As for the justices of the peace throughout that era, what can be said? As the name of the office implies, their main function was to keep the peace and they failed miserably to do that. Not only that, but it is apparent that they were all too often the ones who breached the peace. This ought not to be surprising because of the ongoing remnants of feudalism. The nobility always had the means of raising an army and often kept the core of a standard army as their retainers. When a member of the nobility moved from 'A' to 'B', he took his cavalcade with him- the medieval equivalent of an offer which was difficult to refuse. If a retinue of 100 or more men armed to the teeth pulled up in front of your house and invited you to join them on their enterprise, it was not easy to refuse, particularly if you were fond of your life, family and home. Knights, from whose ranks the justices of the peace were largely drawn, often had close historical ties with the nobility through their former feudal obligations. The warring nobility might be your landlord. He might be the one who recommended your appointment as a JP. For these and similar reasons, not only did the justices turn a blind and impotent eye to the transgressions of the nobility, they often felt constrained to join them.

> "The justice of the peace presiding at Quarter Sessions...was closely associated with the local Lord, probably one of his retainers and in need of his protection." [59]

Then what, if anything, did the justices do during these centuries? They did hold regular sessions, but mostly stayed clear of tackling the nobility. On the occasions when they did summons the nobility, or even merely a retainer of the nobility, to answer for their sins, the session was likely to be greeted with a few hundred thugs hired for the occasion to ensure a favourable verdict.

---

[56] The enclosures phenomenon is dealt with more fully in later chapters. See pages 19,62-69, 73, 82, 91, 92, 106.
[57] See pages 62-69,73,83-84,85,92,93,108.
[58] See page 57.
[59] Marion Yass: *The English Aristocracy*, Wayland Publishers, 1974, p. 24.

What the magistrates did during this period was to keep their foot firmly planted on the neck of the general populace, the hoi polloi, to allow the gentry and nobles to transgress without their interference. In this they were largely successful, if we overlook the peasants' revolt of 1381 and Jack Cade's rebellion of 1450, and Robert Kett's rebellion of 1549.

Magistrates' powers as at the time of the Justices of the Peace Act, 1361

By 1361, the justices had accumulated the following powers, either by the Justices of the Peace Act, or their commissions, or the Ordinance and Statute of Labourers of 1349 and 1351.

- Power to hear and determine all criminal charges except treason.

- Power to make preliminary enquiries into criminal offences, and put suspects up for trial.

- Power to arrest suspects.

- Power to require all persons to enter into a recognisance to keep the peace or be of good behaviour, and to punish for breaches. Power to take all necessary steps to prevent breaches of the peace.

- Power to fine for "trespasses done by any person".

- Responsibility over the standards of coinage, and supervision over weights and measures, with power to punish transgressions.

- Power to regulate wages, and to set maximum wages and to punish breaches of the standards set.

- Power to restrict the movement of labourers and indeed, of anyone but themselves and the nobility.

- Power to deal with monopolies, such as forestalling (buying a commodity, usually grain, on its way to market, with a view to cornering the market and forcing up prices), engrossing (buying a standing crop, same intent), and regrating (buying large quantities at a market with a view to resale at a profit).

Increases in Magistrates Jurisdiction after the Justices of the Peace Act, 1361, to the Tudors

During the remainder of the shambles from the 1361 Justices of the Peace Act to the ascension of Henry Tudor to the throne in 1485, the justices were given the following additional powers, either by acts of parliament or their commissions.

- Power to deal with fraud in the wool market, specifically selling wool at the incorrect weight.[60]

- Power to regulate the selling of cloth, and to punish for breach of the regulations. They were given power to appoint 'searchers', the middle-

---

[60] 1389, 13 Rich. II, c.9

ages equivalent of modern factory inspectors to look for any breaches. Breaches could be heard and determined by a single justice.[61]

- Legislation regulating the tanning of leather and the manufacture of shoes gave power to the justices to punish breaches.[62]

- Power to punish for the manufacture of blunt arrows.[63]

- Power to punish manufacturers of inferior quality silver, and vendors of expensive candles.[64]

- Power to regulate the price of food and other essential commodities.[65]

- Fugitive servants were to be imprisoned and branded on the forehead with the letter 'F', and put to death for a second offence.[66]

- Power to punish beggars and vagabonds.[67]

- Power to regulate and even prevent apprenticeships. (Children of landless labourers could not be apprenticed. This was aimed at mitigating the shortage of labour following the Black Death).[68]

- Games such as football, cricket, tennis, quoits and dice were forbidden. The only pastime permitted was practice with bow and arrow. Breaches of the laws against games were to be punished by six days' imprisonment originally, but this was upped to 2 years in 1474. Magistrates policed this.[69]

- Hunting and gaming became the exclusive province of the rich under acts passed in 1364 and 1390. Punishing poaching became one of the favourite pastimes of the justices.[70]

- By various statutes, justices were made the enforcers of regulations as to what the poor could eat, drink and wear.[71]

- By the 1483 Act, 1 Rich. III, c.3, justices were given the power to bail persons charged with felony, a power which, according to Griffith CJ in

---

[61] By various statutes: 13 Rich II, cc. 10 and 11; 11 Hen. VI, c. 6; 4 Edw IV, c.1 and 17 Edw. IV, c.4.
[62] 1389, 13 Rich. II, C. 12, and 1423, Hen. VI, c.7.
[63] 1406, 7 Hen. IV, c. 7
[64] 1423, 2 Hen. VI, c. 17 (silver); 1432, 11 Hen. VI, c.12 (candles).
[65] 1390, 13 Rich. II, st.1, c.8 and 1476, 6 Hen. VI, c.3
[66] 34 Edw. III, c. 11.
[67] Many statutes: see pages 62,63 under the heading 'Vagrancy and the Poor Laws' for a list of those statutes to the time of Elizabeth.
[68] 1406, 7 Hen. IV, c. 17.
[69] Various laws, including 12 Rich. II, c.6; 11 Hen. IV, c. 4 and 17 Edw. IV, c.3.
[70] 37 Edw. III, c. 19 and 13 Rich. II, st. 1, c. 13, and see pp 128-131.
[71] An unparticularised statute cited by Skyrme op cit volume 1, pp. 59, 60.

Huddart Parker v. Moorehead (1908) 8 CLR 330 at 356, was regularly abused.

Office of Justice of Peace not adopted simultaneously throughout Britain

The office of justice of the peace was not adopted uniformly in 1361 throughout Britain. Justices of the Peace were not introduced, for example, in the county palatinate of Chester until the reign of Henry VIII; in Wales, at any time between 1361 and the Tudors (it varied in different parts of Wales); in Scotland, not until the reign of James VI (James I of England), that is, until sometime after 1603; and in Ireland, it is anyone's guess, but the title appears in Irish legislation of the year 1410 (See Hazeltine's general preface to E G Dowdell's work: *A Hundred years of Quarter Sessions*). Town charters issued after the creation of justices of the peace usually had a provision enabling the council to appoint a recorder to conduct its Quarter Sessions. Petty Sessions were conducted by its justices of the peace.

Domesticated Violence and Forced Marriages in the 15th Century

Wife beating was a recognised right of man, and was practised without shame by high as well as low. The woman's defence was her tongue, sometimes giving her mastery in the household, but often leading to muscular retort. One of the 15th century English translations of the fashionable manual of the Knight of La Tour Landry thus describes the proper treatment of a scolding wife:

> "He smote her with his fist down to the earth. And then with his foot he struck her in the visage and brake her nose, and all her life after she had her nose crooked that she might not for shame show her visage it was so foul blemished [...] therefore the wife ought to suffer and let the husband have the word, and to be master.'"[72]

The alternative for the overuse of the wifely tongue is set forth in the later paragraph: 'Power of the Magistracy – Petty Sessions', involving the use of the cucking stool (see p. 106). But it is almost certain that this device was used only upon 'the low' and never 'the high.' Trevelyan continues:

> "Similarly, the daughter who refused to marry the gentleman of her parents' choice was liable to be locked up, beaten and flung about the room without any shock being inflicted on public opinion. Marriage was not an affair of personal affection but of family avarice, particularly in the 'chivalrous' upper classes. 'For every need,' complains a member of the noble family of Scrope, 'I would fain to sell a little daughter I have, for much less than I should have done by possibility.' Betrothal often took place while one or both of the parties was in the cradle, and marriage when they were scarcely out of the nurse's charge. It was sometimes difficult to get a little fellow to say the necessary words of the ceremony, before running back to his toys."

---

[72] Trevelyan op cit p. 260,261.

Chapter 3

The Tudors: 1485-1603

Henry VII (1485-1509): His growing reliance upon the magistracy

After the battle of Bosworth Hill in 1485, things did not settle down immediately. There had been too many centuries of fighting and too many dispossessions from land to allow this. The dispossessed or their descendants wanted their land back or alternatively, vengeance.

Henry's claim to the throne was tenuous. He was only a great-great-great grandson of Edward III. It is likely that there were many others of similar or better lineage. But none of them had just won the battle of Bosworth, or were surrounded at the time by a retinue of similar size.

A peculiarity of Henry's reign was that, from time to time, someone or other bobbed up, claiming to be one or other of Edward IV's sons. The sons had previously been locked in the Tower of London by their 'protector', Richard III, but disappeared, presumed murdered at Richard's behest to enable him to usurp the throne.

One factor that saved Henry was the extent to which the nobility had been reduced by the time Henry was crowned. They were down to 29 in number.[73] Of that 29, only two had joined Henry at the battle of Bosworth, both of them at that time exiled from England.[74] Henry mistrusted the nobility for good reason. He could not, and did not, rely upon them to assist him to govern England. He was forced to rely upon the gentry in the guise of justices of the peace.

Apart from the sharp diminution in their numbers, the War of the Roses had wellnigh bankrupted the nobility and the nation as well. Henry could not rely upon a paid bureaucracy, because there was no money to pay them, at least in the early years. On the local level, government was left to the justices of the peace. For central government, he selected a group of persons, preferably not from the nobility, and henceforth called the Privy Council, to advise him.

> "He preferred to govern through intimates rather than through the great men of the land. He did not exclude the aristocracy from his council, but he did not place his whole trust in them. Instead, he

---

[73] Trevelyan op cit, p.279 fn.
[74] Ackroyd, volume 1, op cit p. 427.

surrounded himself with a retinue of self-made men, who all owed their loyalty to the King. He preferred lawyers to magnates, and listened to the advice of great merchants, rather than great Lords."[75]

Henry went further and had laws enacted against livery and maintenance.[76] L and M require a word of explanation. It will have been noted that the system of feudalism under which England had suffered at least from the conquest, required the nobility, in effect, to keep standing armies. Theoretically, they were to be 'maintained' by the Lords to be ready to answer the call of the King to assist him to overcome his enemies. The danger of this system was that if the King fell out with his Lords, or one or a combination of them, they could use their retainers against him. They would often use their retainers against other Lords or anyone else with whom they had a falling-out. If you look carefully at the list of problems besetting England over the years since the conquest, you will appreciate that the maintenance by the nobility of these private armies was the cure for some of the troubles, but the cause of many more of them.

Each Lord decked his retainers out in uniforms (called 'livery') to distinguish them as his retainers from those of other Lords. The retainers of each Lord were usually divided up into household servants, Knights and soldiers. Since Henry distrusted his Lords, he issued laws against the maintenance of the soldiers, because he feared, with some justification, that they could be used against him. These laws were referred to as laws against livery and maintenance. The laws were not wholly successful. Lords surely had the right to employ personal servants, and deck them out in uniforms, and it was sometimes difficult to appreciate the difference between the wardrobe-keepers, the bottle-counters and the fart-catchers on the one hand, and the soldier thugs on the other. In any event, the Lords were all justices, and the gentry, from whose ranks the bulk of the nation's justices were drawn, were closely allied, and owed allegiance to the nobility, or were overawed by them. There was, for example, an Elizabethan feud between a Lord Burghley and the Earl of Leicester (a boyfriend of Elizabeth), when many of the justices of the peace openly wore Leicester's livery.[77] Justices were not very successful at upholding the new laws against livery and maintenance.

Henry used the justices of the peace aggressively to take oaths of loyalty and good behaviour from, amongst others, the nobility. Over time, this strategy began to work. At the beginning of his reign, there was much hostility directed at Henry, but as time went by, these attacks lessened. Often now, the Lords directed their anger at each other, or at others who did not belong to the nobility. The gentry too were attacking each other. These private feuds continued well into the future, throughout the Tudor period and the Stuart era, including the Commonwealth. The consequences of picking the wrong side in a fight, greed and land dispossession last long.

---

[75] Ibid p. 430.
[76] 4 Hen VII, c. 12.
[77] Skyrme op cit at p. 182.

Henry introduced an institution, the Lord Lieutenant, one for each county, the senior noble, as head sherang of the county. He was responsible for calling out armed men (the militia) to defend the realm when directed to do so by the King. He was also appointed to be head of the justices of the peace for each county. It came to be that it was upon the Lord Lieutenant's recommendation that people were appointed as justices of the peace, with the exception of the chartered towns, where the town council nominated its own justices.

As to the finances of the country, Henry forfeited and re-sold the estates of all those who had fought against him at Bosworth. He declared that his reign began the day *before* Bosworth, meaning that anyone who fought against him was guilty of high treason for opposing the King, and their property was forfeited!

His real ingenuity as a fundraiser was his invention of the catch-22 of taxation. If landholders lived frugally, that meant they had money stashed that belonged more appropriately in Henry's bank account. If, however, the landholder was seen to be living high, splashing money around like a drunken sailor with three arms, then even more obviously he had money to contribute to the royal coffers. Towards the end of his reign, Henry became obsessed with money: he truly was the monarch highlighted in the old nursery rhyme (Sing a song of sixpence): "The King was in his counting house, counting out his money."

Henry relied upon his magistrates to keep the peace and carry out the other duties they had been allotted before 1485. He made little change to this aspect of government.

Not long after his ascension to the throne, he had legislation enacted to try to curb enclosures.[78] Such measures were not particularly successful, because "these measures did not receive the support of the justices."[79] This is because the justices themselves were profiting from the enclosures.

An act of parliament[80] gave justices the power to supervise the fishing industry, and another act[81] the power to punish importers of wine, unless the wine was imported in English, Irish or Welsh ships (frog wine: yes; frog ships: no!). Magistrates were given power to suppress disorderly or useless ale houses.[82] Justices were required to enforce an act regulating the use of longbows and crossbows.[83]

Laws repressing the 'lower classes' from hunting were to be enforced by the justices, who *were* allowed to hunt.[84] An incentive to be merciless was dangled

---

[78] 4 Hen. VII, c. 16.
[79] Skyrme op cit, volume 1, p. 141
[80] 11 Hen. VII, c. 23.
[81] 1 Hen. VII, c. 8.
[82] 11 Hen VII, c. 2; 19 Hen. VII, c. 12: A useless alehouse was presumably one which yielded little or no revenue to the Royal coffers, or served bad beer.
[83] 19 Hen. VII, c. 4.
[84] 1 Hen. VII, c.7 and19 Hen VII, c. 19.

by allowing the magistrates to pocket one-tenth of the fine imposed for breaches. Offenders were imprisoned until the fines were paid.

Legislation giving justices further power over weights and measures and coinage was passed.[85]

Another duty that came the way of the justices was as a consequence of enclosures of land.[86] Landless labourers lost their jobs and place in society. Laws in Tudor times created an alternative niche for these people by labelling these displaced persons 'vagrants', and making their very existence a criminal offence.[87] They were punished cruelly over the next 400 years by the justices.[88]

By the time of Henry VII, magistrates had gradually picked up jurisdiction over a whole range of offences from felonies with a jury and the death penalty, to less serious matters dealt with out of sessions by one or more justices without a jury.

Henry had turned to the justices of the peace to help him rule because there was no one else to whom he could turn. The vast bulk of the criminal justice system was handled by justices. In this limited sense, justices were in control of the judiciary, and this, combined with their constabulary duties placed them fairly and squarely in charge of law and order. They dominated the legislature and the executive arms of government. With the exception of foreign affairs, they ruled England. This remained the situation until the mid 19th century.[89]

Until the Tudors, acts of parliament were, in effect, petitions to the King, and did not receive force of law until agreed to and signed off by him, usually after consultation with his council. This remains the situation even until today, but the difference is that hitherto it was no foregone conclusion that the monarch would agree to sign off, but in the Tudor era, he or she usually did. Today, it is compulsory for the monarch to sign legislation passed by parliament, notwithstanding that he or she might personally disagree with the legislation. More and more of the law of the land was being initiated and passed through parliament, a parliament that gained in strength and power throughout the Tudor era, to the point that, by the end of Elizabeth's reign, it was arguably supreme. The Stuarts disagreed, but that is another story.

> "Imperceptibly, the House of Commons was becoming the instrument through which the will of the landed classes could be heard, and not an obliging organ of royal control. In Tudor political theory, this was a distortion of the proper function of parliament, which was meant to beseech and petition, never to command and

---

[85] 7 Hen. VII, c. 3 and 19 Hen. VII, c. 4.
[86] See pp. 18-19.
[87] 3 Hen VII, c. 9 and 19 Hen. VII, c. 12
[88] This is dealt with in more detail at pp. 62-69,73,83-84,85,92,93,108.
[89] Holdsworth, *History of the English Law*, volume 1 p. 294, said of the justices that they had 'no small influence in gaining for parliament its supremacy in the state.'

initiate. Three things, however, forced theory to make way for reality.

First was the government's financial dependence on Commons, for the organ that paid the royal piper eventually demanded that it also call the government tune.

Second, under the Tudors, parliament had been summoned so often and forced to legislate on such crucial matters of church and state – legitimising and bastardising monarchs; breaking with Rome; proclaiming the Supreme headship (governorship under Elizabeth); establishing the royal succession; and legislating in areas that no parliament had ever dared enter before – that Commons got into the habit of being consulted. Inevitably a different constitutional question emerged: if parliament is asked to give authority to the Crown, can it also take away that authority?

Finally, there was a growth of a politically conscious and economically dominant gentry; and the increase in the size of the House of Commons reflected the activity and importance of that class."[90]

The EB points out that under Henry VIII, the House of Commons numbered 298 members. By the end of Elizabeth's reign, this had increased to 433. It also points out that the gentry, represented by the Commons, had become more important than the Lords, both economically and politically.

The Commons attacked Elizabeth on her claim of the royal prerogative to grant monopolies, and she was forced to give way. However, she refused attempts to reform the Anglican Church at the behest of the Puritan controlled parliament.

The legislative arm of the government was controlled by justices of the peace. The Lords were all justices, and a substantial majority of the Commons were justices. The Commons consisted of four members from each county and two from each borough. By 1559, 80% of the county members of the Commons were justices and 34% from the boroughs were justices, and by 1593, those percentages had risen to 90% county and 36% borough.[91] Since the very early parliaments in the 13th century, parliament was dominated by guardians or justices of the peace. This remained the situation until the late 19th century.

The King in council could, of course, promulgate laws called edicts, ordinances or proclamations without consulting parliament. If he or she did this, s/he usually consulted his or her council first. This latter type of law remained an option throughout the Tudor and Stuart eras and indeed, up to the present day, but it is usually confined these days to matters of minor significance, by-laws, regulations and the like. Concerning the King's council in the time of Henry VII:

---

[90] *Encyclopaedia Britannica*, 15th edition, volume 29, p. 56.
[91] Skyrme op cit, volume 1, p.108

"A dramatic new development took place in the shape of direct surveyance of the justices by what began to be called 'the Privy Council'. This Tudor innovation was a select inner body of the larger council of the King and was composed exclusively of members chosen personally by the Sovereign. They included no hereditary peers of long standing and were selected on their merits from among the new men who had risen to eminence through their own ability. This was in contrast to the earlier council, which had included almost all the leading nobles, and had suffered from constant bickering between the leading factions. The men who now formed the Privy Council were far removed from the ignorant, self-seeking and often incompetent Lords who were responsible for governing the country before the arrival of the Tudors. The new able and dedicated servants of the Crown were to turn England into a world power, while at home they governed the land through the justices, most of whom were of similar social standing to themselves. The members of the Privy Council themselves were placed on the commissions of the peace throughout the country, thus enabling them to keep in close personal touch with local affairs and also strengthening the authority of all the justices in the eyes of the rest of the population."[92]

One way or another, either through the executive (Privy Council), or the parliament, it was justices of the peace who determined what the law should be, and it was they who enforced it through their sessions.

As for the 3rd arm of government, the situation was not quite so clear-cut. Justices of the peace had civil jurisdiction only in the limited sense that they conducted all the business that would today be handled by local government: roads and bridges, etc. They were also in control of the constabulary, and by the end of the Tudor era, they were responsible under the Lord Lieutenant for the raising and training of the militia in times of crisis. But they did not handle private disputes of the *Smith v. Jones* variety. That was left to the common law courts. Small claims under £10 began to be dealt with by Courts of Request in the 16th century, but they were not run by justices of the peace.

As far as the criminal law was concerned, by the time of the Tudors, there were four different court systems dealing with crime. The foremost in the hierarchy was the King's Bench and its travelling arm, the Assizes courts. The King retained the right to hear prosecutions outside the normal court systems, and this was done through a court that came to be called the Star Chamber, an offshoot of the Privy Council. Previously, this court had been an offshoot of the King's Bench, but under Henry VIII and Cardinal Wolsey, became a branch of the Privy Council, with Wolsey presiding. HThis court dealt with civil and criminal matters, but without a jury. It was unable to impose the death penalty, and used imprisonment and torture in lieu thereof. It was used by Wolsey to bring the

---

[92] Skyrme op cit volume 1 p. 110.

nobility to heel, and to discipline the justices of the peace. It is not necessary to go into the history of this court in any detail, and in any event, it was abolished by act of parliament in 1641.[93] During its time, however it did deal with evolving statutory offences such as perjury, conspiracy and attempt. It summoned and punished members of the nobility who were untouchable by the other court systems because of jury rigging – the Star Chamber was immune from juries. The third court system was the Ecclesiastical Courts, dealing with ecclesiastical matters and naughty priests. The fourth was the system run by justices of the peace. Although subordinate to both the Star Chamber and the King's Bench, these courts handled by far the greater bulk of the criminal cases, including felonies.

Appeals, Instruction and Discipline

The Star Chamber and the King's Bench both exercised discipline against justices of the peace, gave them instructions and sometimes reviewed justices' decisions. There was no appeal from decisions of justices sitting out of sessions until 1597.[94] That was an appeal to Quarter sessions. There was no appeal, as we know appeals today, from decisions at Quarter Sessions or other sessions, nor from the Assize courts, until 1907. The King's Bench could carry out reviews of justices' decisions by way of the prerogative writs of certiorari, prohibition and mandamus. These however were ferociously expensive and cumbersome and beyond the means of the great mass of the English population. For perhaps two centuries, until the Stuarts, justices of the peace were instructed in their duties by either the Chief Justice of the King's Bench, through the Assizes Courts, or the Star Chamber, by letter. Sometimes the justices were admonished directly by letter from the sovereign.

The chief justice of the King's Bench gave the instructions to the Assizes judges about to set off on their twice yearly visit. On the first day of each court sitting in a particular county, each of the justices of the peace for that county was expected to attend, when the Assize judge would pass on those instructions.

These instructions might be an admonishment for not doing their job properly, or advice as to new laws. For example, during times of food shortage, justices might be instructed to intercept a ship of grain, appropriate part of its cargo and distribute it at a reasonable price amongst the local inhabitants.[95] The Nottinghamshire justices were instructed to send two justices to London for a Royal bollocking for failure to raise troops for service in Ireland.[96] Justices of Essex were instructed to examine (probably on the rack), the parson at Haydon, who was supposed to have expressed sympathy with the Jesuits. All justices in each county were instructed to punish recusants in 1582.[97]

93	16 Car. I, c. 10.
94	By 39 Eliz., c. 3, s. 6.
95	Acts of the Privy Council, 1596-1597, 59-60.
96	APC ibid, pp. 6,7.
97	APC 1581, p. 451.

From time to time, justices were instructed by the Star Chamber/Privy Council to take steps to minimise an outbreak of the plague, to secure the national defence, to deal firmly with riots, sedition and that overriding and perpetual menace to the nation, the poor, in the shape of vagabonds. Sometimes these missives to the justices chided them for an excess of zeal and sometimes for not exercising more of that commodity. A letter of general admonition was sent to all justices direct from Henry VIII in 1539. After a broadside about their slackness, he specifically complained that they were not punishing Catholics enough, that they were spreading rumours about him and the state of the nation, that vagabonds were getting off too lightly and that the justices were not suppressing games sufficiently.

The Assizes only visited each county twice each year, and for a limited time. The magistrates in the various counties were sitting more or less continuously in Quarter, General, Special or Petty Sessions, and consequently dealt with the vast bulk of crime in England, including felonies attracting the death penalty, as well as less serious offences.

Did the justices always obey these instructions, and if not, why persist with justices?

Mostly, they did, but not always. They did not enforce the laws against enclosure for the simple reason that they were the ones enclosing, making profits, expanding or creating their country estates. Nor were the justices successful in enforcing the new laws against livery and maintenance.[98] Later, many justices, particularly in the north of England, were reluctant to enforce laws from Henry VIII's time against Catholicism, because they were still Catholics themselves, or friends with those who were. However, when individual justices were thought not to be doing their duty, their commissions were simply not renewed when they expired each year. Justices were on a yearly term, which had to be renewed if they were to remain justices. By and large, they were retained in office because they satisfied the needs of that part of the nation that consisted of the nobility and the gentry.

Moir says:

> "...the Queen had issued injunctions commanding uniformity in religion and that it was incumbent upon justices to see that they were obeyed.
>
> But what did all this amount to? Statutes, orders, exhortations, threats – if the counties were so disposed they were faithful and willing servants of the Crown; if they disagreed with the dictates of Westminster they resisted them or, equally effectively, neglected them. The early Tudor policy against enclosure and eviction touched the pride and the pockets of the landowners rather too closely, and practice fell far short of the fine parade of principles of social justice inscribed upon the statute book. The phrases

---

[98]   See p. 45.

concerning uniformity and supremacy sound magnificent, but in a predominantly Roman Catholic county such as Lancashire sympathetic magistrates sheltered their neighbours and allowed them to practice their Popish worship comparatively unmolested. In conception the Elizabethan Poor Law presents an impressive code of social welfare; in practice it was waived whenever local magistrates found its claims too demanding."[99]

From the 16th century onwards, textbooks on the duties of justices began to appear, books by Anonymous, Lambard, Fitzherbert, Dalton, Bohun, Shephard, Burn and others. One of the sources of justices' instructions and discipline disappeared with the abolition of the Court of Star Chamber in 1641. In 1631, Charles I issued his *Book of Orders* for justices, giving them detailed instructions on their duties. Not long after, the country descended into chaos and then the civil war broke out in 1642 (until 1653). Whether it was the plethora of instructions by way of texts and the King's instructions, or the chaos that followed the *Book of Orders*, instructions and supervision from the Assizes courts ceased and were never taken up again. Review of decisions by prerogative writ remained an option, but it was still beyond the means of the ordinary citizen to pursue.

The result was that the justices of the peace went on their merry, unsupervised way, with results examined in later chapters. Text books could never replace a good public bollocking backed by the authority of the King or Queen.[100]

Summary to the end of the Reign of Henry VII

In short, whether through their judicial, executive or legislative powers, by the time of the Tudors, justices of the peace ruled England.

The justices kept the lid on the poor in the counties, and sometimes tried, without a great deal of success, to restrain the excesses of the nobility and the gentry, and to carry out the numerous tasks foisted upon them by themselves by way of acts of parliament and their commissions.

It would be wrong to assert that Henry VII's reign (1485-1509) was entirely peaceful – it was not. But uprisings and invasions were less frequent and less intense than during the previous 100 years, and were easily dealt with.

This was a country locked in private feuds rather than rebellion against the government.[101] Nobility vs nobility. Nobility vs gentry. Gentry vs gentry. These feuds came about from centuries of land forfeited and redistributed, particularly the land redistributed during the War of the Roses and the early part of Henry VII's reign. The losers or their descendants wanted their land back or alternatively, retribution for their loss. The feuds lasted beyond the Tudor era and well into the Stuart era and may well have been partly responsible for the civil war of 1642-1649. These feuds were conducted by the very people who were

---

[99] *The Justices of the Peace* Penguin, at p.50.
[100] For example, Henry VIII's admonitions, referred to at p. 51.
[101] Moir *The Justice of the Peace* pp. 26-28.

charged with the maintenance of law and order. The justices of the peace were representative of these groups. Far from stopping or attempting to stop these riotous conditions, they were responsible for many of them and participated freely. A motive for becoming a magistrate was to gain advantage over a rival. The magistracy was more than a mere status symbol to flaunt at a rival, it was often used to humiliate the rival with criminal charges against the rival direct, or his servants.

There were riots and crime by the poor and homeless, but they at least had the excuse they were hungry, desperate, cold and disorganised. They were easily beaten into submission. It was far more difficult for the justices to instil any sense of order into their own ranks. But at least there were neither invasions nor insurrections.

Henry VII was able to concentrate on enforcing taxes and attempting to reinforce the rule of law. He strengthened his administration and his wife produced heirs.

> "He bequeathed to his son something quite new in English History: a safe throne, a full treasury, a solvent government, a prosperous land, and a united kingdom. Only one vital element of the past remained untouched, the independent Catholic Church, and it was left to the second Tudor to destroy this remaining vestige of medievalism."[102]

The land may have been prosperous, but two-thirds of its inhabitants remained poor.

The great unpaid?

One of the myths about justices of the peace is that they volunteered their services out of some form of altruism, and were unpaid. They often referred to themselves as 'the great unpaid.' Skyrme, for example, says:[103]

> "A notable feature of the system was that it was based upon the voluntary, part-time, unpaid services of the landed gentry..."

Moir says:[104]

> "There is something extraordinary about an office held by unpaid amateurs..."

As Ita Buttrose[105] might say: 'Horth thhit!' It might be notable and extraordinary if justices were in fact unpaid, but the fact is they *were* paid, and paid quite well for their services.

In 1388, the parliament, dominated by justices, passed a law providing that they be paid 4 shillings per day for each day of each session.[106] They were paid for

---

[102] *Encyclopaedia Britannica*, 15th edition, volume 29, page 50.
[103] At p. Xx of his introduction to volume 1 of his *History of Justices of the Peace*.
[104] Op cit at p. 9.
[105] A well known publisher of Australian women's' magazines. She had a lisp.

three days' attendance provided they showed up for the first day, and it didn't matter if they were absent for the 2nd and 3rd days. The amount was increased to 5 shillings each day for duties in connection with the Artificers, Labourers, Servants of Husbandry and Apprentices Act.[107] They were paid 2s 6d per each enrolment of land, and one shilling for each recognisance taken, for example, from an innkeeper. To get this in perspective: 4 shillings was 16 times the daily wage fixed for an agricultural labourer. There was a period of time when magistrates were the only authorised marriage celebrants in England (during the Interregnum 1649-1660), and they pocketed the fees for this duty. They were entitled to pocket a portion of the value of goods confiscated to pay for fines. Many acts gave them a percentage of fines levied for various offences. Justices of the Peace were for many centuries the representatives of the landed gentry, and ensured that only laws that suited the financial ends of the gentry were passed through parliament, for example, the Corn Laws of 1815. Then there were the bribes... There was some significant money to be made out of the office.

It has been suggested that that sum was pooled at sessions and used for conviviality purposes. Indeed, Richard Burn writing in 1776 speaks of sessions where the justices seemed to have arrived at the Tavern first, for they never reached the court at all.[108] The practice of heavy dining and liquid lunches remained a feature of justices' gatherings for centuries. It probably still is. But the wining and dining were not paid for out of the 4s per day, but out of sessions' funds, which were supposed to be earmarked for the poor, or other public purposes.[109]

Edmund Bohun said:

> "In 1693 there was a complaint to the Privy Council of justices who came and take the King's wages and before half the business is done betake themselves to a tavern."[110]

Henry VIII (1509-1547)

Henry VIII's reign was dominated by his three main characteristics: his greed, his ambition and his ruthlessness. These were all apparent in his extra-marital bonking, his property gathering and spending, his attempts to conquer France and his killings.[111] The overthrow of the Catholic Church was a result of his concern to boot home a legitimate male heir. Many of his killings were directed at any who opposed his overthrow of the church; many were aimed at those who thought Henry's reforms did not go far enough; most were directed at vagrants. The overthrow of the Pope led to the seizure of monasteries and convents, their resale for profit, and the resistance of people who wished to adhere to the Catholic faith.

---

[106] 12 Rich. II, c. 12.
[107] 5 Eliz, c.4
[108] Burn: *Justices of the Peace and Ecclesiastical Law.*
[109] Skyrme op cit Volume 2, p. 42, note 10.
[110] *The Justice of the Peace: His Calling and Qualifications.*
[111] There were 72,000 executions during Henry's reign, an average of 5 per day.

These things are relevant to the story of the gentry, the justices, and the poor of England. The King's greed, ambition and ruthlessness are relevant to this story, as they set the background to the work of the magistrates during this period, and for centuries to come.

Henry's father had left England with a full treasury and a solvent government. Henry set about reversing this situation with his extravagance, greed and ambition.

He married Catherine of Aragon, the widow of his deceased brother, about the time of his ascension to the throne in 1509, but he continued bonking others. He began with one of Catherine's ladies in waiting, Anne Stafford. "Other royal liaisons may have gone unrecorded".[112] The wife of the court goldsmith, Mistress Amadas claimed Henry was bonking her.[113] A five year affair with Bessie Blount began in 1512. Henry Fitzroy was the product of that union. Henry VIII began bonking Mary Boleyn in 1520. That relationship continued until Henry's eyeball fell on her sister Anne in 1525. She became pregnant in 1532. Henry was unfaithful to Anne, and presumably to his wife Catherine, during that pregnancy, although "the identity of that woman is not known."[114] In 1536, while still married to Anne Boleyn, he began bonking her successor, Jane Seymour. In fact, he married Jane Seymour the week after Anne's head was removed from her shoulders.

It is interesting to compare Henry's extra-marital behaviour with his argument to Catherine of Aragon, trying to get her consent to a divorce on the ground that "they had been living in mortal sin all the years they had been together."[115] Henry's argument was based upon an obscure passage from Leviticus to the effect that it was wrong to bonk your brother's wife, and overlooks Deuteronomy, which makes it compulsory to bonk your brother's widow.[116] (Henry was not bonking his brother's wife; he was bonking his brother's widow). Apparently it was perfectly in order for Henry to bonk his way through the opposite gender of England, but both Anne Boleyn and Katherine Howard (wife number 4) were beheaded on allegations of reciprocal behaviour. Truly, the King could do no wrong.

Henry soon bankrupted England. He declared war on France in 1513 for no apparent reason other than to feed his overwhelming ego. His extravagant invasion of France ended in ignominious withdrawal. 'The cost of the brief war was enormous, comprising most of the treasure that Henry VII had bequeathed to his son."[117]

112	Acroyd op cit p. 5.
113	Ibid p. 6.
114	Ackroyd op cit p.77.
115	Ackroyd op cit p.43.
116	Deuteronomy, 25, v.2-5
117	Ackroyd op cit p. 12.

Henry's failed sojourn in France and consequent emptying of the treasury coincided with a run of bad harvests in England. Henry was obliged to have his government pass an Act of parliament imposing a tax on every adult male in England.

It was in the spring of 1516 that Henry's chancellor, Cardinal Wolsey, took over the Star Chamber. Wolsey was not a lawyer. He was the Archbishop of York. He used the Star Chamber ruthlessly to bring the nobility and gentry of England to heel, and to suppress disorder and riots. He thus, to an extent, undermined the work of the justices of the peace, which in any event was fairly ineffectual to that point. Indeed, he also used the Star Chamber to target non-performing or mal-performing magistrates. He ordered them to do their duty. Wolsey and the Star Chamber were generally successful in breaking the iron grip of the nobility upon the country. His main aim was to reduce the numbers of fighting retainers. From the point of view of the Crown, fighting retainers of the nobility were not as essential as they were in medieval times. There was no standing army. Necessary wars were to a large extent fought by mercenaries. Certainly, a ruthless Star Chamber under a determined and competent Wolsey was in a far better position than fragmented justices of the peace to carry out the law passed under Henry VII[118] against livery and maintenance. Wolsey was not bound by the same history of feudal obligations that the justices felt to the Lords, and the Star Chamber had no jury that could be suborned or intimidated. The Star Chamber was not wholly successful in stamping out the fighting retainers of the nobility, but it certainly lessened the threat.

In 1521, the Pope conferred the title of 'Defender of the Faith' on Henry after the publication of his treatise 'In Defence of the Seven Sacraments'. The treatise was dedicated to the Pope and acknowledged that the Pope was the supreme head of the Church. A few years later, when Henry coveted Anne Boleyn as a potential breeder for the Tudor dynasty, and the Pope refused to annul Henry's marriage to Catherine of Aragon, Henry declared that he, and not the Pope, was the supreme head of the church in England. This was in 1530. In 1532, Henry impregnated Anne Boleyn and hectored a convocation of clergy to pass a resolution that his marriage to Catherine of Aragon had been invalid. Henry married Anne in January 1533 and the then Archbishop of Canterbury, Thomas Cranmer, issued a decree that Henry's marriage to Anne Boleyn was lawful. The final break from the Catholic Church came in 1534 with the Act of Supremacy whereby parliament agreed that Henry was the head of the church in England.

The break from the Catholic Church left the bulk of the population in a dilemma. Did they remain faithful to the Catholic Church, or did they die? It was very dangerous to give voice to any protest, or to refuse to tag along with Henry's divorce from the church. Henry began his intimidation of the clergy in 1530. Fourteen senior clergy, including 8 bishops and 3 abbots were accused of colluding with Wolsey to block the annulment by the Pope of Henry's marriage to Catherine. Then an information was lodged against <u>all</u> the clergy of England,

---

[118] 4 Hen. VII, c. 12.

accusing them of the offence of praemunire, that is, colluding with a foreign power; the Pope.[119] Henry let it be known that the transgression would be overlooked if (a) they paid him £100,000 and (b) if they acknowledged him and not the Pope as head of the church in England. Most of the clergy capitulated. Those who did not were put to death.

The would-be reformers too had to pull in their collective heads. If they looked to Henry for doctrinal reform, they looked to the wrong person. In 1539, he more or less forced parliament to endorse his 'six articles of faith', the first of which provided the death penalty by fire for anyone who denied the doctrine of transubstantiation (the belief that the communion bread and wine changed substance during the mass into the actual body and blood of Christ).[120]

The justices of the peace of England were not immune from this dilemma. By a series of acts of parliament,[121] they were required to enforce the new regime. Some refused and were put to death. Most of them actively supported Henry. It's amazing how persuasive a death threat can be. But they had other reasons to support Henry. They were able to purchase cheap land confiscated from the monasteries and convents of England.[122]

In 1534, local justices of the peace were tasked with watching bishops to see if they "do truly, sincerely and without all manner of cloak, colour or dissimulation execute and accomplish our will and commandment."[123] "At the same time, the King and Cromwell were reforming local government by placing their trusted men in the provincial councils."[124]

Rebellions against the break from the Catholic Church were put down by troops assembled by justices of the peace.

> "Yet there was no way of mitigating the wrath of the King. He ordered the Duke of Norfolk to 'cause such dreadful execution to be done upon a good number of every town, village and hamlet... as may be a fearsome spectacle to all others hereafter that would practice in any like matter, which we require you to do, without any pity or respect."[125]

He did.

---

[119] Ackroyd op cit pp. 62, 63.
[120] Ackroyd op cit pp. 141-143.
[121] 27 Hen. VIII, c. 7; 28 Hen. VIII, c.10; 31 Hen. VIII, c. 14; 32 Hen. VIII, c.7.
[122] See the section headed 'Henry's seizures of monasteries etc' at page 66.
[123] Ackroyd op cit, p.89.
[124] ibid
[125] Ackroyd op cit p. 115.

Henry VIII was known as 'the great killer', and it is said that 72,000 people were executed during his reign, an average of 5 per day.[126] **The strata of society in the Tudor Era: Class division**

Class division was rigorously enforced. While there was some intermarrying between the nobility and the gentry, any such liaison between those two classes and 'the lower classes' was simply not on. There were consequences for belonging to the lower strata and here are one or two examples. Travel was forbidden to anyone not a member of the nobility or gentry, unless you had a specific licence from a justice of the peace.[127] An act of parliament of the same year[128] made it a criminal offence to possess or use a crossbow unless defending your home, or unless you were a Lord or person owning at least 200 marks freehold. The bible could be read by the nobility and the gentry, but no women, artificers, apprentices, journeymen, serving men under the degree of yeomen, nor husbandmen nor labourers might read it.[129]

The Nobility

- King or Queen, Prince, Princess, in that order.
- Anyone whose first name was 'Lord', in order of precedence, as follows: Duke, a title first created under Edward III; Marquis (1st appointed 1551 during the reign of Edward VI); Earl, Viscount (1st appointed 1550, under Edward VI) and Baron.
- Ecclesiastical nobility: Cardinal (extinguished along with the last holder in England of that title, Cardinal Pole in 1558), Archbishop, Bishop.

The gentry

The gentry were a loose conglomerate of wealthy land owners, next in rank behind the nobility, often with the first name of 'Sir'.

> "They were technically those large landowners to whom the College of Arms had granted the right of gentility-ie the right to bear a coat of arms."[130]

Justices of the peace were exclusively appointed from the nobility or the gentry. Later, they came to be appointed from the ranks of wealthy industrialists or miners, but usually after they acquired country estates and had become recognised as gentry. Also, many town-dwelling, well off men were appointed as justices to dispense justice in the bigger cities, but often, although they lived mostly in the cities, they too had country estates and were sometimes recognised as gentry. Conversely, many of the country squires had a house in London, in

---

[126] William Eden's *Principles of Penal Law*, pp. 177,178; William Harrison's *Description of Britain* (1577).
[127] Vagrants Act, 1503, 19 Hen. VII, c. 12.
[128] 19 Hen VII c. 4.
[129] Ackroyd op cit 159.
[130] *Encyclopaedia Britannica* op cit Volume 29 p. 57.

addition to their country estate. They chose to live in the country most of the year, but moved to London for 'the season', (spring, summer). This often caused problems in getting a quorum for sessions in their home county at that time of the year. Many edicts were issued over the years by the Privy Council urging these temporary town dwellers to get back to their counties and do their duties as justices.

At the end of Elizabeth's reign, society consisted of two predominate classes: the rich and the poor. There was the beginning of a middle class: in the towns, the shopkeepers and tradesmen; in the country, the yeomen. The poor made up about two thirds of the population. The rich had many sub groups: the nobility, the Dukes, Barons and Earls, who reached the top stratum simply by the act of being born. There were the landed gentry from whose numbers the justices of the peace were usually drawn. These were the descendants of those who had clawed their way to land ownership by various means. Usually, the gentry did not earn their land or money; they inherited it. The difference between the gentry and yeomen seems to be that the latter generally worked the land themselves, whereas the gentry got someone else to work it for them. Then there were the successful commercial people; the financiers, manufacturers, merchants, shopkeepers, tradesmen and artisans most of whom lived in the towns. By Tudor times the make-up of these various strata of 'high society' could change, and often did. Many of the merchants acquired country estates. Their daughters married into the gentry and indeed, the nobility. Younger sons of the gentry usually wound up with their collars on back to front (clergy), or joined the army or the navy as junior officers, but sometimes they resorted to trade and commerce, or overseas adventure.

A member of the gentry, a 'gentleman' or 'Squire' had an income of a minimum of £300 per annum.[131]

Yeomen

Yeoman was a description given to small landholders who worked their land themselves with help from their families and paid seasonal agricultural labour.

Middle class

There was as yet only the beginning of a discernible middle class. Patrick Dillon, speaking of the emerging middle class of the early 18th century, estimated their earnings at between £40-50 per annum.[132]

The poor

'The poor' was one of the politer titles given by the nobility and the gentry to the majority of the population. It is important to understand the way in which the nobility and the gentry regarded the poor. The politer terms were 'the poor' and

---

[131] Patrick Dillon, 'The Much Lamented Death of Madam Geneva', Review, 2002, introductory author's note.
[132] ibid

'the ordinary people' (from Daniel Defoe, author of *Robinson Crusoe*). Less polite terms were:

- 'The common people'[133]
- 'The lower populace'[134]
- 'Maidservants and the lower class of women'[135]
- 'Scandalous wretches.'[136]
- 'The poorer sort of people.'[137]
- 'Loose, idle people.'[138]
- 'The inferior sort of people.'[139]
- 'The lower, poorer sort of people.'[140]
- 'Our lower class of people.'[141]
- 'Persons in low life.'[142]
- 'These lower sorts.'[143]
- 'The common people.'[144]
- 'The mob.'[145]

---

[133] Charles Davenant in 'Essay on ways and means of supplying the war' p. 133; Henry Fielding, author of *Tom Jones*, justice of the peace, and an early stipendiary magistrate. The Rev. Zouch, chairman of the West Riding (Yorkshire Bench) said: 'It is found by long experience that when the common people are drawn together upon any public occasion, a variety of mischiefs are certain to occur.' (Webbs': *Parish and the County*, p.357).

[134] Saucerre, *A Foreign View of England*.

[135] Robert Campbell in *The London Tradesman*.

[136] *The Tavern Scuffle* 1726.

[137] Sir John Gonson, long-time chairman of the Middlesex and Westminster benches of magistrates, a founding member of the Society for the Reformation of Manners, scourge of prostitutes and gin. London Metropolitan Archives, Middlesex Orders Book, MJ/OC 1 fol.s. 126-128. See also pages 94, 121.

[138] Gonson, ibid.

[139] A Middlesex magistrate, MLA, Middlesex Sessions papers, 1721, May 2.

[140] Sir Daniel Dolins, chair of Middlesex Quarter Sessions, 10/ 1725 in 'Two charges of Sir Daniel Dolins.' (Dolins was also a member of the Manners society.)

[141] Daniel Defoe in 'Augusta Triumphans'; *London Daily Post*, 22/10/1736 and 2/11/1736.

[142] Report of Middlesex magistrates, led by Thomas Lane, LMA, Middlesex order book, MJ/OC 4 fols. 54-57.

[143] By none other than the Prime Minister, Sir Robert Walpole, in a letter to his brother, Horace Walpole in 1736.

[144] Walpole, again.

- 'Common townsman.'[146]
- 'Great number of idle and disorderly people.'[147]
- Swinish multitude[148]

According to Moir, during the reign of Elizabeth,

> "... 'the poor' was the collective title by which the lower orders of society were known. These formed 3.3 million out of a total population of 5.5 million. They were the underprivileged, the common, the anonymous; they ranged from small shopkeepers, tradesmen and artisans through mechanics, labourers and cottagers to paupers, vagrants, thieves and beggars. They were neither all destitute, nor destitute all the time, but a large proportion was potentially destitute, and over them hung the threat of poverty, unemployment and starvation, either when times were bad or as they grew old and could no longer support themselves. To keep alive they must either turn to crime, depend upon charity – or receive the support of the state."[149]

Unlike the nobility and the gentry, the poor were unable to meet together in order to confer and put forward their needs and aspirations. The nobility met regularly in the House of Lords. The gentry's representatives met in the House of Commons, and also through the justices of the peace, met regularly at sessions, and sessions' dinners. If the poor attempted to meet together in like manner, the meeting was almost invariably declared a riot by a justice of the peace, acting under the terms of the Riot Act, first enacted in 1550.[150] The poor had no means to draw attention to their grievances.

It was during the Tudor era that the poor began to occupy much of the time of the justices of the peace. The wrath of the justices was particularly aimed at that branch of the poor that was mobile: the vagrants.

A hard-working poor man earned £10-15 per annum.[151] Most of the farm labourers and women earned far less than this.

Vagrancy and the Poor Laws

---

[145] Lord Egmont's diary; Sir Stephen Hales, from the diaries of Thomas Wilson 1/11/1736; Dudley Bradstreet in 'The life and uncommon adventures of DB.' p.78; Henry Fielding in *Covent Garden Journal*, 20/6/1752.

[146] Attributed to one Uffenbach in Porter's *English Society in the 18th century revisited*, p. 254. The context is Uffenbach's comment on hearing that a 'common townsman' had dared to stand for parliament in opposition to a member of the nobility!

[147] *London Daily Post*, 2/11/1736.

[148] Edmund Burke, cited in Schama: *A History of Britain*, 1776-2000: 'The Fate of Empire.'

[149] Moir *The Justice of the Peace*, Penguin, p. 59.

[150] 3 and 4 Edw. VI, c. 5, see pp.79-80.

[151] Dillon, ibid.

Vagrancy itself progressed through its own name-calling. One began as 'idle and disorderly', moved on to being a 'rogue and vagabond', and if you were sufficiently dedicated to the cause of vagrancy, you might end up an 'incorrigible rogue', often with fatal consequences.

Vagrancy defies a precise definition. The word has connotations of a wanderer, a person who will not settle in one place and who has no apparent means of support. The authorities at the time justified their treatment of such people by saying they must be stealing in order to survive, and there is some truth in that suggestion, but it does not explain the whole story.

The vagrants who filled the institutions were variously described. The Statute against Vagrancy 1572 defined them thus:

> "The able bodied labourer who refused to work, workmen on strike, the poor scholar at university (unless he be fully licensed), the shipwrecked mariner, fortune tellers and collectors of subscriptions."

Blackstone in his commentaries described them thus:

> "Such as wake on the night and sleep on the day, and no man wot from whence they come, or whither they go."

The *Encyclopaedia Britannica*[152] makes it plain that there is no fixed definition of vagrant, and it is rather an elastic concept. In its purest form, a vagrant is a person of no established home (no 'settlement', to use 18th century English), who drifts from place to place without visible or lawful means of support. Traditionally a vagrant was thought to be one who was able to work but preferred not to work. This, however, could not be used as the definition of a vagrant, since it is a description that fitted the majority of the nobility and gentry and the justices of the peace of England. None of them worked. Others 'did' for them.

The concept of a vagrant was more elastic than someone with no fixed place of abode: the *Encyclopaedia Britannica* points out that it often applied to a person who had a fixed habitation, but pursued a calling condemned by the law as immoral, such as prostitution and gambling. Again, since gaming was an activity much favoured by the idle rich, and the said idle rich were the main source of income for the prostitutes, this definition is unsuitable and smacks of hypocrisy.

The EB then suggests that vagrancy is a "tool for police and prosecutors to proscribe a wide range of behaviour", and gives examples of "political demonstrations, the obstruction of streets and walks, riotous activities and loitering". Since from time to time, the gentry have indulged in all of these activities, this definition will not do either. The main enclosers, hence obstructers, of land in England were the gentry.[153] It was often the magistrates who turned otherwise peaceful demonstrations into riots by unnecessarily sending in the constables or military to break up the demonstrations – the magistrates ran the

---

[152] 15th edition, volume 12, p.231.
[153] See next heading 'Enclosures and Vagrants.'

country and wanted it kept the way it was. Hazeltine refers to the Cornish justice of the peace from 1451, who doubled up as a pirate when not sitting on the bench: "It must not be thought that he was the only man who represented both law and lawlessness."[154]

In summary, the following have all come under the vagrancy or poor laws: the underprivileged, the common, the anonymous, small shopkeepers, tradesmen and artisans, mechanics, labourers, cottagers, paupers, vagrants, thieves, beggars, the lame, the blind, the infirm, the sick, the mentally ill, the brain damaged, the elderly, the unemployed, the idle, prostitutes, bowlers, tennis players, drinkers, gamblers, rogues, vagabonds (for example, Gypsies and tinkers), travelling salesmen, striking workers, political demonstrators, poor scholars at universities (unless licensed), shipwrecked mariners, fortune tellers, collectors of subscriptions, insomniacs, strangers, orphans, neglected children, itinerant preachers, obstructers of streets and walkways, robbers, rioters, loiterers, disorderly persons, the desperate, and organisers of fairs. The nobility and gentry were apparently exempt from these laws.

In practice, vagrants were anyone the justices said were vagrants. It didn't pay to be a stranger or to look different.

Persecution of vagrants was later wrapped in a package which pretended to help 'the poor.' Until Tudor times, it had been left to parishes of churches to do what they could to help the poor within their parish, on a voluntary basis. An act of parliament placed the onus upon the parishes of helping the poor, but also upon a voluntary basis.[155]

Parliament then made it obligatory on each parish to strike a poor rate and assist the poor by providing accommodation and weekly "reliefe and pencion."[156] This was to be done by overseers of the poor who were appointed by the justices of the peace and worked under their supervision.[157]

In fact, the persecution of vagrants began long before the pretence of aiding the poor. There was the establishment of debtors' prisons under Edward I; the original Justices of the Peace Act of 1361, warning justices about vagabonds and requiring them to be kept in custody until they found sureties; the petition against vagrants, rogues and beggars of 1376; the statute of 1388 12 Rich. II, c.3, requiring any person found outside his territory to be put in the stocks; a statute forbidding the children of landless labourers from being put into an apprenticeship (1406, 7 Henry IV, c. 17), to ensure a cheap supply of labour for the gentry;[158] a statute of 1389, 12 Rich II, c. 6, forbidding the poor from playing such idle games as tennis, football, quoits and dice, a breach attracting a sentence

---

[154] In the general preface to Dowdell's book: *A Hundred Years of Quarter Sessions, 1660-1760*
[155] 27 Hen. VIII, c. 25.
[156] 1572, 14 Eliz. c.5
[157] This theme is taken up in the notes on the reign of Edward VI, at pp. 72-73.
[158] Introduction pp. xiv, xv, and xxi to Judge Parry's *Vagabonds All* (Cassel and Co).

of 6 months' imprisonment. Then there was the Vagrants Act of 1503, 19 Hen. VII, c. 12 requiring harsh treatment of vagabonds (whipping and stocks) and making it an offence for anyone to house them; the Vagrancy Act of 1530, 22 Hen VIII, requiring vagrants and beggars to be whipped and forcibly sent back to their place of origin. The whipping consisted of being publicly whipped through the streets on market days, the severity of the whipping (i.e. the number of lashes) depending upon the seriousness of the vagrancy and/or begging. For a second breach of this act, the offender's right ear was to be cut off, and he was to be placed in the stocks. Third offence: other ear and pillory. Under 1 Edw. VI, c. 3, any labourer or apprentice who left his master was, on apprehension, brought before two justices, branded on the cheek with the letter 'v', and adjudged to be a slave to his master for two years. A second absconding earned a branding with the letter 's', signifying he was thereafter a slave to his master for life. By statutes of 1550, 1554 and 1563, gypsies were to be put to death, and this death penalty was not removed until 1820 (1 Geo. 4, c.116).

The numbers of vagrants increased significantly under Henry VIII by virtue of two main factors: more enclosures of land (see next paragraph) and Henry's seizures of the monasteries and convents (see pp. 66-68). Before then, vagrants came from three main causes: gypsies or people who simply liked to wander; travelling salesmen operating in competition with merchants of fixed abode; and those rendered homeless by enclosures, looking for food and shelter.

Enclosures and Vagrants

Enclosure of land has been briefly touched upon at pages 18-19 and 39-40, but since it is a key to vagrancy and therefore the source of much of the attention of justices of the peace, it needs some elaboration. There was usually only one reason for the enclosure of land before the Agricultural Revolution of the 18th century, and that was to convert it from crop-growing to sheep-raising, and the most usual result was that the tenant farmers were ejected and became vagrants. Enclosure meant fencing or hedging property that had previously been available for others to use, such as commons, so that the encloser could use the land for his own purposes to the exclusion of those others.

Enclosures began some time after the Black Death (1348), when agricultural labour was in short supply, and advances in wool processing suggested a solution for untilled land in England. Instead of labour-intensive crop-raising, sheep-raising became more profitable and far less labour intensive (1 shepherd for 20 agricultural labourers). Landlords simply took over abandoned lands, enclosed them with hedges and employed shepherds to rear sheep. Initially this had little effect on the agricultural labourer, since the sheep-raising took place on land abandoned following the decline in population caused by the Black Death.

When, however, all the abandoned land was re-occupied and enclosed, and it had become apparent that sheep-rearing was profitable, the Lords and gentry looked for other land to use for the same purpose.

The first method of enclosure was the simplest: brute force. Landlords simply seized and enclosed for their own use lands that had previously been village common lands. Those lands had been previously used by all the villagers for their own crops and stock. A variation on this theme was that the landlords did not renew arrangements previously in place for generations whereby land had been let to particular tenant families, and enclosed the land to raise sheep.

There was very little that the dispossessed could do. It was not much use appealing to your local manor court; that court was presided over by the landlord who had just evicted you. Quarter Sessions could have taken action to restore the seized land to the villagers, using laws against enclosure enacted during the time of Henry VII[159] but the justices often refused to do this, because they, or their fellow justices were the ones profiting from this practice. The writ of Novel Disseisen could have been employed, but that involved employing London lawyers and a trip to the Royal Courts of justice in London. This would have been prohibitively expensive for a villein or subsistence land-holder. Another possibility was a complaint to a local justice of the peace and, if he found a case to answer, a reference would follow to Quarter Sessions. Since the complaint was made about the actions of the local nobility or gentry, it would be unlikely to strike a responsive chord within the local justices of the peace. This type of enclosure equated might with right and generally stuck.

In Bland, Brown and Tawney's colourful work, *English Economic History* (Bell, 1914), the authors explain a series of documents on rural conditions thus:

> "But their peculiar interest consists in the light they throw on the grievances of the peasants. They suffer from enclosing, from excessive fines and from rack renting. They are gravely prejudiced by the land speculation following the dissolution of the monasteries. They are too poor and too easily intimidated to get redress even when they have a good case. The justices who ought to administer the Acts against depopulation depopulate themselves".

The upshot was that the villages emptied of all bar a few of the remaining landholders, some shepherds and perhaps an agricultural labourer or two. Those ejected took on a new title: vagrant. Their very act of moving away from the village became a criminal offence under the Justices of the Peace Act of 1361, as well as some earlier and later legislation.

Another legal, if more surreptitious, form of enclosure was labelled 'engrossing.' Engrossing means cornering the market or getting a monopoly, and usually applies to the acquisition of goods, but can and did apply to land as well. What happened was that a wealthy landowner acquired more and more land, usually by purchase or inheritance, until he had a monopoly on all or most of the surrounding arable land. As he went about the acquisitions, there was usually an understanding that he would continue to employ local agricultural labourers in crop raising. Then the day came when the landowner switched from growing crops, enclosed the land with hedges to keep others out, and took up grazing

---

[159] 4 Hen. VII, c.16.

sheep. The agricultural labourers became vagrants. It is true that the encloser employed shepherds to do the actual work, but it is estimated that one shepherd took the place of 20 agricultural labourers.[160]

"The sheep were now eating the people, rather than the reverse."[161]

Not all land in England was seized by the rapacious nobility and gentry for sheep-raising. England still needed crops: wheat for bread, barley for beer and vegetables for eating and feeding livestock. But so much was seized as to empty many villages and create a greater class of poor and many more vagrants. There was less land available for crops, leading to scarcity and galloping inflation. Henry VII had laws passed to curb enclosures[162] but justices of the peace steadfastly refused or neglected to enforce this legislation. It was the nobility and the gentry who were enclosing, and the justices of the peace, drawn exclusively from those strata, were not about to rat upon their own class. If justices of the peace acted together as a body in matters such as enclosures, livery or maintenance, there was not much the Privy Council or anyone else could do about it.[163]

So enclosures continued for centuries until the mid-1800s, and the vagrancy class increased accordingly. The nature, purpose and method of enclosure had changed by the late 1700s, early 1800s. It became part of the Agricultural Revolution which was in turn part of the Industrial Revolution. This later type of enclosure was achieved by private acts of parliament (thousands of them) and later, by general acts of parliament passed in 1801 and 1845. This type of enclosure is dealt with at pages 134-137.

Henry VIII's seizure of monasteries and convents and its affect upon the numbers of vagrants

Henry VIII reigned from 1509 to 1547. That the Catholic Church wielded power can be gathered from the fact that his chief administrator until 1529 was Cardinal Wolsey. Wolsey's international policies badly misfired. When the going got tough (that is, when Henry tired of Catherine of Aragon and coveted Anne Boleyn), Wolsey was unable to orchestrate the necessary divorce, and he was dismissed from office. The Pope steadfastly refused to declare Henry's marriage to the daughter of the King of Spain null and void. The impasse was more a matter of politics than religion. It took until Anne was six months pregnant to declare Henry's previous marriage ended. Elizabeth, clearly of the wrong gender, was born in 1533. Still, it was hoped the new Queen might do better next time around.

Two acts of parliament followed in 1534. The first was the Act of Succession, making it an offence punishable by death to assert that Henry was not legally married to Anne Boleyn. (Two years later, there was another law making it an

---

[160] Ackroyd's *The History of England*, volume 2, p.22
[161] Thomas More's *Utopia*.
[162] 4 Hen. VII, c.16.
[163] Skyrme op cit p.115,116.

offence punishable by death for anyone to assert he ever had been lawfully married to Anne Boleyn).

The other act of significance of 1534 was the Act of Supremacy, proclaiming that Henry was, and always had been, supreme head of the Church of England.

By this act, England divorced itself from Rome and in the years following proceeded to divvy up the matrimonial property. The newly established Church of England itself retained most churches but the monasteries, convents and priories were sold to anyone who had the money to pay for them, especially the landed gentry. This boosted the state revenue, and at the same time gave the most powerful class of Englishmen reason to support the ouster of the Catholic Church and the recognition of the Church of England.

According to Andro Linklater[164]

> "The greatest real estate sale in England's history occurred after Henry VIII dissolved a total of 400 monasteries which had been acquiring land for centuries. He justified his action on the grounds that the houses of prayer had grown depraved and corrupt, but tales of drunken monks and lecherous nuns served to conceal a more mundane purpose – Henry needed the money."

The land sold consisted of one sixth of the English land mass.[165] The purchasers were land-hungry owners, mostly Lords and Sirs, but they included "small landlords who had done well from the rise in the market value of wool and corn."[166] These no doubt included descendants of former villeins and cottagers who had got their leg in the real estate door following the Black Death. It may well have included some first time land owners.

> "The greater part of the monastic lands were sold to the highest bidder or the highest briber; many went to the local gentry or to newly rich merchants who were eager to secure their status in a society based solidly on land ownership. It was a way of binding the rising families both to the cause of the reformation and to the Tudor dynasty."[167]

When Henry appropriated this real estate, the majority of the monks and nuns were sent packing and thus the number of vagrants was swollen. Further, since the monasteries included villages which had grown up on land belonging to the monasteries and included arable land tilled by tenants who rented from the monasteries, most of the monastic farmers had to join the unemployed and become vagrants.

Inflation during the reign of Henry VIII caused prices to double and this added to the misery of the poor as a whole, and the vagrants in particular.

---

[164] *Measuring America*, Harper Collins, 2002, p.6.
[165] Ackroyd op cit p.121.
[166] Ibid p. 6.
[167] Ackroyd, ibid.

It was the greed of the nobility, gentry and Henry VIII in particular which created this class of vagrants. The grossly severe and unfair punishments devised for the vagrants by a parliament controlled by justices of the peace and mercilessly carried out by them in sessions is probably a reflection of magisterial guilt feelings for helping to create this class in the first place.

The situation continued for centuries until the mid to late 1800s when parliamentary reforms began to take effect.

Enclosures did not go unprotested. Resentment aimed at the gentry turned into an ugly attempted revolution led by Robert Kett in 1549. Kett's petition is reproduced in *English Economic History* op. cit. at pages 247-250, and specifically accuses justices of the peace of concealing the extent and evils of enclosure. Kett's rebellion was put down with great loss of life. Justices of the peace took part in its suppression. There were a few, very few, occasions when enclosure was successfully resisted by recourse to the courts.[168] Nor did the divorce from the Catholic Church go unprotested. There were numerous and bloody outbreaks of rebellion under both Henry VIII and his son, Edward VI, all savagely put down by nobility and gentry who had greatly profited from the land carve-up. When the Catholic Church was briefly restored under (Bloody) Mary (1553-1558), the same people resisted this restoration and eventually triumphed with the death of Mary and the return of the Church of England under Mary's half-sister, Elizabeth. The struggle for supremacy over the church is not the subject of this book, but it is necessary to consider some of the consequences, since justices of the peace were given the job of combating recusancy and heresy.

Other legislation during the reign of Henry VIII affecting magistrates

- Four justices of the peace sitting together had power to deal with decayed bridges.[169]

- Justices of the peace were ordered to supervise gaols.[170]

- (This was the nearest justices of the peace came to acquiring civil jurisdiction). They were given power to arbitrate in certain disputes (1) clearing of woodland and supervising partitions between landlords and commoners;[171] (2) Disputes between farmers and butchers over the price of beef.[172]

- Extra sessions were authorised for justices of the peace in between Quarter Sessions.[173] In 1545, justices were authorised to hold sessions whenever they thought fit.[174]

---

[168] Cantrell v. Church (1601) B. And M. 588 is one of the few examples.
[169] (1530), 22 Hen. VIII, c. 2.
[170] (1531), 23 Hen. VIII, c. 2.
[171] 35 Hen. VIII, c. 17.
[172] 32 Hen. VIII, c. 1.
[173] 33 Hen. VIII, c. 10, s.1.
[174] 37 Hen. VIII, c.7.

The effect of the last dot point was that sessions were held more or less continuously throughout the year.

Procedure at sessions of justices of the peace; Juries; Accused denied opportunity to give evidence, or have legal representation, or call witnesses; British Justice?

Sessions usually started with local government concerns: bridges, roads, wages, prices and the like. Then the juries were called. There were three juries. The first was drawn from the "same class as constables."[175] This jury told the assembled justices of all the nuisances, defaults and minor offences occurring in their areas. This was supplemented by reports from constables.

The next jury summoned was 'the grand jury', drawn from Knights and leading landowners (income of at least 40 shillings per annum, raised to £10 per annum in 1692).[176] Evidence was then presented to the grand jury of alleged felonies. If the grand jury thought the evidence constituted a prima facie case, the charge became a formal indictment against the accused, to be determined by a petty jury. The petty jury was then selected from freeholders of land of lesser standing than the grand jury, but greater standing than the first jury. Having heard the evidence presented to the grand jury, there wasn't much left for the petty jury to do except to pronounce on the guilt or innocence of the accused. The finding was usually the former. Having heard the great of the land endorse a case to answer, it would take a brave petty jury to gainsay that.

It was shortly after the time of Henry VIII that the task of the petty jury was made even easier and quicker. The courts ruled that an accused person could not give evidence on her or his own behalf.[177]

Further, to render their task even quicker and easier, a person accused of felony was not allowed legal representation, nor to call witnesses on her or his behalf.[178]

---

[175] Skyrme op cit, volume 1, p. 136.

[176] By 4 Will. And M, c.24.

[177] Holdsworth, *History of English Law* Volume IX, p. 195. Holdsworth believed that the rule came into force in the latter half of the 16th century. Stephen, *History of English Criminal Law,* volume 1 pp 439-442 says that the rule commenced with the 'glorious revolution' of 1688. Stephen is possibly mistaken about that, as the rule appears to have been well settled before that: *R. v. Coleman* (1678) 7 ST 65 and *R. v. Colledge* (1681)8 ST 681. This rule remained in force until as late as 1898, when it was abolished by The Criminal Evidence Act, 61 and 62 Vic. c. 36.

[178] In his *Commentaries*, Blackstone explained the rule against calling witnesses on behalf of the accused: "As counsel was not allowed any prisoner accused of a capital crime, so neither should he be suffered to exculpate himself by the testimony of any witnesses." This seems to be a non-sequitur. The rule against an accused calling witnesses was abolished in 1702, by 1 Ann. St. 2, c.9. The rule against legal representation for an accused remained in force until The Prisoners Counsel Act, 1836, 6 and 7 Will. IV, c. 114. However, towards the end of the 18th century, judges began to allow rich prisoners very

The justification for the rule against allowing an accused to give evidence was based upon the "probability that persons interested were likely to commit perjury."[179] It would never do for a jury to actually believe what the accused said, and acquit her or him. Juries were "much more in the habit of counting witnesses than of weighing their credibility."[180]

The denial of the right to give evidence to the accused, or for the accused to be allowed legal representation, or to call witnesses, is proof of the denial of a fair trial: the judges, including justices of the peace, did not want the truth getting in the way of a conviction. This sorry state of affairs remained in force until abolished by the Prisoners Counsel Act 1836 (in the case of legal representation) and the Criminal Evidence Act of 1898 (61 and 62 Vic. C. 36) (in the case of giving evidence).

Edward VI (1547-1553)

Henry VIII was succeeded by his son Edward VI, a by-product of the union between Henry and his third wife, Jane Seymour. Edward was 9 years old when crowned. He never reached his majority, and died of tuberculosis at the age of 15.

Unlike his father, and his grandfather Henry VII, Edward never exercised power over the nation. For the first few years, the country was under the rule of a dictator, the King's uncle and protector, Edward Seymour. He was Edward VI's mother's brother, the Duke of Somerset. The Privy Council was dominated by Somerset, who was supported by the next most powerful man in England, the Archbishop of Canterbury, Thomas Cranmer.

One of the hot topics of the five and a bit year reign was, of course, religion. Whilst it is true that Henry VIII had sacked the Pope, he had stuck, theoretically at least, to the beliefs of the Catholic Church, although in practice he did not always adhere to its commandments. Edward, his protector Somerset, and the Archbishop Cranmer all embraced Protestantism. Churches were stripped of their ornaments, Catholic ceremonies were banned, and Henry's six articles of faith were abolished. In 1549, Cranmer produced the *Book of Common Prayer*, and made it the only legal form of worship, by the Act of Uniformity.[181] Far from unifying society, the act was the trigger to divide it. It is worth commenting at the outset that you can't alter a person's mind, a person's beliefs, by an act of parliament.

---

limited legal representation, limited to arguing a point of law or to cross-examination of prosecution witnesses. The barrister could not address the jury directly, comment upon the evidence, or lay out the client's defence. (Langbein: *'The Origins of Adversary Criminal Trial'*).

[179] Holdsworth op. cit. p. 196. Holdsworth says, in effect, that the courts did not trust juries to bring in a correct verdict.
[180] Ibid.
[181] 1549, 2 and 3 Edw. VI, c.2.

In fact, England was already riven by factions in 1549, even before the passage of the Act of Uniformity. There were four causes: high inflation, low wages, enclosures and religion.

Between 1547 and 1549, inflation caused prices of commodities, including food, to double. Wages remained fixed by orders of justices of the peace at pre-1547 levels.

Enclosures continued to add to the misery and resentment of the labourers, small landholders and the poor. A series of uprisings took place aimed at enclosures, prices, landlords, Lords, the gentry, justices of the peace, Knights and graziers. Rebellions broke out in Wiltshire, Oxfordshire, Sussex, Hampshire, Kent, Gloucestershire, Suffolk, Essex, Hertfordshire, Leicestershire and Worcestershire.

The King's protector, Somerset, blamed the rioters, rather than look for the true causes of the disquiet. He issued a proclamation aimed against all:

> "Lewd, idle, seditious and disordered persons... posting from place to place... to stir up rumours or raise up tales."

The upshot was the Riot Act of 1550,[182] the first of a series of Riot Acts enacted over the centuries. The Riot Act was a baseball bat wielded by justices of the peace to prevent any coming together of the poorer two-thirds of society and used from 1550 onwards to break up disturbances. Justices were authorised to call in the militia and all constables to attack any gathering, and under the Acts, justices were not responsible for any deaths or injuries caused by the attack.

Upon the publication of the *Book of Common Prayer* backed up by the Act of Uniformity, more riots and demonstrations broke out in 1549. Under Edward's immediate predecessor, his father Henry VIII, anyone who denied the doctrine of transubstantiation was to be burned as a heretic at the stake. This was the first of Henry's six articles of faith, and it was promulgated in 1539, and a law that remained in force until repealed by the Act of Uniformity of 1549. It is asking a lot of people to believe one thing one day, on pain of being burned at the stake, and the next day, to believe the opposite. These changes of belief were dictated to bewildered and unwilling people by a remote government in London.

Rebellion broke out over the religious changes in the south-west of England, Devon and Cornwell, in 1549. This rebellion was unable to be squashed by the local justices of the peace, and Somerset was obliged to send in the army, which consisted of foreign mercenaries. Many thousands of rebels died at the sword.

Shortly after the south-west flames were extinguished, Robert Kett led a rebellion in Norfolk. This was not aimed at religion, but rather, at enclosures and the gentry/justices of the peace. This was a serious rebellion and for a while looked like it might succeed. However, it too was put down with much slaughter by foreign mercenaries under the direction of the Earl of Warwick. The gentry and the enclosers still called the shots.

---

[182]   3 and 4 Edw. VI, c. 5.

Robert Kett's manifesto is republished in Bland, Brown and Tawney's book *English Economic History*.[183] In it Kett specifically blames justices of the peace for hiding the extent of the rural problems in general and enclosures in particular.

The outcome of all these rebellions was that Somerset was sacked as the King's protector and from the Privy Council, and replaced by the Earl of Warwick. Warwick was promoted to become the Duke of Northumberland. Somerset was executed.

Vagrants

In the first year of Edward's reign, parliament passed a new Vagrancy Act.[184] This provided that if a labourer left his master, he was to be adjudged a slave to that master for two years. As a permanent record of that fact, the miscreant was to have the letter 'v' for vagrant branded upon his cheek, and was adjudged a slave to his master for two years. If he absconded again, he was adjudged a slave to his master for life, and he was to have the letter 's' branded upon his cheek. A third absconding attracted the death penalty. The provisions of this act were to be carried out by any two or more justices acting on the evidence of two witnesses and presumably their own observations of the accused's cheeks.

The Poor Laws and the Origins of the Sentence of Imprisonment

In 1552, the Bishop of London, Bishop Ridley, preached a sermon to a congregation which included the 14-year-old King Edward VI. Its theme was: 'something must be done to help the poor.' The King took up the suggestion in the time-honoured method by handballing the problem to somebody else, in this case, the Lord Mayor of London. The mayor did what any self-respecting mayor in that situation would do, he formed a committee. In due course, the committee's report categorized the poor into three sub-species:

1. The poor by impotence;
2. The poor by casualty;
3. The thriftless poor.

In turn, each of these was broken down into three sub-sub-species.

The poor by impotence:

- The fatherless or poor man's child;
- The aged, blind and lame;
- The diseased person, by leprosy, etc.

The poor by casualty:

- The wounded soldier;

---

[183] Op cit, at pages 247-250.
[184] 1 Edw. VI, c.3.

- The decayed householder (i.e. the elderly);
- The visited with grievous disease.

The thriftless poor:

- The rioter that consumeth all;
- The vagabond that will abide no place;
- The idle person, as the strumpet and others.

The committee could have, but did not, include a fourth category:

4. The homeless, so rendered by the illegal enclosures of the nobility and gentry, and the confiscation, sale and enclosures of the monasteries and convents under Edward's father.

Unfortunately, those many thousands dispossessed by the author's imaginary category 4 were simply lumped in with the category 3 thriftless poor, as if it was *their* fault that they became homeless by enclosure

The committee recommended that the first two categories could either be accommodated in hospitals such as Grey Friars' Christ's Hospital, St. Thomas' Hospital or St Bartholomew's Hospital or, in the case of the decayed householder, in her or his home and given 'weekly reliefe and pencion.' These recommendations were taken up and incorporated into the Poor Laws. Funds necessary to fund this poor relief were to come from parish funds. Parish funds were a commodity much in demand. Apart from the obvious need to maintain the church and the minister and family, they were also to be used for the repair of bridges, the construction and maintenance of roads and gaols etc. It was unfair to spread these burdens amongst the entire population by way of a tax upon the parishioners. The money ought to have been raised by a tax on luxury goods, or an income tax upon the wealthy nobility or gentry to fund these expenses, but the nobility and gentry were in charge of the ball game and insisted the money come from parish rates.

Before these particular poor laws, the impotent poor had been cared for by voluntary funds raised in those parishes which could afford to do so. In other words, if they were to be cared for at all, the poor were to be cared for by that most fickle of philanthropists, charity. An act of parliament[185] placed the onus on parishes of supporting the poor 'by voluntary alms.' This was all very well but presupposes that parishes throughout England were all full of philanthropic wealthy donors, when plainly, they were not. Many parishes had wealthy gentry, but the wealthy seemed hell-bent upon hanging on to and increasing their wealth, rather than spending it upon people whose existence they tried to ignore.

When the laws recommended under Edward finally came to fruition under Elizabeth[186] they imposed an obligation on the parishes, by requiring each

---

[185] 27 Hen. VIII, c. 25.
[186] 5 Eliz. c. 3.

household, rich and poor alike, of paying a fixed amount or 'rate.' The fixed amount was a pittance to the wealthy, but beyond the means of the average householder. The act and the collection of money were to be enforced by justices of the peace. It will be seen that there was an 11 year gap between the suggested poor relief and its implementation to assist the first two categories of the poor. However, immediate action was taken against the 3rd category, the thriftless poor. Since these people had previously been categorised as vagrants, there were already some laws in place for dealing with them.[187] The government decided that the time was right to try something new.

Edward VI, then in his last year, donated Bridewell Palace in London to be the repository for London's thriftless poor. Over the years, more 'Bridewells' were constructed in other places, or existing gaols took on the nickname 'Bridewell'. The point to notice is that the first practical implementation of the London Council's plan for aiding the poor was to lock them up, and it took a further 11 years, until 1563, before legislation was passed aimed at forcing the poor in the parishes to assist 'the deserving poor.'

There have always been gaols or rooms set aside in a castle to incarcerate people. But, until the advent of Bridewells on the scene in 1553, they were rarely used as a punishment for crime. Serious and not so serious crimes, felonies, only had one official punishment: death. In medieval times, banishment as a punishment in the tradition of 'abjuring the realm', lapsed centuries earlier, and was not re-introduced as an alternative to the death sentence until well into the 17th century.[188] Serious crime included minor theft, and it was only very minor crimes and in particular, the new-ish vagrancy laws, that were categorised as 'misdemeanours,' and enabled an accused to cop an alternative to the death penalty such as imprisonment, usually with a whipping.

Prior to 1500, gaols were only used to incarcerate debtors; accused waiting for trial; the convicted awaiting execution; and for non-payment of a fine. Gaols were, very infrequently, used for fixed terms of imprisonment.

As to the gaols themselves, they were all privately run under licence from the government. Debtors were mixed in with accused awaiting trial and the convicted awaiting execution or, in a few years, transportation to the Americas. Males were mixed in with females. There was usually a tap room dispensing alcohol. Of Newgate, the largest of the gaols, Charles Dickens would later describe it as "this gloomy depository of the guilt and misery of London." The invariable practice for these gaols was for the gaolers to demand money for services, such as supplying food. If the money was not forthcoming, the prisoner was clapped in chains and starved to death. In 1729, the Ogelthorpe Committee said:

> "When the miserable wretch hath worn out the charity of his friends, and consumed the money which he hath raised upon his

---

[187] For example, the Beggars Act, 1536, 27 Hen. VIII, c. 25; the Vagrants Act, 1530, 22 Hen. VIII, c.12.
[188] See pp 105.

clothes and bedding, and hath eaten his last allowance of provisions, he usually in a few days grows weak for want of food, with the symptoms of a hectic fever; and when he is no longer able to stand, if he can raise threepence to pay the fee of the common nurse of the prison, he obtains the liberty of being carried into the sick ward and lingers on for about a month or two (on charitable rations) and then dies."[189]

The prisoners' behaviour was uncontrolled, and there were constant orgies, riots and brawls. Gaol fever was rampant. In what one might call just retribution, during the 'Black Assizes' in 1750, 2 judges, the Lord Mayor and 40 barristers and court officials all caught the fever from the prisoners and died. A ventilation system had to be constructed to try to extract foetid air from Newgate, but 7 workmen employed in its installation succumbed to the fever.[190]

A King's edict of 1285 provided one years' imprisonment for a lawyer who misled a court. Another edict of 1361 made the stealing of a hawk punishable by two years' imprisonment. An act of parliament of 1406[191] prescribed imprisonment for the manufacturer of blunt arrows. Breaches of the Statute of Labourers[192] were punishable by imprisonment. But as far as imprisonment for offending went, until 1553, that's it. Anything else was punishable in the case of a felony by death, and in the case of a misdemeanour,[193] to be punished with whipping, branding, the pillory, stocks, cutting off of various bits of the anatomy, the tumbrel, the cucking stool, fines or recognisances.[194]

Bridewells (the original institution in London retained its name, others adopted it) became the repository of the dross of England. In addition to beating the bejesus out of the idle poor, Bridewells were also used to house orphans. These children were educated and apprenticed.[195] The Bridewells were run by Courts of Governors containing a sprinkling of justices of the peace. The orphans were supplied by various parishes and hospitals, and vagrants brought in by Bridewell officers, with no trial. They were simply rounded up, and locked up. Sometimes vagrants were sent in by magistrates' sessions.

---

[189] This was the report of a committee set up to enquire into the state of the prisons. John Howard wrote his treatise on the state of the nation's prisons in 1773, with similar conclusions to the Ogelthorpe Committee. Ogelthorpe went on to found the state of Georgia in the USA, which he settled with pauper migrants.

[190] Babington: *The English Bastille*, page 97.

[191] 7 Hen. IV, c. 7.

[192] 1349, 23 Edw. III

[193] Usually, the Act of parliament creating the offence specified if it was a felony or misdemeanour. If the Act was silent upon this point, the courts treated the offence as a misdemeanour.

[194] These are explained later, see pages 103-105.

[195] Apprenticeships are considered separately, see p. 92

The Bridewells were not the beginning of a more sustained sentence of imprisonment for crime. They were its prelude.[196] None of the inhabitants of the various Bridewells had committed a crime; they merely answered a particular description that brought them within the vagrancy laws.

The original Bridewell was soon stuffed full of "rioters who consumeth all; vagabonds that would abide in no place; and idle persons, as the strumpet and others," plus a smattering of orphans and illegitimate children. The Bridewell officers were authorised to go out into the streets of London and apprehend persons who were found in "taverns, alehouses, dicing places, bowling alleys, tennis plays (sic) and all other suspect places and houses of evil resort." A member of parliament, William Fleetwood, caught and imprisoned in the Bridewell 146 'vagrants' in just one week! It is said that the rest of London's vagrants fled panic-stricken to the country.[197] So many strumpets were locked in the London Bridewell that in 1559, there was a determined and wholly understandable attack upon it by the men of London in an endeavour to release them.[198]

In 1570, an act of parliament[199] ordered other counties to set up 'Houses of Correction' under the local justices of the peace, modelled upon the original London Bridewell. In popular language, the Houses of Correction were called 'Bridewells.' The idle poor of the Bridewells were thus put to hard labour or, in the case of children, into schooling and apprenticeships. The strumpets were probably put to a different use. The local parishes were required to find the necessary funds to pay the staff and feed the inmates. The same act of 1570 directed justices to provide the necessary materials to enable the idle inmates to work: wool, hemp, iron, flax and 'other stuff' also paid for out of parish rates. Bridewells generally had a poor reputation.

It is necessary to remember that vagrants had not necessarily committed any crime: they had merely answered a description, and a committal in the Bridewells was not necessarily as a result of a trial. The vagrants were usually apprehended by Bridewell officers and incarcerated without trial.

Apart from the Houses of Correction, England had an assortment of other 'houses' over the centuries. Some parishes had a poorhouse in which it housed its homeless. Sometimes they were merely 'dosshouses', but in any case, the inhabitants were free to come and go, or at least as free to come and go as the increasingly restrictive vagrancy laws would allow. Of the poorhouses, Moir said:

> "They proved disastrous in a populous district, when it had to have 50 or more."[200]

---

[196] Imprisonment in England for crimes began in England only in the early 1800s: see pp. 133-134, 147-151.
[197] Thomas: *Prisons and Prisoners in England 1500-1800*.
[198] ibid
[199] 18 Eliz. c. 3.
[200] *The Justice of the Peace*, Pelican, p. 95

In 1696, these poorhouses were renamed 'Houses of Industry', popularly called 'the Workhouse,' and the inmates were required to earn their keep. But again, they were free to come and go, subject again to the vagrancy laws. Of the Workhouses, Moir said:

> "Whatever the special design or purpose for which they were founded, whether education, gainful employment, medical treatment or attention to one class of pauper alone, they soon degenerated into the general workhouse, indiscriminately housing and maintaining all destitute persons, irrespective of age, sex or condition."[201]

The amended Poor Laws of 1834 made it compulsory for anyone who applied to the parish for relief to surrender themselves to the workhouse, and this time it was forever. Conditions inside these latter-day workhouses were deliberately kept bad to discourage anyone from applying for relief. Then, of course, there were the alehouses...

Two centuries after the Bridewells entered the English system of government, their experience was used when it was decided to introduce an alternative to the death penalty for relatively minor crimes. The alternative chosen was sentences of imprisonment in prisons or penitentiaries.[202] Another alternative, for both felonies and misdemeanours came into being in the early 17th century, involving transportation as slave labour to the Americas.[203]

Bishop Ridley had collaborated with Edward VI and his protector, the Duke of Northumberland, in setting up the Bridewell and the early implementation of the Poor Laws. None of them lived long. Edward died, probably of tuberculosis, in 1553. Henry VIII had nominated his daughters Mary[204] and Elizabeth,[205] in that order, to succeed Edward, and that nomination had been accepted by parliament.[206] However, Bishop Ridley had proclaimed both Mary and Elizabeth illegitimate, and Edward nominated Lady Jane Grey as his successor. She was a great niece of Henry VIII. The Duke of Northumberland in fact had Lady Jane Grey installed as Queen. She lasted 9 days before being deposed by forces loyal to Mary. Lady Jane Grey, her husband, Bishop Ridley and the Duke of Northumberland were all put to death.

The Riot Act

The earliest Riot Act was passed in Edward's reign, in 1550.[207] This gave power to a single justice of the peace to take assistants with him to the scene of the Riot

---

[201] Ibid.
[202] Dealt with in more detail at pp. 133-134, 147-151.
[203] See pp. 105, 110.
[204] Daughter of Catherine of Aragon.
[205] Daughter of Anne Boleyn.
[206] By the 3rd Act of Succession, 1544.
[207] 3 and 4 Edw. VI, c. 5.

and read the following proclamation to the assembled multitude:

> "The King our sovereign Lord charges and commands all persons being assembled to disperse themselves and peaceably depart to their habitations or to their lawful business upon pains contained in the act lately made against unlawful and rebellious assemblies: God save the King."

If the order was disobeyed, the justice and helpers could arrest those present, using such force as was necessary. If, as frequently happened, in the ensuing affray, anyone was killed, the justice and his helpers were exonerated. The offence of failing to disperse was specifically labelled a felony, therefore punishable by death.

'Riot' came to be interpreted by the justices as any gathering of people, the people not being of the nobility or gentry classes. Later acts required there to be twelve or more persons assembled to constitute a riot.[208]

Trevelyan said of justices in the 15th century:

> "The law breakers were the justices of the peace and some of the worst 'ambushes' were committed by royal judges and nobles high in office."[209]

The reading of the Riot Act 100 years later did little to alter that situation.

Mary I (1553-1558)

Random characteristics of Mary's reign:

- She was Catholic, so the people of England were required to change their beliefs once again.

- She acquired the title 'Bloody Mary' in her attempts to enforce her beliefs in others.[210] Those who spoke out against her burned at the stake; some 300 of them.

- She married Phillip, son of the King of Spain, in 1554. Parliament insisted she rule in the name of her husband and herself. Thus, after her marriage, acts of parliament are cited as e.g. 1 Phil. and M. C.13.

- Phillip could not have liked Mary, because he soon left England, never to return. They had no children.

- Ackroyd is of the opinion that at the time of her reign, Catholics in England outnumbered Protestants:

---

[208] 1714, 1 Geo. I, st. 2, c. 5.
[209] *History of England* op cit p. 259.
[210] This is one person on average for every 5 days of her reign, compared with 5 every day of her father's reign.

> "To gauge the true faith of England is impossible. It is clear enough that only a minority of the people were committed to the new faith, and that a slightly larger number now espoused full Catholicism."[211]

- The relevance of the above dot points is that they set the background of continued turbulence against which the justices of the peace operated.
- Uprisings against the Catholic Church were put down.
- When the Pope's representative, Cardinal Pole, arrived, he attempted to have the former monastic lands which had been sold off under Henry VIII and Edward VI restored to the Church. This was a step too far. The gentry were very attached to their land, even when acquired under such dubious circumstances. They were not about to stand by and let the land be reclaimed by the Catholic Church. The Protestant faith suddenly seemed more attractive.
- Papal supremacy was never really restored.

> "Mary remained the supreme head of the Church in England, and only lip service was paid to the doctrine of Papal supremacy... it simply could not be imposed once more."[212]

- Mary and her Council set about executing those who preached against the Catholic Church. They were executed by being burned at the stake, some 300 of them. Calculated to terrorise the population into an acceptance of Catholicism, it seems to have had the opposite effect.
- Major legislation affecting justices of the peace and 'committal proceedings' were passed by parliament during her short reign.

Committal Proceedings

Alleged felons were put up for trial after an investigation into the crime by one or more justices. If the 'examining justices' were satisfied that a prima facie case against the accused existed, the accused was either bailed to appear before the next Quarter Sessions or remanded in custody to appear there. The examining justices sent a document called an indictment to the Quarter Sessions so that the justices there assembled would know what the accused was alleged to have done.

The gathering of evidence by the examining justices was usually rough and ready, and any confession of guilt from the accused was likely to have been extracted, voluntarily of course, with the aid of thumb screws or a good stretching on the rack. Written records of these proceedings by the examining justices were spasmodic and not usually forwarded to Quarter Sessions.

The power to grant bail on a committal proceeding originated in 1483.[213] If, as sometimes happened, the accused did not answer his bail at Quarter Sessions, but

---

[211] Op cit p. 247
[212] Ackroyd op cit p.266.

went into hiding, what were the Quarter Sessions justices to do? They could issue a warrant, but often that was ineffectual, the horse having bolted. Sometimes they were reluctant to issue a warrant without knowing anything about the charge except the bare bones of it contained in the indictment. They knew nothing of the evidence to support the charge or the strength or weakness of the prosecution case. Accordingly, justices lobbied for an act of parliament, and it was duly passed.[214] This provided that before admitting a suspect to bail, the examining justices should make a written record of the evidence, and forward it to Quarter Sessions. The justices at Quarter Sessions found the paperwork so useful, they had a second act of parliament[215] passed requiring examining justices to take and transmit to Quarter Sessions a written record of all committal proceedings. These were the first laws regulating committal proceedings.

Roads, Highways, Bridges

In 1555, responsibility for all public roads, bridges and highways was given to the parishes through which the roads passed.[216] The inhabitants had to provide the labour, material and equipment. The parish was responsible for appointing one or more of its inhabitants as surveyor of highways for one year, the appointment to be ratified by the justices of the peace. The position of surveyor was unpaid. All able-bodied persons in the parish were to work on the roads for four consecutive days (increased to six in 1563). Persons who failed to contribute had to be reported to the justices of the peace, who would impose a fine.

Elizabeth I (1558-1603)

The initial years of Elizabeth's reign were preoccupied with re-establishing the Protestant religion, and Elizabeth herself warding off attempts to marry her off for the purpose of bearing her successors. She was not particularly concerned about the form of the liturgy, or the tenants of the faith.

> "There is only one Jesus Christ. The rest is a dispute over trifles."[217]

Catholics were purged from office. The *Book of Common Prayer* was reintroduced.

> "Protestantism became the acquired faith of the majority of the people; they may have conformed out of fear or indifference, but the conformity became by degrees the traditional religion of England."[218]

As to marriage, Elizabeth remained happily unmarried for her entire life.

213	1 Rich. III, c. 3.
214	1554, 1 and 2 Phil and M., c. 13
215	2 and 3 Phil. and M., c.10
216	2 and 3 Phil. and M., c.8.
217	Ackroyd op cit p. 292
218	Ackroyd, op cit p.324.

In 1562, justices were given the power to impose a compulsory levy upon each household to give to the poor.[219] If any householder neglected to do so, he or she was referred to the next session of the local justices, who imprisoned them until they did. This was followed in 1572 with another act: "An act for the punishment of vagabonds and for the relief of the poor and impotent."[220] The justices showed more enthusiasm for the former than the latter.

It is an unfortunate fact that no measure to aid the poor was unaccompanied by measures to beat the shit out of vagrants. The unfortunate poor became indistinguishable from vagrants, at least in the minds of the parliamentarians and the justices of the peace. No thought seems ever to have been given that vagrants were vagrants because they were poor.

> "The only measures at all consistently pursued by the courts [...] were those designed to repress or restrict certain activities which were thought to conduce to pauperisation as well as to immorality – drinking, especially gin drinking, gaming and the like.
>
> In the absence of general principles and of systematic administration, it was impossible to prevent the continuance of a body of able-bodied poor who, if they had more opportunity or incentive, could to a great extent probably have found work for themselves."[221]
>
> "The justices were more concerned with suppressing vagrancy than the relief of the impotent poor."[222]

These two acts gave justices the power to arrest, imprison, whip and burn a hole through the right ear of any person they judged to be a rogue, vagabond or sturdy beggar found begging or simply wandering. A second offence was punishable as a felony – by death. The purpose of the hole through the right ear was as a form of mobile court record, so that the justices could determine by a contemplation of an accused's right ear, whether or not he had a previous conviction.

In 1562, parliament passed the Statute of Artificers, Labourers, Servants of Husbandry and Apprentices. This act repealed previous acts on the same subject and substituted a new code. Justices were again given power to fix wages. The stated purpose of the act was to dissuade employers and employees from giving or receiving more than the maximum fixed wage. If they did pay more, employers were subject to 10 days' imprisonment and a fine of £5. Workers were to be imprisoned for 21 days! Apprenticeships were fixed at 7 years for both males and females. The real purpose of the legislation was to ensure a plentiful supply of cheap farm labour for the landed gentry.

---

[219] 5 Eliz., c. 3.
[220] 14 Eliz., c. 5.
[221] Dowdell, EG, *A Hundred Years of Quarter Sessions* 1932, p. 86.
[222] Skyrme, op cit, volume 1, p. 225.

In 1570, an act of parliament[223] gave justices of the peace the extraordinary power of hearing a treasonable offence: the importation of a Papal Bull. (A Papal Bull was the Catholic Church's equivalent of an act of parliament). The English legislation was in answer to a Papal Bull excommunicating Elizabeth with the added exhortation that the faithful were duty bound to kill the person excommunicated. The 1570 Act was followed by another act in 1581,[224] giving justices of the peace power to hear and determine at Quarter Sessions a charge against anyone who attempted to entice a person away from the Church of England. This, too, was a treasonable offence, punishable by hanging, drawing and quartering, and forfeiture of estates. This act also gave power to a single justice to fine £20 for anyone who did not attend church on a Sunday.

In 1571, justices of the peace in general came in for an official bollocking from Sir Nicolas Bacon in the presence of the Queen and parliament.

> "A justice should by his oath and duty set forth justice and right, yet he offered injury and wrong [...] specially chosen amongst a number by a Prince to appease all hardships and controversies, he became a sower and maintainer of strife and sedition, by swaying and leading of juries according to his will, acquitting some for gain, indicting others for malice..."

Skyrme comments:

> "Nicholas Bacon's rebuke appears to have had little effect as it was felt necessary to deliver a further speech on very similar lines at the end of sessions four years later."[225]

The majority of Elizabeth's reign was concerned with religion, specifically keeping both Catholics and radical reformers at bay. She spent much time and energy avoiding matrimony. There was the occasional invasion of France by England, and England by Spain (the Armada). There was a constant weeding out and warding off of plots against her. Mary Queen of Scots plotted once too often against her, and lost her head on Elizabeth's warrant. (Mary QOS, however, had the last laugh. All subsequent Kings and Queens of England are descended from her, not Elizabeth).

Throughout all these recurring embuggerances, the justices of the peace were gradually purged of Catholics and Puritans and they continued with their allotted tasks, including keeping the population in subjection. The enclosure of lands came to haunt the gentry when, from 1594, for four years there was insufficient flour to feed the people. The price of flour had tripled in those four years.

> "In the latter years, real wages plunged lower than at any time since 1260. The proportion of families without sufficient land to feed themselves was growing all the time; the number of vagrants,

---

[223] 13 Eliz., c. 2.
[224] 23 Eliz., c. 1.
[225] Skyrme, op cit, volume 1, p. 183.

forced to wander in order to find work, also increased. Many people did not have enough money to buy food; the dearth caused famine and created the conditions for diseases such as typhus and dysentery on a wider scale than had previously been seen in this country."[226]

Enclosures by the nobility, the gentry and justices of the peace led directly to insufficient land being available for the national staple, grain. As a result, many people starved. This led to a genuine fear of insurrection of the poor against the rich, similar to those insurrections under Wat Tyler in 1381, Jack Cade in 1450 and Robert Kett in 1549. This fear resulted in consolidations of the Poor Laws in 1597, [227] and 1601.[228] Once again, more emphasis was placed upon punishment than assistance:

> "Every rogue, vagabond or sturdy beggar which shall be at any time [...] taken begging, vagrant, wandering or misordering themselves was to be stripped naked from the middle upwards, and shall be openly whipped until his or her body be bloody."

These consolidations remained in force for the next 250 years until 1834. Under them, justices were to strike a parish poor rate to fund pensions for the deserving poor. They were to appoint an overseer of the poor for each parish, who was also responsible for the running of the parish workhouse. The overseers were to be overseen by the justices. Many parishes were simply unable to raise the funds to support these people and the temptation remained for the justices of the peace to view the impotent poor as vagabonds. Time and time again, the justices succumbed to this temptation.

The Militia

Prior to the Tudors, necessary armies were supplied by troops from private standing armies kept by the nobility. These were supplemented by mercenaries recruited from abroad. Often, particularly during the War of the Roses, these private armies were used against the King. The Tudors set about rectifying this situation by passing laws against livery and maintenance.[229] Justices of the peace were supposed to enforce these laws, but either lacked the clout or the will to do so. Under Henry VIII, however, his chancellor Wolsey used the court of Star Chamber to good effect to enforce the laws and the practice of the nobility keeping such private armies was considerably lessened.[230]

This left a vacuum in the event an army became necessary to defend the realm against threats from abroad or within. To overcome this, the Privy Council would issue Commissions of Muster to the Lords Lieutenant, their deputies and the justices of the peace for the counties. The deputies and the justices would jointly

---

[226] Acroyd, op cit, volume 2, p. 448
[227] 39 Eliz., c. 2. And 3
[228] 43 Eliz., c.2
[229] See pp. 45, 49-50.
[230] See p. 56.

carry out the muster and train and equip the resulting 'militia.' Persons so impressed into the militia were not allowed to desert. Desertion was a felony punishable as any felony, by death.[231] Justices of the peace were responsible for raising the funds necessary to prepare the militia.

Summary to the end of the Tudor era

Justices of the peace ruled England. They owned parliament, which was the superior, but not yet supreme, arm of government. They were well represented in the Privy Council. They, together with the Lords lieutenant in the various counties, were responsible for law and order, in that they were jointly responsible for summoning the militia in times of crisis, and alone, supervised the police system. They were responsible, again through the justices, for administering the vast bulk of the criminal justice system. They carried out all local government functions.

Queen Elizabeth, like her sister and brother, had no heirs. There were no more legitimate descendants of Henry VIII, and a replacement monarch had to be found amongst the descendants of Henry VII. James VI of Scotland, a great-great grandson of Henry VII, was the one chosen to replace Elizabeth. He was a son of Mary Queen of Scots who had been executed under Elizabeth's warrant. He became James I of England, the first of the Stuart dynasty.

The fact that England and Scotland shared a sovereign brought the countries closer together, but did not unite them. This had to wait another 100 years until the Act of Union in 1706-1707.

---

[231]   3 Hen. VIII, c. 5.

Chapter 4

The Stuarts (1603-1714)

James I (1603-1625)
Charles I (1625- 1649)
Commonwealth Interregnum (1649-1660)
Charles II (1660-1685)[232]
James II (1685-1688)
William III (1689-1702), jointly with Mary II (1689-1694)
Anne (1702-1714)

Overview

When Elizabeth fell off the perch in 1603, England had to cast about for a successor. In fact, ever since it had become apparent that she would never bear children, the council and parliament had been eyeballing potential successors. The burden ultimately fell upon King James VI of Scotland, a great-great grandson of Henry VII. He was also the son of Mary, Queen of Scots, former arch-rival to Elizabeth for the throne of England, but James had long since fallen out with his mother over the monarchy of Scotland. She was styled 'Queen of Scots;' he was in fact King of Scots. He became James I, King of England, as well as James VI of Scotland. This paved the way for the unification of the two countries 100 years later.

The next few Kings and Queens are easily explained. Charles I was the son of James I. Charles II was the son of Charles I. Charles II had no legitimate children, so the next King was his brother James II. Mary was the daughter of James II, and she ruled jointly with her husband, who was also her first cousin, William of Orange. Both Mary and William were grandchildren of Charles I.

Mary and William had no children, and when William died, the throne went to Mary's sister, Anne. She had 17 children, but none of them survived into adulthood. The Stuart dynasty came to an end in 1714. Parliament and the Privy Council again had to cast about for a new dynasty. Some favoured 'the

---

[232] Sometimes backdated to 1649, as if there was never any interregnum.

pretender', James, the son of the 'abdicated' James II. The problem was, he was a Catholic. Under the Act of Settlement of 1701, the new dynasty to take over was the Hanover family. George I was a great grandson of James I. Enough already of this groping in the cesspits of European royalty!

Even before Elizabeth's death, her Chief Minister entered into negotiations with James VI of Scotland. These negotiations were carried out in secret. Since they were successful, it seems that Sir Robert Cecil had the authority of the Privy Council and probably parliament as well, for the accession of James as King of England went off without a hitch, and no particular opposition. What started off with goodwill and harmony deteriorated soon enough, for James and his immediate successors believed they were appointed by God, rather than more earthly institutions.

At that time, England was governed by a loose conglomeration of parliament dominated by the gentry and the justices of the peace, and the Privy Council headed nominally by the King, but in reality by its Chief Minister, Sir Robert Cecil. The first four Stuarts failed to grasp the fact that the dominant rulers would no longer brook a veto on their decisions, nor would they tolerate a denial of the opportunity to make those decisions. The gentry thought that the importance, legitimacy, purpose and place of parliament in the government of England had been firmly established for many years before the Stuarts. The battle became the divine right of Kings to rule versus the divine right of the gentry to rule. Government could have benefited had there been a bit of give and take, an occasional compromise. No one, and in particular the first two Stuarts, was in the mood to compromise. Apart from the parameters of power of the contending parties, religion and finance proved to be insoluble problems for England, and were not wholly sorted by the Civil War, nor the rolling of Charles' head into the basket. Both James I and Charles I thought the simplistic solution to the argument of the supremacy of parliament versus the supremacy of the Crown was to dissolve parliament and not recall it. Parliament only sat for four and a half years between 1603 and 1629, and not at all between 1629 and 1640. Once Charles I was forced by a desperate need for money to recall parliament in 1640, civil war was inevitable. The gentry would not be ignored again.

The dispute between King and parliament was not the only cause of the Civil War.

> "One thing is becoming increasingly clear, that the perspective is distorted if attention is focused mainly upon London and upon politics at the national level. The localities hold the key to any true understanding of events, for local loyalties and local feuds were the very stuff of life to the 17th century nobility and gentry. Parliament might be the ultimate arena for constitutional debate, but it would be a mistake to take parliament as a mirror of the nation [...] The mainspring of government was the Privy Council with its

executive, the justices of the peace. The county gentry were the political nation."[233]

Moir went on to make the point that at that time, the counties of England were individual, independent shire states, each "with its own ethos and loyalty." So many of the justices of the peace in the counties were members of parliament, however, that one cannot consider the London situation in isolation from the county situation, and vice-versa. This is particularly so when it is recalled that parliament was not sitting at all in the years leading up to the war, and its disgruntled members had dispersed into the counties.

Moir also points out that while the dominant families in some counties lived harmoniously, this was by no means universal. Many of them were deeply riven by ancient and even recent feuds. She instances Leicestershire and Somerset. The implication is that when the quarrel over the control of government in London reached a stalemate, it only needed a spark or two from the counties to ignite the Civil War. If faction 'X' in Somerset opted to back the King, it was a safe bet that faction 'Y' would side with parliament. The Civil War resulted in a parliament/ puritan/gentry victory and, for the time being, a kingdom without a King. There was a commonwealth interregnum instead. Oliver Cromwell became the 'Lord Protector.' After a number of years under an apparently dismal regime, there was a very strong movement to restore the monarchy. After Cromwell died in 1658, and his son acknowledged his inability to govern, Charles II accepted an invitation to take over the reigns.

During the 11 years of the interregnum, England was divided up into a number of military districts, each ruled by a Puritan Major-General. For the time being, these officials took over many of the administrative functions previously performed by the justices of the peace. These functions were returned to the justices in 1660 on the restoration of the monarchy. The monarchy was restored upon vague conditions set out in the declaration of Breda: these included promises to allow liberty of conscience, and to honour laws passed by parliament, and amounted to very little. It took until the 'Glorious Revolution' of 1688 for the place and importance of parliament to be acknowledged by royalty.

As it was, the Anglican Church faction held sway in England under Charles II, and the Corporation Act of 1661 prevented all but practising Anglicans from holding political office. Dissenters (Puritans, Quakers, Catholics and the like) were outlawed from professional advancement in England. These people were severely persecuted throughout the 17th century, and many fled the country. This had the unexpected consequence of the colonisation of the Americas, bits of the Far East and ultimately, and indirectly, Australia and New Zealand. It may seem odd to categorise the flight of refugees as 'colonisation,' but while the government was content to rid itself of what it saw as troublemakers, it only did so on condition that each settlement was approved and governed by a Royal Charter, as a colony belonging to England.

---

[233] Moir, *The Justice of the Peace*, Penguin, 1969, pp. 54, 55.

The development of these places and the part played by justices of the peace is considered briefly later.[234] This is merely an overview.

The founding of the various colonies also had consequences on the sentences handed down by the courts, both for felonies and misdemeanours (minor crimes). For the first time with felonies, an alternative sentence became available: transportation as a slave to the Americas. Previously, the only penalty for felonies, which included offences as trivial as minor assaults and thefts, and repeat offences of vagrancy, was death. Transportation as a slave also added to the available penalties for misdemeanours.

The reigns of the last three Stuarts (William and Mary jointly, and Anne) were comparatively peaceful unless you were Irish.

Religion

The form of worship was a bone of contention in England even before Luther published his thesis for reform upon the church door at Wittenberg in 1517. Puritanism grew in strength during the reign of the later Tudors, and continued to grow, particularly among the gentry and the mercantile class during the reign of the early Stuarts. They came to dominate parliament on the few occasions it met during the reigns of James I and Charles I. Queen Elizabeth had found herself vexed by these 'zeley people,' and so did her successors. Then there were the closet Catholics, much feared by the majority of the gentry. James II was openly Catholic and brought about his undoing by his not-so-subtle attempts to restore that faith, or at least have it tolerated in England. The official religion was that of the Church of England (Anglican), established by the Acts of Uniformity of 1549, 1552 and 1559 with its faith embodied in the Book of Common Prayer. The Quakers were founded by George Fox in 1646 and therefore could not have influenced the outbreak of the Civil War. Quakers were described as "the extreme left wing of the 17th century English Puritan movement."[235]

Who then were the Puritans?

> "[They were] independents, Presbyterian, Baptists and some Puritan sectarians, but not Anglicans, Catholics or licentious people.
>
> What set a Puritan off from other Protestants was the literalness with which he held to his creed, the discipline with which he watched his soul's health, the militancy of his faith, and the sense that he was somehow apart from the rest of corrupt humanity."[236]

Being 'somehow apart' did not prevent Puritans from imposing their beliefs on others, as they did during the interregnum. Their beliefs included the duty of living a joyless existence: no games, no sports, just work. After a few years' rule, England seemed glad to be rid of them, and welcomed the restoration of 1660.

---

[234] See pp. 109-110.
[235] *Encyclopaedia Britannica*, 15th edition, volume 5, p. 10
[236] *EB*, 15th edition, volume 29, pp. 56 and 63.

People were probably becoming tired of the different religions. Consider the following.

Under Henry VII, the official religion was Catholicism, with all its attendant beliefs and forms of worship. Under Henry VIII, it was the same: Catholicism minus the Pope. Under Edward VI, it was Low Church Anglicanism, with the *Book of Common Prayer*. It was back to Catholicism under Mary. Under Elizabeth, it was the Church of England, but with variants from High Church to Low Church. This more or less remained the same under the first two Stuarts, but with increasing pressure from the 'zeley people.' Under the interregnum, the official religion was Puritanism. After the restoration in 1660, the official religion was that of the Anglican Church. Indeed, other forms of religion were discouraged: the Corporation Act of 1661 restricted political office to Anglicans only and the 'Clarendon Code'[237] came down heavily on dissenters.

The long parliament of 1640 dismissed all clergy from the ranks of justices of the peace, and a number of royalist supporters were dismissed during the interregnum. On the restoration in 1660, this was reversed, and clergy were again appointed as justices of the peace and Roundhead justices were purged in favour of royalist supporters.

Society under the Stuarts

The author of the *Encyclopaedia Britannica*'s section on the history of England[238] spent almost 700 words describing Stuart society in detail: its numbers, the monarchy and its council, the aristocracy its numbers and hierarchy and the gentry, with definitions and details. It also mentions the commercial society of financiers, manufacturers, merchants, shopkeepers, tradesmen and artisans who lived in the towns, but emphasises that these people sought and bought country estates and married their daughters off to the gentry and the aristocracy. There is not one mention about the remainder of the population, the vast majority, the other two thirds. It is almost as if they did not exist.

No doubt this omission accords with the views of the 17th century ruling class of England: those people did not count.

The following points emerge from the EB's dissection.

1. The gentry formed less than 6% of the population.
2. 1,000 knighthoods were sold by James I.
3. The era began with 30 members of the nobility. James I doubled their size to 60 by selling lordships to the highest bidder or the highest briber.
4. The House of Lords thus had 60 lay members, plus 26 Bishops. The House of Commons had 433 members.

---

[237] A series of Acts of parliament passed in the early 1660s.
[238] 15th edition, volume 29, p. 57.

5. England was ruled by an organisation representing less than 6% of the population: hardly a democracy.
6. The rest of the population is not worth mentioning.

The first 80 years of the Stuart Era consisted of a monumental struggle for supremacy between parliament and the Crown. This was settled only temporarily by the Civil Wars of 1642-1652, and more permanently by the Bill of Rights of 1689. The main issues between King and parliament, other than supremacy, were money and religion. The main sufferers during that 80 year period were the vast majority of the population other than the nobility, the gentry and the financiers etc.

The gentry class more than doubled during the 17th century.[239] The total population also increased, but the point is that the proportion of the gentry class to the rest of the population probably increased to, say, 10%.

> "Membership of the commission (being a JP) was of even more significance than it had been in the previous (16th) century. The justices of the peace were a select class even under the first Stuarts, and by the end of the century their elitism was a pronounced and established feature of society."[240]

In so far as the Poor Laws had ever provided relief to the deserving poor, that task became so much more difficult, if not impossible, by a vast increase in the number of supplicants: widows, orphans and wounded soldiers, together with the sucking up of funds which might otherwise have been used to help the poor, being used for the opposing armies in the Civil War. It was all very well for the justices to make orders for the relief of these people, but it was an altogether different task to find the money to implement the order. The Civil War also provided an alarming increase in vagrancy in the shape of wounded, displaced or unemployed soldiers and orphans. The justices of the peace continued their attack upon this group in their out of sessions work.

Badges

In 1694, without any legislative mandate, the Middlesex justices in Quarter Sessions ordered all pensioners within their area to wear badges, about 3" by 3" in size.[241] The only purpose of the badges was to act as a mark of shame, to further humiliate those who were probably beyond humiliation. No doubt the justices hoped this public shaming would discourage others from applying to the parishes for relief.[242] The badges were similar in size to those which Jewish people were forced to wear in medieval times as well as later under the Nazi regime in occupied Europe in the 1930s and 1940s. Parliament subsequently

---

[239] Skyrme op cit, volume 1, p.207.
[240] Ibid, p. 208.
[241] MSB 10/1694, p. 570.
[242] There were 9 parishes in Middlesex.

adopted this idea for other parts of the country.[243] This practice was finally outlawed in 1810.[244]

Gypsies, Tinkers and Travelling Salesmen

Off their own bat, and without any specific act of parliament to back it, the Middlesex Quarter Sessions ordered that all persons travelling with packs on horses were to be arrested as vagrants.[245] Those people caught wandering with Scotch or Holland cloth were to be whipped.[246] Many of the Middlesex justices held commissions for other areas of London and were of dubious character – 'trading justices.'[247] Such orders were without any legal justification whatsoever, and the orders were aimed solely at protecting the interests of the justices, many of whom were in similar trades themselves, and those who were not may either have had shares in their fellow justices' businesses, or were simply looking after the interests of their fellow justices: the 'you scratch my back, and I'll scratch yours' principle. The only possible justification for the orders was that the travellers were vagrants, but obviously they were not. They had visible means of support. One of the main essentials of vagrancy was that one had no visible means of support.

Destitute Children

Children became destitute from one of two reasons: the parents were destitute, or they were non-existent, that is, the child was an orphan or abandoned by its parents. If the cause was that the parents were destitute, the child was allowed to stay at home with the parents and the parish gave relief money to the parents to help support the child.

Unfortunately, this was not followed up in any way by the parish, the overseer of the poor or the justices who made the order. Particularly in London in the late 17th, early 18th centuries, the likelihood was that the parents were caught up in the gin craze that swept the country, and the relief money was spent on gin, and the child neglected unto death. The gin craze is considered in more detail in the next chapter at pages 118-121.

If the child orphaned or abandoned was an infant, it was farmed out to a nurse, who was paid a lump sum out of parish funds. Again, there was no supervision or follow-up on that baby. A nurse could make a large profit by taking on many babies, with no guarantee that she would actually look after the children. In 1694, Mary Compton was convicted of murdering several babies who had been entrusted into her care. She simply took the lump sum and killed the babies. This

---

[243] 1697, 8 and 9 Will. III, c. 30
[244] 1810, 50 Geo. III, c.10
[245] MSB Jan 1683, 1684, p. 29.
[246] MSR, April 1684.
[247] See next chapter under the heading 'trading justices' at pp. 122-125.

scandal did not result in any change in the justices' practices, not any increase in supervision of the nurses.[248]

> "Poor newborn infants were given the virtual death sentence of being dispatched (by the magistrates) to one of the London wet nurses in the slums of St. Giles."[249]

Orphaned or abandoned children, or children of poor parents who applied to the parish for relief, who were over 5 years of age, were placed in the Bridewell (if in London), or the workhouse (if elsewhere), until the magistrates could arrange an apprenticeship for them: the girls were put into domestic service and the boys into a variety of apprenticeships. If the justices nominated a particular tradesman or household, the master had no choice but to acquiesce. It was an offence to refuse to take on an apprentice nominated in such circumstances. The welcome mat was not always put out for the apprentice.

The status of the apprentice was that of slave. He or she was unpaid. The apprentice was obliged to obey his master's commands and failure to do so was a criminal offence. Running away was punishable by a whipping and branding.[250]

> "The apprentice could not expect very considerate treatment. The only incentive for the master to keep the apprentice alive was the use of his labour. Ordinary apprentices had no easy or comfortable life. We hear a great deal of cruelty to such children. A majority of the worst cases of oppression never reached the ears of the law."[251]

Rumpy-Pumpy and all that

In 1691, two years after 'The Glorious Revolution', a group of magistrates in the Tower Hamlets of London formed the Society for the Reformation of Manners, meaning thereby 'Morals.' The Charter of the society began:

> "An agreement of divers gentlemen and citizens in and about London for promoting the execution of laws made against profaneness and debauchery... and the suppression of sin and vice."

Membership of the society spread throughout England from its beginnings in London. Not only were the magistrates stepping outside their jurisdiction into the realms of religion, the means they used to achieve their aims were alarming. They set up a fund from the fines they received to pay informers to bring sinners to their sessions. They published an annual blacklist to further shame those they considered to be offenders against morals. By 1725, 90,000 sinners had been dragged to court by their informers.[252] The society railed against:

---

[248] Dowdell: *One hundred years of Quarter Sessions*, Cambridge University Press, 1932, p. 54.
[249] Schama, *A History of Britain*, volume 3, p 40
[250] See page 72.
[251] Dowdell, op cit p. 55.
[252] Dillon, *The Much Lamented Death of Madam Geneva*, Review, 2002, p. 45.

> "...delight in idleness, excessive vanity, revellings, luxury, wantonness, lasciviousness and whoredoms." [253]

The society was not without its detractors:

> "Neither has the Magistrate the right to direct private behaviour of men."[254]

The aristocracy and the gentry and their offspring were apparently exempt from supposed breaches of the morals of the country, even though they were the main customers for the various brothels in and around the country and London in particular. The magistrates only ever had the prostitutes arrested and dealt with, not the customers. Two of Hogarth's caricatures of the seamy side of London depict the number one moral campaigner and zealot, Sir John Gonson, personally leading raids on brothels and arresting the prostitutes.

> "You annual lists of criminals appear,
>
> But no Sir Harry or Sir Charles is here."[255]

> "We don't find the rich drunkard carried before my Lord Mayor, nor a swearing, lewd merchant punished."[256]

Events such as fairs, held in England since time immemorial, were banned. The justices believed them to be:

> "...the encouragement of vice and immorality and to the debauching and ruining of servants and apprentices and others, as well as to the disturbance of the public peace by occasioning quarrels, riots, tumults and other disorders."[257]

Accordingly, the Middlesex justices ordered their constables to prevent:

> "...a concourse of disorderly persons from assembling upon the pretext of holding a fair."[258]

On one occasion, the avenging constables were themselves set upon by persons dressed as soldiers (they probably *were* soldiers). Several constables were wounded, one of them fatally, as they tried to stop the May Fair at St Martin-in-the Fields near Hyde Park.[259] Dowdell said:

---

[253] Shoemaker, 'Reforming of the City, the Reformation of manners Campaign in London', in Davison, Hitchcock, Kiern and Shoemaker: 'Stilling the Grumbling Hive,' p. 101.
[254] The London Journal, 20/1/1721.
[255] Daniel Defoe, cited in Dillon, ibid at p. 57.
[256] Attributed by Dillon, ibid, pp. 57-58, to a 'poor man's plea', presumably to a bench of magistrates.
[257] Dowdell, *One Hundred Years of Quarter Sessions*, op. cit p. 29.
[258] Middlesex Sessions Books, May 1697, p. 35
[259] MSB May 1702, p. 35.

> "It is very probable that, to members of the poorer classes, this campaign appeared as an attempt to deprive them of one of their very few diversions. The campaign for the suppression of plays was waged mainly in the belief that ordinary people should have no public entertainment."[260]

There was no legislation justifying the magistrates' actions, and in suppressing fairs, plays and the like, they were acting illegally. It was not just the justices of London acting in this way. Gloucestershire justices forbade plays, revels and other disorderly meetings.[261] Middlesex justices directed constables to apprehend, as rogues, vagabonds and sturdy beggars, the actors in a play.[262] In June 1752, one John Scudamore was dealt with by the Middlesex justices:

> "...for being a lewd person and for keeping a certain booth for dancing on ropes and other unlawful exercises in Well Close whereon he is an actor with other lewd persons his servants who use much obscene and profane language, by means whereof many idle persons assemble, from whence proceeds many tumults and disorders, to the great disturbance of His Majesty's peace."[263]

Even poor old Morris dancers who, generally speaking, don't do much harm, earned a bucketing from the Warwick justices in 1655.[264]

The Society for the Reformation of Manners died its death in the 1730s, but the good work was carried on by its former members under the guidance of Sir John Gonson, a magistrate with extraordinary and long-lived righteousness, the scourge of prostitutes, sinners and drinkers, together with his sidekick, Sir Daniel Dolins. Sir John was on the bench of justices for more than 50 years. Their largely unsuccessful attempts to eliminate extra-curricular rumpy-pumpy and other sin and vice lasted well into the Hanover era, and is taken up in the next chapter.

Ascendancy of the gentry and justices of the peace: Decline in central government

The sale of peerages led to a loss of prestige of the nobility. [265]

> "This greatly weakened the effectiveness of the House of Lords as a mediating body between the King and the House of Commons. The decline in prestige of the nobility had been preceded by a financial crisis among the aristocracy from about 1590 to 1610 as a result of a shrinkage of their landed wealth. A member of the

---

[260] Op cit, p.32.
[261] Gloucestershire Quarter Sessions Minutes, Epiphany and Easter 1710, Epiphany 1718, Easter 1752.
[262] MSB July 1709, p. 49.
[263] MSR June 1752.
[264] Warwick Records Office, 1642-1660, volume 11, p. 1427.
[265] EB, op cit, Volume 29, p. 57.

nobility claimed in 1628 that the Commons, which was made up mostly of gentry, could buy up the Lords three times over."[266]

This situation had occurred by the acquisition of more and more land by the gentry, and by enclosures. An analysis of 300 manors in 1640 showed that 80% were owned by squires (gentry), less than 7% by peers and only 2% by the Crown.[267]

> "...whereas under the protectorate, the justices of the peace had occupied a subordinate position, from 1660 onwards both the JSP and the squirearchy as a whole regained their influence and became of even greater significance than before. The Stuarts and the Commonwealth had tried to override the squires and the chartered corporations and had failed. The central government's influence in local affairs declined throughout the period and by the end of the century was far weaker than it had been under Elizabeth. The Justices of the peace were a select class even under the first Stuarts, and by the end of the century, their elitism was a pronounced and established feature of society."[268]

Emergence of political parties

The political parties, Whigs and Tories, emerged out of the Civil War and its aftermath. In broad terms, the Tories were the King's supporters, the old Cavaliers whose main platform was their hatred of the Roundhead/Puritans. The Whigs were would-be reformers, former Roundheads and Puritans. Depending upon which party had the majority in the House of Commons, the other party had its members struck out as justices of the peace, who were replaced by members of the dominant party.

Supervision of magistrates and the abolition of the Star Chamber

Until 1641, justices of the peace had received instruction and discipline from the Privy Council, either through the Assizes courts or the Star Chamber.

It will be recalled that the Star Chamber was taken over by Cardinal Wolsey during the reign of Henry VIII. His main aim was to disarm the nobility. Justices of the peace had failed to do this.[269] The Star Chamber was particularly unpopular amongst the nobility and gentry, because it had no jury which could be intimidated or suborned. During the reign of Charles I, it took upon itself the task of stopping the land-grab of the nobility and gentry. In their colourful work on *English Economic History*, Bland, Brown and Tawney at p. 276 publish a copy of a document titled 'Complaint of Lands Action on the Commission for Depopulation.' Specifically, the document is a complaint against certain of the gentry of Wiltshire for illegally enclosing lands. It can be inferred from the record

---

266 Ibid.
267 Herbert Heaton, *Economic History of Europe* 1948, pp 310, 311.
268 Skyrme op cit, pp. 208, 229.
269 See page 56.

of the proceedings that the alleged enclosers denied the charges, but that the chairman of the Commission, Archbishop Laud, remained unconvinced of the accuseds' innocence. He referred the matter to the Star Chamber. That very same year, 1641, the Star Chamber was abolished,[270] presumably to prevent the matter from coming on for hearing – it certainly had that result. Not long after, Archbishop Laud himself was arrested and ultimately executed for treason. The moral seems to be: Don't mess with the gentry from Wiltshire! (It is not suggested that the court was abolished and Laud executed solely for this particular case. Indeed, Laud and before him Wolsey and the Star Chamber had given the nobility and gentry many other reasons to separate heads from shoulders and the Chamber's abolition, respectively. The case may have been the last straw.) Supervision of the justices by the Star Chamber ceased there and then. Supervision of the justices by the Privy Council via the Assizes courts ceased the very next year, with the outbreak of the Civil War. It was never resumed. Justices of the peace went on their way unchecked.

Fundraising

The main reason Kings and Queens called a parliament was to raise funds for various purposes dear to the heart of sovereigns. Under the early Stuarts, the 'zeley people' (Puritans) had control of parliament, and each time they were called together, they demanded changes in the form of worship of the church. Specifically, they wanted the bishops to play a lesser role in the running of the church, and elders of the church to be given a greater role. Neither James nor Charles would have a bit of this. When it became apparent to James' parliament that he merely regarded their resolutions as suggestions which he was free to ignore (and he did ignore), parliament dug in its collective heels and told James to accept an annual sum of money (£200,000) in return for foregoing other sources of revenue. His response was to dissolve parliament in 1610. Although he called parliament again several times during his reign, it was dissolved prematurely each time. The same thing happened under Charles. Both James and Charles tried to govern without a parliament. They set about raising money by royal proclamations and decrees. Previously money for government purposes had always been collected by justices of the peace at the behest of parliament. After his impasse with parliament, James turned to the justices to raise money for him without parliamentary approval. In 1614, James wrote to the justices in each of the counties directing them to shake down the county "for plate or money or both." They were to forward it forthwith if not sooner to him. What he mostly got in return were evasive letters, pointing out that hitherto, all fundraising was done through parliament. Justices were accordingly summoned to the Privy Council for a royal bollocking. Even so, enough counties sent *just* enough money to keep the royal cellars stocked for the time being.

When Charles I succeeded to the throne, he too could not bring parliament to heel on the question of necessary funds. When he dissolved parliament, he directed his justices of the peace to put out the begging bowl in manner similar to that ordered

---

[270] 16 Car. I, c. 10.

by his father. This time, the justices collectively told him what type of olives to purchase: 'get stuffed,' they said. Charles was forced to employ special commissioners to travel the country to get cash, but they met with stiff resistance. People would only raise money for the King through parliament. A number of commissioners and justices were committed to gaol by the King for two years.

Religion after the Restoration (1660)

It is unfortunate that religion keeps cropping up, but it was such a dominant theme under the Tudors and the Stuarts that it can't be ignored.

Charles II's declaration of Breda promised religious tolerance, a promise which he was unable to deliver – parliament was in no mood for tolerance. A succession of acts of parliament, 'The Clarendon Code,' restricted political office to practicing Anglicans.[271] A new prayer book was drafted into law.[272] This act:

> "Required subscription by the clergy to the new prayer book, the 39 articles, the oaths of supremacy and allegiance and a new oath of non-resistance to the Crown."[273]

The Conventicle Act[274] forbade Puritans, non conformers or dissenters from assembling in groups of five or more, thus effectively preventing them from holding any alternative form of worship. 2,000 clergymen were dismissed from office.

From time to time, Charles II tried to honour his promise of religious tolerance, but his Declaration of Indulgence, in which he purported to suspend the Clarendon Code, had to be swiftly withdrawn. Parliament then capped its previous efforts with the Test Act.[275] This act required officeholders, civil or military, to take communion according to the Anglican rite, and denounce the Catholic doctrine of transubstantiation.[276]

Justices of the peace were required to enforce these acts. John Bunyan, author of *Pilgrim's Progress*, was sentenced to 3 months' imprisonment by the Bedford Quarter Sessions. By continuing to refuse to conform, he remained in gaol from 1661 to 1672, and again from 1675 to 1677. Some of his best writing was done in gaol.

Some justices refused to do their duty under the code, and a further law was passed making it an offence for a justice to fail to enforce it, punishable by a fine of £100.[277]

Some oddities of the Stuart Era

---

[271] Specifically, the Corporation Act of 1661, 13 Car. II, st.2, c.1.
[272] The Act of Uniformity, 14 Car. II, c. 4.
[273] EB op Cit, volume 29, p. 64.
[274] 1664 16 Car. II, c. 4.
[275] 1673, 29 Car. II, c. 7.
[276] See page 57.
[277] 22 Car. II. C. 1.

Attempted Law Reform during the Interregnum

From time to time, some persons in responsible positions attempted to lessen the horrific results of sentencing, punishment and other legal absurdities. One of the reformers was William Sheppard, the legal advisor to Oliver Cromwell, a lawyer and justice of the peace. He wrote a book in 1656 called 'England's Balme' in which he advocated wholesale reform of the laws of England, civil and criminal. He advocated, for example, the amalgamation of equity and the common law, and the courts of King's Bench with the Chancery court, simplification of civil suits, uniform conveyancing documents, registration of dealings in land and the re-writing of the criminal law. He wanted to lessen the number of capital offences and in particular to abolish the death penalty for petty theft. He sought an easing up on the chopping off of various bits of the criminal anatomy and many other reforms. Sheppard was something of a God-botherer himself, having written many religious tracts as well as 22 legal texts, so it should not come as any surprise that he wanted to up the penalties for Biblical infringements such as swearing and cursing, disobedient children, sexual offences, drunkenness, bankruptcy and rogues and vagabonds. He argued for the abolition of peine forte et dure[278] and benefit of clergy.[279]

It also ought not to come as a surprise that Sheppard's suggested reforms were thrown neck and crop out of parliament controlled by justices of the peace. The number of capital offences continued to grow, from 50 in 1688 to 220 in 1820. Limbs and various bits of anatomy continued to be lopped, and about the only part of Sheppard's reforms to be adopted was the upping of the penalties for rogues and vagabonds.

The Trial of William Penn

William Penn was a Quaker. He had been arrested and imprisoned for his beliefs many times, but his trial by a magistrate, the Lord Mayor of London, Sir Samuel Starling, and a jury in 1670 is notorious. Penn was arrested for addressing a street meeting. He asked the judge if he could see a copy of the charge against him and to know what law it was alleged he had broken. Both of these fundamental matters were refused. The judge did not hear any defence, and directed the jury to bring in a verdict of guilty. When the jury said they were unable to agree upon a verdict, the judge had them locked in Newgate gaol until they did agree; they found Penn not guilty. The judge locked them in Newgate gaol for two more days without bread and water. Eventually the judge had to accept the verdict, but he still sentenced the jury to gaol and fined them, and they had to take out a writ of habeas corpus to secure their release. He also gaoled Penn for contempt of court.

Penn went on to found the colony of Pennsylvania, named after Penn's father, Admiral Penn. The case is cited to illustrate the depths to which the magistracy had sunk, that the authorities tolerated such an unjust bigot as Starling, and not only tolerated him but elected or appointed him as their leader as Lord Mayor.

---

[278]   See p. 103.

[279]   See p. 21, fn 43, and pp.107-108, 154.

The Hanging Judge

'Hanging Judge' Jeffries achieved his record for hangings 15 years after Penn's trial. He was both a judge and a magistrate. During the 'bloody assizes' following Monmouth's rebellion, he ordered the execution of 300 people altogether, and the deportation of nearly 1,000 others. He ordered the death penalty for 144 people over a two day period in 1685, 72 jury trials per day. Assuming each working day lasted 8 hours without any breaks, this means each trial lasted 7 minutes. For his brutality, he was elevated to the peerage.

When his mentor James II did a runner to France in 1688, Jeffries disguised himself as a sailor, and he too attempted to flee the country. He was recognised by 'the mob' and incarcerated in the Tower, where he died.

Stabilisation: The Bill of Rights

The accession of William and Mary to the throne was accompanied by a revolutionary agreement which had the effect of stabilising the country for the benefit of the majority, lessening the powers of the monarch, and strengthening the hand of parliament. The conditions under which they, and subsequent sovereigns, were to hold office were spelled out and agreed in the Bill of Rights.[280]

> "The Bill of Rights affirmed free speech, free elections, and frequent meetings of parliament; it prohibited the levying of taxes or the keeping of a standing army except with the consent of parliament; it proscribed ecclesiastical commissions or courts, and the Royal suspending or dispensing power."[281]

Subsequent legislation fine-tuned much of this, and also provided for a freer press through the repeal of the Licensing Act in 1695. Agreement was reached over the provision of money for the Crown. A new Coronation oath required the sovereign to uphold the Protestant reformed religion established by law, the Anglican Church. The Toleration Act of 1689 permitted everyone except Catholics, Jews and Unitarians to worship as they pleased. The changes did not increase the numbers of those entitled to vote or stand for parliament: running the country was exclusively the province of the elite, the nobility or the gentry. Indeed, the Bill of Rights was designed to protect only those people.

> "Free elections and free speech meant free from influence by the King and the lower orders of society, but not free from influence by the nobility or the gentry."[282]

The Act of Union 1707

This act united England and Scotland politically, with the abolition of the Scottish parliament, and the substitution of 46 seats in the English House of Commons and

---

[280] 1689, 1 Will. And M. St. ii.
[281] EB op cit, volume 29, pp. 65,66.
[282] EB op cit, volume 29, p. 66.

16 in the Lords. Thus began the United Kingdom of Great Britain, consisting of Wales, England, Scotland and Ireland.

Magistrates in the Stuart Era

Twice in this era, moves were made which, had the political situation not changed, might have led to the abolition of the institution of justices of the peace. The first was in the reign of Charles I when he appointed commissioners to collect taxes in lieu of the justices who had refused to do so. The second time was during the interregnum, when Major-Generals were appointed to carry out the functions previously allocated to the justices. The first experiment ended when Charles' head rolled into the basket, and the second was scrapped with the restoration in 1660. From then, the power and prestige of the magistrates grew, and they were unchecked and untutored by the Assizes courts.

The Civil War severely disrupted the ability of the justices to hold sessions, particularly in the centre of England where the opposing forces marched and fought. In some places, sessions ceased to be held altogether. For example, no Quarter Sessions were held in Warwickshire for three years. Similar problems occurred elsewhere. As had been the case during the War of the Roses, magistrates met out of sessions in their own homes. Difficulty was also experienced in enforcing orders made by justices at that time.

One duty not previously performed by justices came their way during the interregnum. Church marriages were banned, and all marriages had to be performed by a magistrate. Some justices charged exorbitant fees for this. Church marriages resumed in 1660.

While the power and prestige of the justices of the peace was assured, their tenure was not. If the Whigs controlled parliament, only justices who supported them were appointed, and Tories found that their commissions were not renewed. If Tories were in power, the position was reversed.

Skyrme was of the opinion that many justices were reluctant to enforce the new laws proscribing any religion but the Anglican Church.[283] An online trawling through the sessions records for the period shows very little such reluctance. The following books suggest enthusiasm on the part of the magistracy in upholding these and earlier laws favouring the Anglican Church.

> "Parliament had re-established the national church under conditions that were to breed constitutional conflicts for the next three decades and to circumscribe the political structure for the next two centuries.
>
> The course of events by which Puritan authority was systematically crushed by militant Anglicanism and communicants of the Church of England came to enjoy a complete monopoly of political power invites a brief review.

---

[283] Op cit, volume 1, p. 233

> A spontaneous movement towards reconstruction gained strength and momentum through the intervention of local magistrates. Those justices of the peace, appointed for their Royalist sympathies in the first months of the restoration, began prosecuting ministers who failed to follow the traditional form of worship.
>
> Hapless Puritans were indicted on charges of sedition on the strength of Edwardian and Elizabethan statutes and during the autumn of 1660 the persecution of non-Anglicans took on a vindictive character. The deliberate misapplication of the old statutes by magistrates...
>
> Many of the non-conformists who were prosecuted in Quarter Sessions and Assizes were faced with rigged testimony, hostile benches, confusing rules of evidence and intentional breaches of correct procedure."[284]
>
> "In 1685, it was discovered that more than 7 people were languishing indefinitely in gaol for recusancy, one of whom had been in custody for more than 4 years."[285]

The following are extracted at random from the records of the Middlesex sessions.

> "Twelve persons were sentenced for recusancy to seven years' transport to Jamaica (to work as slaves on plantations). In addition, they were ordered to pay their own costs of transport."[286]
>
> "In 1764, a woman, Frances Beddingfield, was fined one hundred and eighty pounds for recusancy."[287]
>
> "More than 300 persons were indicted, convicted and fined for recusancy in one session."[288]

Justices of the peace were shaken during the short reign of James II when he sacked 50% of them, and replaced them with Catholics. This may well have been a trigger for the 'Glorious Revolution' of 1688, with Whigs and Tories uniting to invite William of Orange to invade England. He took up the invitation. James fled England and things reverted to normal.

The Book of Orders of 1631

In 1631, the Privy Council issued a *Book of Orders* directed to justices of the peace. This was not only a text book for magistrates – it had the force of law. It

---

[284] Nancy Matthews: *William Sheppard: Cromwell's Law Reformer*, 1984, CUP, pp.241-255.
[285] Dowdell: *A Hundred Years of Quarter Sessions*, p. 38.
[286] MSR, December 1664, pp. 29-31.
[287] MSR, January 1673-1674. In 1763, £180 was an impossibly large sum of money for most people. It is almost certain this woman was gaoled for default in payment.
[288] MSR, April, 1674.

set out the programs of poor laws, peace laws, watch and ward, maintenance of tillage, apprenticeships, regulation of ale-houses and so on. Apparently the book was necessary because:

> "The good laws of the kingdom had not been executed, especially from the neglect of duty in some of our justices and other officers, magistrates and ministers of the peace."[289]

Numbers of Justices

In 1687, there were about 3,000 justices of the peace, of whom only about 700-800 were active.[290]

Capital Offences

There is some confusion about whether justices of the peace were hearing cases in Quarter Sessions which carried the death penalty (felonies) during the 17th century. Both Skyrme and Moir say that Quarter Sessions were regularly remitting such cases to the Assizes Courts for hearing before professional judges, but Skyrme says that if an Assizes sitting finished without having dealt with all its felonies, they remitted them back to the local justices of the peace to deal with.[291] A troll through the online records of the Middlesex Quarter Sessions up to the very end of the 17th century has justices of the peace in those sessions imposing that one sentence bound to cure recidivism, death by hanging, with monotonous regularity. It may well be that those cases were the left-overs from Assizes, in which case we can say with some certainty, there were plenty of left-overs.

Magistrates sentencing options under the Stuarts

Death Penalty

All felonies were punishable by death until the mid-19th century. The number of felonies actually increased as time went by. For example, in 1688, there were 50 capital offences, but by 1820, the number had risen to 220. The power of justices of the peace to inflict the death penalty, at least in theory, was not abolished until the Reform Act of 1832. However, cases likely to attract the death penalty were usually remitted to the Assizes courts from the late 17th, early 18th centuries. (This was not universal. Often Assizes Courts could not finish their lists in time, and

---

[289] From the Book of Orders.
[290] Skyrme, op cit volume 1, p. 231.
[291] Skyrme, op cit, volume 1, p.239: "Although many instances are recorded in county archives of the death sentence being imposed by Quarter Sessions during the first half of the 17th century, a large proportion of these cases had been to Assizes and were remitted to Quarter Sessions only because the judge had not completed his list before he was obliged to move on to the next county...from the second half of the century...there were still occasions when they (Capital offences) were tried at Quarter Sessions because the Assizes ran out of time." See also pp. 110-112. where there are plenty of examples of death penalties by Jsp.

would remit unfinished business, including capital offences to Quarter Sessions for them to deal with).

There might be several add-ons for the death penalty. These included outlawry and forfeiture of the felon's goods, chattels and land. For some felonies and treason, the offender was sentenced to be hung, drawn and quartered, with his entrails to be burned while he was still living. Forfeiture was also retained for any conviction for felony, even if the death sentence was watered down by a transportation order.

Transportation to the Americas is considered shortly under this heading as an alternative to the death penalty. Justices of the peace came to favour transportation over death simply because it was cheaper. It cost £5 to transport a convict, whereas it cost £10 to execute a felon.[292]

Torture

In most cases, except for whipping, the stocks and the pillory, torture was not part of the sentencing regime of justices of the peace, nor any other court for that matter. It was however part of the function of a justice in his constabulary duties to order torture on a suspect to extract a voluntary confession. Peine forte et dure, the rack and the thumb screw were freely used for this purpose.

Alleged offenders sometimes did not plead at all, but remained mute. The reason they remained mute was to avoid conviction – they could not be tried unless they pleaded. If they could not be tried nor found guilty, their estates could not be forfeited. The penalty for failing to plead, or remaining mute was 'peine forte et dure' (hard and strong pain). The prisoner was removed to a gaol, tied to a floor and his chest loaded with increasingly heavy weights, until the prisoner gave in, confessed, pleaded or died. If he managed to die without giving in and pleading guilty, his estate was not forfeited to the Crown, and his widow or children could inherit. This procedure was not abolished until 1772 by the Felony and Piracy Act. Even then, under that act, refusal to plead was to be treated as a plea of guilty. It was not until 1827 by the Criminal Law Act that refusal to plead was to be treated as a plea of not guilty.

Skyrme op. cit., vol. 1 p.267 says that part of the punishment for counterfeiting, a particularly seriously regarded offence, was the infliction of "unbearable torture."[293]

The infliction of the death penalty and the use of torture for whatever purpose were not confined to adults. Children were both tortured and executed.

<u>Whipping, cutting off of various bits of anatomy, branding, burning, stocks, pillory, tumbrel, hurdle, cucking stool and fines</u>

---

[292] Skyrme, op cit, volume 1, pp. 239- 240. The author finds these figures hard to believe.

[293] An oxymoron, if ever I've heard one.

With the possible exception of branding, burning and ear-lopping, the miscellany of penalties in this heading were the smorgasbord of penalties, along with or in lieu of imprisonment and the House of Correction (considered separately), available to justices for offences lesser than felonies (misdemeanours).

Whipping was carried out in public. Men and women were stripped naked from the waist up. Sometimes the whipping occurred with the whippee fixed to a post. Sometimes he or she was led through the town tied by the arms to the back of a cart, being whipped the length of the journey.

Cutting off of ears has been considered earlier in the previous chapter at page 65. Hands could be cut off for theft or seditious writings. Cutting off of an ear was the prescribed punishment for drawing a weapon. Cutting off of a hand was the penalty for striking a blow in the sovereign's palace.

Burning holes in the ear, and branding 'V,' 'F' or 'C' on the cheek or thumb were not punishment: they were the forerunner of modern computer records. A Quaker, James Nayler was branded with the letter 'B' on the forehead for blasphemy simply because he re-enacted Christ's ride into Jerusalem on a donkey (Bristol apparently being the English equivalent of Jerusalem). Nayler also had a hole burnt in his tongue with a red hot iron, a stint in the pillory, a whipping through the streets of London and Bristol, and to round it all off, he was thrown into gaol. Cutting off of ears was also a type of mobile court record. A glance could reveal at what stage the offender was in the criminal justice system. An 'F' branded on the cheek says the offender has previously been convicted of an affray in a church. 'C' branded on the balls (of the thumb) meant the offender had previously been given the benefit of clergy, which benefit can only be enjoyed once.[294] 'B' on the forehead meant you were a convicted blasphemer. One ear off meant either you had been once convicted of drawing a weapon or you had been twice convicted of vagrancy. Two ears off and you had been thrice convicted of vagrancy, and now faced the death penalty.

Stocks and pillory were devices into which a person sentenced could be locked and put on display as a form of public humiliation. The pillory required a person to stand with his head and arms locked into the contraption. The stocks enabled a prisoner to sit and it pinioned her or his arms but not the head. On sentencing, the magistrate would nominate the days and hours when the prisoner was put on public display in these devices. The pillory was abolished in 1816 and the stocks fell into disuse by 1860. They were used in the various states of Australia in the early years. The author of *Robinson Crusoe*, Daniel Defoe, was sentenced to the pillory because of a book he wrote about dissenters. (Defoe also spent time in Newgate prison as a debtor).

Tumbrels and hurdles were another means of public humiliation favoured by justices. More often than not, they were used to convey a person convicted of felony to her or his place of execution, but sometimes a person convicted of a

---

[294] See pp. 197-108.

minor offence could be strapped to a tumbrel or hurdle and dragged around the market place.

Imprisonment

Imprisonment was now used more often than in the Tudor era, especially on the growing numbers of vagrants and recusants. They were cast into the prisons previously the exclusive home of debtors, those awaiting trial, and the condemned awaiting execution or transportation as slaves. In London, the prisons were the Fleet, Newgate or Kings Bench gaols or, in the case of vagrants, the Bridewell. In the various counties, there were already existing gaols or parts of old buildings used as gaols, or perhaps new Houses of Correction.

Imprisonment for felonies (serious crimes), did not begin until 1792 in the USA, and in the early 19th century in England. These modern gaols or penitentiaries are considered later.[295]

Transportation

In Jamestown, Virginia, the first successful attempt in 1607 by the English to colonise America, was the inspiration for forced transportation. In 1611, the free settlers were in a sorry state and on the brink of starvation. Enter a new governor, Sir Thomas Dale, who set about rectifying the situation. First he imposed his 'Lawes Divine, Politique and Martiall'. These laws required the settlers to work under threats of dire punishment. Then he penned a letter to England begging for those criminals condemned to die to be sent instead to Jamestown to be used a slaves.

There was no immediate response to this – reasons of state as well as geography and the radical nature of the proposal delayed implementation of the suggestion until 1617. Then the first convicted felons were sent to Virginia to work as forced labour. It was Hobson's choice for the convict: would you rather be put to death or sent as a slave to Virginia?

There was no legislative imprimatur for this until 100 years later (the Transportation Act of 1718), but the courts justified the practice by reviving the option of abjuring the realm. Alternatively, the convicted were pardoned conditionally by the Crown (the condition being to accept slavery in the colonies).

Thus the justices of the peace at Quarter Session (and the judges at Assizes) were given the first practical alternative to the death penalty. Over the next 150 years the justices at Petty Sessions also sent the vagrant poor to America, although they had not necessarily committed any offence at all. They were treated precisely as slaves throughout the duration of their sentence. Transportation was used in some of the other colonies as they developed. When it became impossible to transport the convicted to the Americas because of the War of Independence, transportation resumed in 1787, this time to Australia.

---

[295] See pp. 132-134, 147-151.

The cucking stool

The cucking stool was a device used mainly for women. It was for a female scold, prostitutes, mothers of illegitimate children and witches. The procedure was that the offender would be strapped to a chair attached to a device like a see-saw, and ducked a specified number of times in a pond. It was a public spectacle in the nature of Saturday afternoon entertainment. Fighting married couples could be strapped back to back and dunked. Dishonest brewers and bakers could also earn an afternoon on the stool.

Recognisances

A recognisance is a promise to do or refrain from doing something, under pain of a monetary penalty should one breach the recognisance. In the context of sentencing, the promise was invariably to be of good behaviour for a specified period of time. A person who breached the recognisance was gaoled until the money forfeited was paid. Recognisance was not much used as a sentencing option.

Fine

This type of penalty needs little explanation. It was often imposed on those with no money to pay the fine. The person fined was incarcerated until the fine was paid.

Other Duties of Justices of the Peace

The various duties of magistrates have been considered in previous chapters as they were allocated. Not a great deal was added during the Stuart era, but there was a considerable amount of consolidation, embellishment and fine-tuning. At the end of the era, they were more powerful than ever. Unfortunately, they were also becoming corrupt, particularly in London. This is considered in the next chapter.

In broad terms, their duties were as follows.

Law and order

They were in charge of maintenance of the King's peace, which they did by taking recognisances to keep the peace, and on occasion, by reading the Riot Act. They were in charge of constables and the justices had powers of arrest, and the raising of hue and cry. They were in charge of watch and ward, instituted along with hue and cry by the Statute of Winchester of 1285. With the Lord Lieutenant and his deputies, they were responsible for raising, training, equipping, maintaining and deploying the militia.

Judicial

Justices sat at Quarter, General, Special and what came to be called Petty Sessions, adjudicating on felonies and misdemeanours, and at the Petty Session level, held preliminary hearings into felony charges which came to be called committal proceedings, and dealt with minor crimes.

Administrative functions

The administration of the Poor Laws involved striking a poor rate, to be paid by the householders of parishes, the resulting monies to alleviate the lot of the poor, and other purposes: roads bridges and the like. The administration of the poor laws also involved sinking the slipper into those the justices deemed to be vagrants. This was usually done at Petty Sessions.

The next aspect of their administrative functions was their local government type work.

The next administrative duty was to strike wages rates for different types of employment, usually done at Quarter Sessions, or General or Special Sessions.

Recusants were dealt with at General or Petty Sessions, depending upon whether the recusancy was thought to be petty or felonious.

Licensing of Alehouses was carried out at General Sessions.

The final administrative duty was collection of special taxes, for example the chimney tax.[296]

Avoidance of Penalties

Some magistrates began to take pains to avoid the brutality dished out by their brethren. The law still required them to hang, flog, torture and export those brought before them, but these more merciful magistrates avoided this by freely adopting fictions, bending the truth and various tricks of the trade.

From early times, a clergyman alleged to have broken the laws of England could insist upon being dealt with by an ecclesiastical court.[297] It was the law that the common law courts had no jurisdiction over the clergy. All a person had to do was prove he was a clergyman, and he did this by reading from a book. The book chosen was invariably the bible. It was said that only the clergy could read, so if he could read, he must be a clergyman. Of course, the authorities realised that was nonsense, after all, they could read, and they weren't clergymen. But they allowed the practice to continue because it was in their own interests to do so – it might come in handy if they were charged with an offence. They did fine-tune the rule so that benefit of clergy could only be claimed once. If it was successfully claimed, the person was branded with a red hot iron on the balls (of the thumb), and each person claiming benefit of clergy by reading from the bible ('seeks the book') had to show his unbranded thumb first. The branding was the forerunner of the modern computer record of convictions.

Over time, the ritual adopted by the merciful magistrates was invariably as follows. The accused took the bible, opened it, sank to his or her knees and recited (or pretended to recite in the case of an illiterate accused with a good memory):

---

[296]   14 Car. II, c. 40.
[297]   See p.21 and fn. 43.

> Have mercy upon me, Oh God, according to thy loving kindness: according unto the multitude of thy tender mercies blot out my transgressions.[298]

If the accused could manage that, he or she was then branded and released. Of course, the hanging magistrates kept changing the reading, so that only the truly literate could use this escape. This farcical procedure was not abolished until 1827.

Another farcical procedure adopted to avoid the death penalty by the merciful magistrates was the alteration of the charge and the evidence to turn the offence into an indictable misdemeanour instead of a felony. The value of goods stolen was crucial in differentiating between a death sentence and an alternative. The value changed over the years. The critical value was one shilling in 1612. By the late 18th century, the critical value had become two pounds, or forty shillings.

Bentham gives the following epitomised example (numerous actual cases are recorded):

> "Case of prosecution for theft: subject matter nine pieces of gold, value thirty-nine pounds sterling – Judge's charge: 'Gentlemen of the jury, find the value thirty-nine shillings.'
>
> The capital penalty prescribed by the law is thus perjuriously averted."[299]

Another way around the death penalty was to pick through the charge sheet and find some minor omission or fault in the wording. An example is *R v. Walcott* (1694) 4 Mod 395. An appeal court examined the order for conviction which ordered hanging, drawing and quartering. It was held to be invalid, because the draftsman forgot to order that the entrails be burned whilst the convicted person was still living! In *R v. Turner and Reader* (1830) 1 Mood.CC 239, the information read:

> "That [the defendants] not having the fear of God before their eyes, but being moved and seduced by the devil, on the 31st March, in the 10th year, with force and arms, at a certain barn of Benjamin Keane, there situated, feloniously, voluntarily and maliciously did set fire to and burn, against the peace..."

In his adjectival zeal, the draftsman forgot to allege that the offence was 'unlawful,' and the indictment was thrown out.

On the one hand by adopting procedures, fictions and devices that were either illegal, or at the very least, against the spirit of the law, the merciful magistrates were failing in their duty. By imposing sentences that were out of all proportion to the offences, and authorising torture, all the 'hanging' justices who participated

---

[298] Psalm 51, verse 1.
[299] Coleman Phillipson: *Three Criminal Law Reformers*, p. 215.

were guiltier than those they sentenced, and it is amazing that the people of England tolerated such a system for as long as they did.

When, to these examples of medieval mysticism and grossly excessive legalism, one adds the lack of opportunity for an accused to defend herself or himself,[300] or to have legal representation, one obtains a fairly accurate notion of British justice, or lack of it, during the 17th century. There was no improvement during the 18th century. Trials only took a few minutes. In fact, the quality of justice deteriorated markedly, with magistrates becoming more and more greedy and corrupt, and with the savage enforcement of the game laws and the laws against vagrancy.

Changes to The Quorum

One of the most significant changes to the justices of the peace during the Stuart era was the fact that knowledge of the law was no longer a requirement for someone to become a justice of the peace. The quorum is explained at page 26, but briefly it meant that no session of justices of the peace could take place unless one at least of the justices was of the quorum. In its early days, it was necessary to have legal training to be on the quorum. By the end of the reign of Charles I, barely a handful of justices of the peace were not of the quorum.[301] Legal training was no longer a prerequisite for the quorum and a bench could consist of amateurs who had no legal training whatsoever. In 1732, solicitors, but not barristers, were specifically banned from the bench.[302]

The Place of the Magistracy in the History of the 17th Century

> "Justices of the peace played an important part in curbing Royal supremacy and in ensuring that attempts by James I, and particularly Charles I, to establish a dictatorship were unsuccessful. The peculiar characteristics [...] of justices of the peace [...] were perhaps the most important cause of the ultimate success of the parliamentary opposition."[303]

Colonisation by the British

It was during the Stuart Era that serious colonisation of other lands (other than France, Scotland, Ireland and Wales) by England, and later, Britain, got underway. There had been an attempt to establish a colony at Roanoke Island, Virginia in 1587, but the colonising party vanished without trace. The East India Company was formed in 1600 during the last years of the reign of Elizabeth. This company established trading posts in India, with the permission of the local rulers, and worked cooperatively with them in peaceful trading during the first few years. Colonisation proper did not commence there until the 18th century.

---

[300] See pages 69-70.
[301] Skyrme op cit p. 209.
[302] 5 Geo. II, c. 18.
[303] Skyrme op cit, volume 1, p. 211, citing Holdsworth: *History of English Law* volume VI, p. 61.

The next attempt to colonise was in 1607 at Jamestown, Virginia, under a Royal Charter from James I. The people who put their hands up for a one-way ticket to Virginia were a mixed bag of adventurers, the get-rich-quick types, and desperadoes: those fleeing persecution for religious beliefs, and the poor seeking a better life.

Such colonies affected the institution of justices of the peace in two ways: it enlarged their sentencing options (transportation in lieu of the death sentence), and the institution itself was transported to the various colonies.

Colonisation of the West Indies was well under way by the time of the Stuarts, but not by England. English had set up outposts in defiance of the other colonising powers, but without official sanction from England. These people were a mixture of agricultural people, traders, smugglers and privateers (buccaneers) operating mainly against the Spanish. Then in 1655, Jamaica was captured from the Spanish, and official recognition of these various settlements was forthcoming.

Jamaica was divided into 11 parishes administered by parish councils. Each parish had a resident magistrate, a paid official, and under him, Petty Sessions Courts run either by the resident magistrate or unpaid justices of the peace. The Resident Magistrates were probably the forerunner of the later institution in Britain of Stipendiary Magistrates.

Random Extracts from Justices Records

Middlesex Sessions of the Peace, held at the Castle, St John's Street, 1 & 2 December 1612:

- Agnes Hill: (Theft) of linen and 26 pounds: guilty to be hanged.
- Edward Abyerre: for robbery of Thomas Knyvette of Middle Temple, gentleman: guilty to be hanged.
- Ursula Woodforde for (theft) of gold and goods: to be hanged, but respited because pregnant.
- John Smyth: to be whipped for (theft) of divers goods.
- Ditto Anne Holmes.
- John Mapis: for theft of a kettle: seeks the book, read, branded.
- Morgan Herreye: to be hanged for being a cutpurse.
- Margaret Maynard: Guilty, to be hanged for stealing a plate.
- William Walker: accessory before and after to Margaret Maynard: Guilty, seeks the book, read, branded.
- Phyllis Roache: guilty for the murder of Magdelen Welch, seeks the book, does not read, therefore to be hanged.

- Thomas Walker: guilty for stealing 4 hogs: value 11 pence, to be whipped.
- Robert Merryton for stealing 5 wethers, guilty to the value of 11 pence: to be whipped.

There were many other cases dealt with on those two days by the same justices, and quite a few were found not guilty. A quick calculation is that each trial, even for capital offences, must have taken less than half an hour. The court also dealt with a plethora of recusants (either religious dissenters, or people who neglected to go to church), and petty offenders – the days seem to contain a mixed bag of Quarter Sessions and Petty Sessions work.

Some commentary on the sentences is in order. Thomas Knyvette, the victim of Edward Abyerre, seems to have been handed preferential treatment. Out of all the cases, he is represented, or more accurately, Abyerre is singled out, by the arrival of a special prosecutor from the Middle Temple, Knyvette's address. Knyvette's address (Middle Temple) and occupation (gentleman), suggests he is a barrister and land owner and therefore possibly a justice of the peace himself. Elsewhere he is described as of a different address and as a yeoman, again suggesting he is a landowner – he was later in the sessions himself prosecuted as a highway defaulter, whatever that might be.[304]

Thomas Walker and Robert Merryton managed to escape the gallows by the amazing coincidence that the goods they stole were only worth 11 pence, in other words, a hog is only worth two and three quarter pence, and a wether only two and one quarter pence. Often the value of the goods stolen is put down at 11 pence, because if worth more, the only punishment was death. In other words, the value of the goods as found by the court is a fiction, and the justices knew it.

Ursula Woodeforde used pregnancy as an excuse to dodge the gallows, a merciful outcome that was denied to Agnes Hill, Margaret Maynard, Phyllis Roache and all the men who were hanged.

Finally, 'seeks the book' means that the offender was claiming a defence of benefit of clergy. If a first time offender was charged, he could plead benefit of clergy, and provided he could read (or pretend to read by memorising in advance) a short passage from the bible, he was able to avoid the death sentence. (Benefit of clergy is elaborated upon under the heading: 'Avoidance of penalties', pp.107-108 and also p.21, fn.43). You will have noticed that several of the offenders successfully passed the test, but that poor old Phyllis Roach failed. It could be said that she was hanged either because she couldn't read, or because she had a bad memory.

The records show numerous persons sentenced to transportation to the West Indies or Jamaica for attending unlawful religious assemblies in mid-century. The

---

[304] Sir Thomas Knyvette and his experiences being pressed by parliament to raise a company to fight in the Civil War is mentioned in P. Ackroyd's *History of England: The Civil War*, volume 3 at p. 242.

'West Indies' in this context can mean either the West Indies, as we know them today, or North America, specifically what we now know as the United States of America.

The Navigation Act

England looked to America as a market for its woollen cloth and other manufactured goods, and a source of raw materials that it might have otherwise to import from other countries. As time went by, the new settlers in America discovered that they could get higher prices for their raw materials by selling them elsewhere, and that they could import goods for a lesser price by buying them from countries other than England. In 1663, the English passed the Navigation Act which compelled the Americans to deal exclusively with the English.

> "[The settlers] could still have carried on a successful trade in obedience to the Navigation Act, but disobedience was more profitable."[305]

This act, along with other English irritants, fostered the 'them against us' attitude among the settlers which ultimately boiled over into the American War of Independence a century later.

---

[305] Blum, Morgan, Rose, Schlesinger, Stamp and Van Woodward: *The National Experience: A History of the United States* 5th Edition, p.45.

Chapter 5

The Hanovers 1714-1815

George I (1714-1727)

George II (1727-1760)

George III (1760-1820)

George IV (1820-1830)

William IV (1830-1837)

Victoria (1837-1901)

Historical Background

The accession of Hanover Kings to Great Britain was not universally welcomed. Many would have preferred the exiled Stuarts. Jacobite rebellions took place in 1715-1716, and again in 1746, but these were quickly extinguished. During the century from about 1700 to 1800, politics underwent several significant changes. The Privy Council was split into the King's advisers and renamed 'The Cabinet.' From then on, the Privy Council confined itself to hearing and determining appeals from Britain's colonies' courts, the Court of Admiralty, and the Ecclesiastical Courts. Robert Walpole was recognised as the first Prime Minister of Great Britain. He presided over the Cabinet from 1721 to 1742. The Kings lost interest and did not attend Cabinet meetings from 1718 onwards. (George I could not speak English). The members of Cabinet were all members of parliament.

During the 18th century, the population of England almost doubled from about five and a half million in 1700 to nine million in 1801 (the year when England conducted its first census).

In 1711, a statistician, Gregory King, divided society up as follows. At the top were the nobility and gentry. Below them were the fast growing middle class, office-holders, merchants, clergy, professional men, freeholders and small farmers. Some of the merchants were wealthier than either the nobility or gentry. Beneath the middle class, occupying the border between the middle and 'lower classes', were the shopkeepers and artisans. The 'lower orders' were the common soldiers and sailors, labourers and servants, cottagers, paupers and our old friends, the vagrants.[306]

The South Sea company gained a monopoly over trade in the southern hemisphere. To gain this monopoly, they paid seven million dollars and undertook to pay two-thirds of the national debt. An over-optimistic boom in share prices, 'the South Sea Bubble,' was followed by the bubble bursting in 1721. Many of those embedded in Kings' population strata changed places as a result.

On the war front, Britain signed peace treaties with the French and the Dutch in 1717.

Friction over trade in the new world between Spain and Britain led to one Captain Jenkins tendering his left ear in parliament as an exhibit, mute testimony to the over-enthusiastic objection of a Spaniard to Jenkin's trading. The 'War of Jenkin's ear' broke out in 1738 between Spain and Britain. This war somehow got mixed up with the 'War of Austrian succession,' and lasted until 1748.

War, this time with France, resumed in 1756. This was over conflicting claims to bits of North America, India and much of the West Indies. Many other European counties were dragged into this war. It lasted until 1763. By this war, Britain gained control over most of North America, Canada, India and much of the West Indies. Jamaica had been wrested off the Spanish in 1655.

The control over what is now the United States of America was short-lived, with the colonies rebelling in 1776 over taxation and non-representation in the British parliament. The war of American independence, which sucked in France and Spain on the side of the rebels, lasted until 1782, with the British forces surrendering to the rebels, and Britain acknowledging the USA as an independent country.

Hot on the heels of the American war came the French Revolution in 1787 and yet another war. It was not an entirely peaceful century.

At the outbreak of the American War of Independence, transport of prisoners to the Americas came to a halt. Prisoners who might have been transported to the Americas were now held indefinitely in the ships which might otherwise have transported them. The authorities were not entirely sure what to do with these prisoners. Until 1782, they still had hopes they might beat the rebels, and transportation to America could recommence. When it became obvious they had lost the war, there was no immediate alternative strategy in place. It took some years for them to decide upon Botany Bay. The dispatch of the first fleet of prisoners in 1787 to Australia coincided with the outbreak of the French Revolution.

The British were still making up their minds whether to support the French Revolution, or to oppose it, when the French made up their minds for them by

---

[306] EB op cit, p. 78.

declaring war on Britain in 1793. Britain and France remained at war on and off until France was decisively beaten at Waterloo in 1815.

On the home front, the gin craze took hold in the early 1700s and held London and other parts of the nation in its grip until about mid-century.

Justices of the peace had become corrupt and were heavily involved in the gin craze, both for and against, and in the lurks and perks of 'trading justices' and the heavy abuse of the game laws. Out of this corruption arose the need for paid incorruptible magistrates, and the institution of stipendiary magistrates was born.

During most of the 18th century, the Whigs ruled England with what amounted to one-party rule. Many of the Tories (Conservatives) had favoured the return of the Stuart dynasty. They had to flee the country into exile with the failure of the Jacobite rebellions of 1715-1716 and 1746. However, by the end of the Napoleonic Wars, the Tories were back in charge, geared for the war, but uncertain what course to take in the peace that followed.[307]

The cabinet left the nuts and bolts ruling of the country to the justices of the peace in the various counties and Burroughs.

Eligibility for any office remained the same. Only property-holders of the Anglican Church need apply. Justices of the peace continued to dominate parliament and the Cabinet. This remained so until the 20th century.

In 1778, there was a movement towards making concessions towards Catholics, which in 1780 resulted in the 'Gordon Riots.'

In 1792, a reform movement seeking universal, but male only, suffrage resulted in a savage government crackdown. Ringleaders were charged with treason, but were acquitted. Thereafter, any agitation for such reform, or any agitation of any kind, was left to the tender mercies of the justices of the peace. The adult suffrage reform movement was abandoned in 1795 and not revived until after Waterloo in 1815.[308]

Rebellion in Ireland was put down in 1798 with the usual savagery, and boatloads of Irish political prisoners were transported to Australia. They fared no better in Australia, thanks to the ministrations of a bigoted cleric justice of the peace, the Rev. Samuel Marsden JP, aka 'The Flogging Parson.' In order to extract voluntary admissions from the Irish as to where they might have hidden some non-existent weapons, he ordered that they each receive 300 lashes of the whip until they revealed where the weapons were hidden.

Ireland was incorporated into the Union in 1801, and allowed 100 representatives in parliament, provided that they were not Catholic.

During the 100 years from the end of the Stuart dynasty (1714) to Waterloo (1815), England underwent a transition from mainly agricultural rural living to

---

[307] EB op cit p.77
[308] EB p. 76.

industrial urban living, because of the Agricultural Revolution, incorporating a new wave of enclosures, and the simultaneous Industrial Revolution.

Slavery

While the extent to which slavery within England extended into the 19th century is a moot point, there is no doubt that the English embraced the institution in the new world. The first boat load of slaves from West Africa was snapped up in Virginia in 1619, delivered by the Dutch. This was about the same time that the first boat load of slaves, direct from England, began to arrive, vagrants and the like. Within the next century, the number of slaves exported from the west coast of Africa rose to about one quarter of a million. The English were the most important importer of slaves in the Americas, both in mainland North America and the West Indies.[309] The institution of slavery took three forms: black slaves snatched from the west coast of Africa; prisoners transported from Britain; and indentured labour.

> "Probably on the whole the situation of slaves was not much worse than that of indentured labourers brought over from Europe."[310]

The most obvious difference is that the prisoners and the indentured had hope: the prisoners' sentences of 7 or 14 years were sometimes successfully completed, and indentured labourers often completed their obligations. For the black slave there was little hope. Even after the British were defeated by the Americans, the black slaves and their progeny remained slaves. The promises of the freedom of mankind embodied in the Declaration of Independence did not extend to slaves.

Britain allowed the slave trade to flourish until purporting to abolish it in 1807. Slavery, however, continued in England under different names. 'Slave' according to the Oxford dictionary is a "person who is the legal property of another, servant completely divested of freedom and personal rights; human chattels; helpless victim; submissive or devoted servant; drudge."

Labourers' and others' wages were fixed by justices of the peace at or below subsistence level to maintain the status quo. The landed gentry and the rich industrialists benefited by cheap labour.[311] This enabled them to entertain with lavish dinner parties costing thousands of pounds, served by a maid whose annual income was a mere £3. As at the late 18th century, the hard working poor man earned £10-£15 per annum.[312] This was slavery.

Any joint attempt by the grossly underpaid labourers to achieve a more reasonable salary was a criminal offence. The nebulous concept of a vagrant to be

---

[309] EB 15th edition, volume 27, p. 233.
[310] Ibid.
[311] Judge Parry in *Vagabonds All* Cassel and Co. P.xiv: "The employers of labour objected to vagabonds because they diminished the amount of cheap and available labour. (at p. xxi): 'This is pure class legislation activated by a desire to uphold the social convenience of a large reserve of cheap labour."
[312] Dillon: *The Much Lamented Death of Madame Geneva*, author's introductory note. Others, for example female domestic servants, received much less.

whipped and imprisoned by the justices was another example of slavery. Moving from one place to another to try to get work to avoid starvation was an offence. This was slavery. Leaving your master, and thereby earning a branding and an official adjudication that you were a slave to your master, is self-explanatory. If a destitute person sought assistance from the authorities, he or she was locked in the workhouse and forced to work. This is slavery. Persons thrown out of their work and home by enclosures became vagrants and a target for the authorities to punish. This is slavery. Transporting orphans and poor children en masse as 'apprentices'[313] for factory fodder was slavery.

The nobility, the gentry and to a lesser extent, the emerging middle class, believed that their task in life was to control the other two thirds of the population, and they did this by keeping them in subjection, in varying degrees of slavery. It was all very well abolishing slavery abroad, but why was it necessary to keep it at home?

Transition from Rural Agrarian Society to Industrial Urban Society

Since Kett's rebellion in 1549, a rebellion against the failure of justices of the peace to enforce laws against enclosures,[314] something of a balance seems to have been struck between sheep and grain. In a speech to parliament in 1601, a member draws attention to the fact that corn is now cheap.[315] He continues:

> "If we debar tillage, we give scope to the depopulator, and then if the poor, being thrust out of their houses, go to dwell with others, straight we catch them with the Statute of Inmates. If they wander abroad, they are within danger of the Statute of the Poor, to be whipped."[316]

This means that, despite corn being plentiful, or perhaps because of it, people were still illegally enclosing lands. We know that because of a complaint against enclosures in 1641, against certain gentry of Wiltshire.[317] We know that it was the gentry who were illegally enclosing land from a number of sources. One of these is a return from the justices of the peace of Lincolnshire of 1637, which named 9 persons found guilty of enclosure and depopulation. Of these nine persons, six had the first name 'Sir', two of them had the last name 'Esquire', and the 9th had the last name 'Gentleman.'[318] The report concluded that the 9 depopulators were fined and pardoned.

Despite the enclosures, it seems that there was still sufficient land to raise grain and feed the population, or those who could afford it, at least in the good years.

---

[313] Apprentices did not get paid.
[314] See page 68.
[315] Bland, Brown and Tawney: *English Economic History*, op cit, p. 274.
[316] Ibid page 275. It is assumed that the 'Statute of Inmates' is the Statute against Vagrants, 1503, 19 Hen VII, c. 12, see pages 63-64. This offence was illogical because the very act of housing a vagrant made that person no longer a vagrant!
[317] See pages 95-96.
[318] Bland, Brown and Tawney, op cit p.275.

It seems likely that there was an easing off in the profitability of wool and sheep in the latter half of the 17th century and the early 18th century. Wool at last had serious competition from imported cotton from Egypt, India and North America.

> "By 1664, the East India Company was importing a quarter of a million pieces of cotton cloth into Britain... Wool continued to dominate the European market, but cotton prints were introduced to Britain by the East India Company in the 1690s. Imports of calicoes, cheap cotton fabrics from (Calcutta) found a mass market among the poor. By 1721 these calicoes threatened British manufacturers and parliament passed the Calico Act that banned calicoes for clothing or domestic purposes. In 1774, the Act was repealed..."[319]

Wool also had increasing competition from linen (flax) and hemp (cannabis).

Whatever the cause, by the early 18th century, there was a glut of grain. England remained an agrarian country until about 1850, when it became more urban and industrial.[320] The 'Gin Craze' was invented to assist the grain-growing gentry.

The Gin Craze

It seems likely that the gin craze was imported into England along with William of Orange in 1689. He certainly enjoyed a drink.[321]

> "Martial William drank Geneva, yet no age could ever boast a braver Prince than he."[322]

James Stuart had fled the country for France, where he was given sanctuary and where he spent his time plotting a return. William and England quickly declared war on France and brandy became illegal. The dead hand of the Puritans had kept England tolerably sober during the Interregnum, but the restoration allowed brandy to be imported and consumed. With its banning, Geneva (or 'gin' as it became known) was the substitute. Parliament passed an act in 1690 "for encouraging the distilling of spirits from corn." 'Corn' meant any one or more of the grain crops, wheat, barley, rye or oats. Malted, mashed, filtered and double or triple distilled, the end result was a ghastly mixture of raw alcohol. When flavoured with 'Geneva' (juniper berries) it became almost palatable, and a cheap trip to oblivion. Even the poorest quality grain, which would not normally be harvested, could be used to make gin.

---

[319] http://en.wikipedia.org/wiki/History-of-cotton. Once again, the parliament dominated by the justices of the peace sees its duty as helping the rich at the expense of the poor.

[320] EB op cit p. 77.

[321] Patrick Dillon: *The Much Lamented Death of Madam Geneva*, Review, 2002, pp. 5 and 6.

[322] Ibid p.5, citing Blunt: 'Geneva: a poem. Addressed to the right honourable Sir R-W-, 1729.'

> "If the aim was to get the English drinking corn spirits, William's legislation had to be rated a spectacular success."[323]

Once again, parliament had delivered legislation with one aim in mind: to enrich the landed gentry regardless of the damage to the nation. The idea was to boost the profits from the land which they owned, and others worked for them at a pittance.

> "Government had declared free trade in a powerful new drug. It had done everything it could to promote its manufacture and sale. It had flooded London in spirits; now Londoners were only too happy to consume them."[324]

Harvests failed in 1699, leading to a shortage of corn, an escalation in the price of bread, and a (very) temporary ban on the distillation of corn. Londoners survived somehow on the importation of rum from the West Indies.

The rather sad reign of 'Dram-Shop Annie' (apparently she, too, liked a drink), resulted in another act "For encouraging the consumption of malted corn," the real purpose of which was to promote distilling.

Gin had its enemies: the do-gooders, the God-botherers and the brewers of ale. They got to work. They had to. "To call the early 18th century a hard-drinking age would be something of an understatement."[325]

> "But it wasn't only because gin was cheap and easily accessible. The lives of the poor had always been hard. When they dreamed up a new market for English corn, no one had pictured dram shops in every basement and Londoners sprawled drunk in the streets. Something else was going on. Something had changed in the city where Madam Geneva had made her home. London, brash, sprawling and chaotic, was fertile ground for her. The Glorious Revolution hadn't just shaken up the drinks trade. The changes which it triggered had created a chaotic and insecure city, vulnerable to a new drug, thirsty for gin."[326]

This was the world inherited by the Georges. Under normal circumstances, one would expect the justices of the peace to step in and restore order. The problem was, not all of them wanted to step in. The vast majority of the justices were still country-dwelling, land-owning gentry. They had a vested financial interest in the sale of excess and poor quality grain, and they were unconcerned by the population lying in the gutters of London.

Some of their London brethren looked on in impotent horror. There was little they could do to cure the drunkenness of London. They lobbied hard for changes to the law, either to have spirits like gin banned altogether, or for it to be priced out of

---

[323] Dillon, op cit p.10.
[324] Ibid.
[325] Dillon, op cit, p. 17.
[326] Dillon, op cit, p.23

reach. The remnants of the conspicuously unsuccessful Society for the Reformation of Manners, such as Sir John Gonson and Sir Daniel Dollins, became voices crying in the wilderness for something to be done. The problem was that what they were trying to do was the equivalent of endeavouring to urinate into a fairly stiff hurricane. The people of London wanted their gin. Their country brethren were against them, and they were the ones who still ran parliament. Parliament had twice legislated to promote gin, and while there was money in it for them, they were not about to change their minds. Many of their London brethren were corrupt "trading justices," [327] and couldn't have cared less. Therefore, appeals to disorder in the streets, drunks in the gutters, morals, manners, God, religion, all came to nothing.

The beginning of the end of the gin craze came about when George II became King in 1727, but it took about 25 more years for things to calm down. It was not that George II was anti-booze. He preferred someone other than Walpole as Prime Minister and was minded to get rid of him. Walpole called the King's bluff by promising a substantial increase in the civil list, a polite term for the King's wages. That did the trick. Walpole suddenly seemed less objectionable, and remained as Prime Minister. He then had to figure out how to raise the money to keep this promise, and decided upon a substantial tax on gin. The result was the Gin Act of 1729. It never succeeded because it imposed the tax on gin sellers, 6,187 of them in Middlesex alone.[328]

The sellers proved difficult to track down. They sold gin from grocers' shops, the shoeshine boy, the washerwomen, all emerging from cellars to peddle their poison. The next problem was that gin was defined as "spirits to which had been added juniper berries, or other fruit, spices or other ingredients." The obvious response was to hold the juniper berries and just sell the raw spirit: 'parliamentary brandy' as it became known. The tax was axed in 1733. Juniper berries were popped back into the mix.

Once again the moralists sprang back into action, with furious lobbying and propaganda. The result was that another Gin Act was passed in 1736. The main controlling measure was the imposition of a licence-to-sell fee of £50 per annum for retailers. Out of the estimated 10,000 sellers in London, only two paid the fee.[329]

The magistrates swung into action. They met as a group at the house of the Court Justice,[330] Thomas de Veil. There they plotted the best way of enforcing the Act against all the 'idle vagabonds.'

> "From Thomas de Veil's house they sent out instructions to their constables. The magistrates agreed to meet at several vestries once or

---

[327] See heading: 'Trading Justices,' at pp. 124-127.
[328] Dillon, op cit, p.88.
[329] Dillon op cit, p.150.
[330] See next heading: 'Court Justice.'

twice a week, to receive information against all offenders, and to punish 'em with the utmost severity.

The result was shocking. The enforcement drive didn't make any difference at all. All the magistrates achieved was to fill up the Houses of Correction. Two weeks later, the *London Daily Post* reported that "gin is still sold about the streets every morning about six or seven o'clock by women and shoe-blackers." The paper found it "very surprising, considering what numbers are now in gaol for retailing that liquor." Another morning, they described how "last night and for several nights past, gin was publicly sold by women and ordinary fellows, on the bulks of Ludgate Hill, and about Fleet Ditch, and there are running shabby fellows that still sell it about the streets." Other vendors had simply moved out of town. "The skirts of the town are pestered with great numbers of walking distillers" reported the *Daily Post* on the 19/11/1736, "inasmuch as no less than six of them were taken up yesterday on Southwark side [...] for retailing the same in the fields."

Two months into prohibition, a horrible realisation began to dawn on the authorities. They had feared uprising, riot and overthrow of the state, but something far worse was happening. They were being ignored."[331]

Once, two informers brought a gin-seller to de Veil's house. 'The mob' surrounded the house; there were more than a thousand of them. De Veil read them the Riot Act, but they did not disperse. De Veil recognised the ring-leader and had him arrested for a breach of the act, a capital offence. Someone stumped up the cash for a lawyer to represent the accused, an exceedingly rare event in those days. (Legal representation was not then allowed for an accused, unless, as here, there was some special point of law to argue, such as insanity). The upshot was that the accused was acquitted on the grounds of insanity. In his after-trial speech, the accused claimed that he had "wit enough to prove myself a fool." "For the authorities, this was a devastating blow."[332]

It took until 1751, and a much more detailed and thoughtful Gin Act to put the brakes on the trade, and to bring gin drinking under some sort of control. In 1752, Henry Fielding claimed that the new law was a success.

"Which, if it had not been abolished, hath very considerably lessened the pernicious practice of gin drinking."[333]

Court Justice

---

[331] Dillon, op cit, p. 158, citing the *London Daily Post and General Advertiser* 2/11/1736.

[332] Dillon, op cit, pp189.

[333] Covent Garden Journal, 10/3/1752. The novelist Henry Fielding is regarded by many as the first stipendiary magistrate: see the later heading 'Stipendiary Magistrates'. According to the dust jacket on Dillon's work, op cit, Fielding said in 1751: "Should the drinking of this poison be continued in its present height during the next twenty years, there will be by that time few of the common people left to drink it."

The mysterious office of court justice began in the 17th century. In addition to the powers of an ordinary justice of the peace, it would appear that the court justice was a spy. He was supposed to report to the government on matters pertaining to "the maintenance of order in the capital, with special regard for the safety of the sovereign."[334] These officials received a stipend and were the precursors to the office of stipendiary magistrate. The ideal of separation of powers had not yet penetrated the English institutions. Some of the court justices were:

1670s: Sir Edmund Berry Godfrey;

1681-1689: Sir John Reresby;

1720s: Nathaniel Blackerby;

1729-1746: Thomas de Veil;

1748-1753: Henry Fielding;

1754- 1780: John Fielding (Henry's blind brother);

1761- 1780: John Hawkins.[335]

Trading Justices

The typical justice of the peace over the centuries and into the Georgian era was the country squire, recommended for the commission by the county Lord Lieutenant. There were not many country squires living full-time in London and the other big cities. A 'lesser class' of person had to be appointed. The quality of justices varied considerably in London, as indeed it did in the country. The various boroughs that make up London all had the right to nominate their own justices of the peace, as did all towns with a Royal Charter. There was always a level of corruption in the magistracy. In order to qualify to be a justice of the peace, one had to acquire sufficient land bringing in sufficient income, and the land was acquired, kept and expanded by fair means or foul, often the latter. In the typical case the justice was wealthy enough not to have to work – he lived on the rent monies he received by letting his lands to others to work. This left him free to carry out the duties of a justice. He was rewarded for this.[336] It was the one shilling fee for recognisances that led to the most corruption, particularly in London.

A recognisance is a form of contract entered into between an individual and the Crown. The person promises, under pain of forfeiture of money (or imprisonment in the event of non-payment), to obey some conditions spelt out in the recognisance. For example, a person wanting to run a tavern had to get a licence from justices of the peace. In order to get that licence, he had to pay one shilling for the recognisance, and promise that he would run the tavern properly, peacefully and in accordance with the law. It was rare for a justice to refuse such an application – if he did, he would not get the one shilling fee. Another form of

---

[334] Skyrme, op cit, Volume II, p.139.
[335] http://www.londonlives.org/static/Pretrial.jsp.
[336] See section entitled: 'The great unpaid?' at pp. 53-54.

recognisance for which a fee of 2s.4d. was payable was a bail recognisance. A person arrested was kept in custody, guilty or innocent, until the trial finished, unless the magistrate granted him or her bail, that is, let them go free, with conditions. Again, there was a strong incentive for the justice of the peace to grant bail – the 2s.4d fee. This may not sound much, but it all added up when the justice was dealing with dozens of such matters per day. Other recognisances attracting rewards for the justice of the peace were promises to be of good behaviour, or to keep the peace. While these extra earnings were no doubt welcomed by the country squire, they were probably insufficient to bankroll retirement on the Cote D'Azure. But it was a different proposition entirely for the London beak.

> "When the writer Henry Fielding took his place as Westminster's senior magistrate in 1749, he complained that 'a predecessor of mine [he was no doubt referring to Thomas De Veil, see next heading 'Stipendiary Magistrates'] used to boast that he made one thousand pounds a year in the office.' A thousand pounds a year put the canny magistrate in the bracket of the most successful doctors and top businessmen. There were plenty of ways for a 'trading justice' to wring money out of the bench. The trick with whores was simple. 'The plan used to be to issue warrants,' as a House of Commons committee was told, 'and take up all the poor devils in the streets, and then there was the bailing them, 2 shillings and 4 pence, which the magistrate had; and taking up 100 girls, that would make, eleven pounds thirteen shillings and four pence.'"[337]

By the early 18th century, there was a common simile: "As corrupt as a Middlesex justice."[338]

> "In 18th century London, some justices, known as 'trading justices', turned the task of issuing recognisances into a business, with some even reputedly encouraging custom by granting warrants on credit or employing a clerk to stand outside their door, touting for business.
>
> In a city where there were dozens of active justices, access to this type of law was relatively easy for anyone who could afford the cost of a warrant (one or two shillings) to bring the accused before a justice."[339]

The corruption of London justices was not confined to the tricks referred to by Dillon, Fielding and Shoemaker. Another title for them was 'Basket Judges.'[340] The basket was the receptacle in which bribes were supposed to be placed. Half a dozen chickens here, a bottle or three of wine there... According to Skyrme:

---

[337] Patrick Dillon, op. cit, p. 55.
[338] Robert Shoemaker: *The London Mob*, Bloomsbury Publishing, p. 233.
[339] Shoemaker, ibid
[340] Skyrme, op. cit, vol. 2, p.135.

> "In May 1780 Edmund Burke said in the House of Commons that the Middlesex justices were 'the scum of the earth; brickmakers, shoemakers, some of whom were notoriously men of such infamous character that they were unworthy of any employ whatever, and others so ignorant that they could scarcely write their own names.'
>
> It is not surprising that the justices failed abysmally in the performance of their task and that the situation deteriorated to a state bordering on anarchy.
>
> As the reputation of the Middlesex and Westminster justices deteriorated, men of the right quality became increasingly reluctant to undertake the office, but there were a few exceptions. One of those who held the office of Court Justice in the mid-18th century was Thomas de Veil who is often regarded as the immediate ancestor of the chief magistrate at Bow Street [...] The room of the present Chief Magistrate contains a plaque which shows de Veil as the first holder of the office [...] what distinguished him from his fellows were the efforts he made to improve the office of magistrate."[341]

Skyrme's exemption of de Veil from the description of trading justice is strange, given that Skyrme was well aware of Fielding's description of de Veil's activities.[342] Further, Skyrme himself went on to describe de Veil:

> "He was a flamboyant character, vain, arrogant and extravagant and his morals left much to be desired even by contemporary standards."[343]

That description appears to fall within Edmund Burke's description of Middlesex justices. Another perspective of de Veil comes from a combination of the works of de Veil's biographer and Patrick Dillon:

> "De Veil worked a 24 hour day, 7 days a week. The harder he worked, the more business came his way and the more money he made. Enemies called him a trading justice; De Veil reckoned himself a professional. 'Though he did much of the ['trading justices'] kind of business,' as his biographer put it, he 'did it in another manner; so that though his office was profitable, yet it was not liable to any scandal.'
>
> That wasn't quite true. There may not have been scandals about money, but money wasn't Thomas De Veil's weakness. 'His greatest foible,' his shamefaced biographer admitted, 'was a most irregular passion for the fair sex.' And when it came to women, he

---

[341] Skyrme, op cit, p.137-139.
[342] Ibid, p. 140
[343] ibid

was quite prepared to abuse his office. If whores were brought in, Thomas De Veil made sure to get their address, whether their house had a back door, and when was a good time to visit them. He was adept 'in distinguishing ladies of a certain character.' 'You see, madam,' he would say as he led women out of his study after a 'private examination', that 'I am capable of being particularly diligent and expeditious in doing a lady's business.'"

It could be said that de Veil got on top of this particular problem.

The reputation of the Middlesex and Westminster justices must call into question the characters of those who led them during this period, including Sir John Gonson, Sir Daniel Dolins and de Veil.

An act of parliament in 1792 brought the era of trading justices to an end.[344] This act provided that justices in Middlesex, Westminster and certain parts of Surrey (which together covered London) could no longer charge nor receive any fees for services. It also officially created a new class of magistrates, stipendiary magistrates, based around Bow Street Magistrates Court. (This group was already in existence, but the act gave them official recognition: see next heading). Seven other permanent magistrates' courts were set up around London, manned by stipendiaries. Any fees charged by these new courts went straight into general revenue. Trading justices faded away.

Stipendiary Magistrates

A stipendiary magistrate is a justice of the peace who is paid by the state. The first stipendiaries appeared in the eleven parishes into which Jamaica was divided in the late 17th century. They were paid public servants and called 'Resident Magistrates.' Not long after their appearance came the 'Court Justice' in London, also in the late 17th century.[345] The court justice was paid as a spy rather than for the work he did as a justice, but not only did the court justice 'report on matters pertaining to the maintenance of order in the capital,' he also engaged in the enforcement of orders by swingeing use of criminal and poor laws. Certainly de Veil purported to lead the other London Justices, with meetings at his home, but that may simply have been a matter of geographical convenience. De Veil, the Fielding brothers and their successors are more accurately judged as laying the foundation for the institution of stipendiaries. The first official Chief and Stipendiary Magistrate is probably Sir Sampson Wright, who served as the beak at Bow Street both before and after the Metropolitan Police Act of 1792.

Enough has been said about de Veil. His successor was Henry Fielding, an unsuccessful barrister and successful novelist (he was the author of *Tom Jones*). His earlier character is summed up by Dillon as follows.

> "By the late 1740s he was broke and ill, disappointed and nearing the end of his life [...] the legal career [...] had never prospered. He

---

344 The Metropolitan Police Act, 32 Geo. III, c. 53.
345 See p. 124.

was always in debt [...] He was paying the price for a youth spent in coffee houses and theatres, too much drink and too much good food. 'Fielding continues to be visited for his sins' reported the young poet Edward More, 'so as to be wheeled about from room to room... his disorder is the gout and intemperance the cause.' Another visitor found him 'a poor, emaciated, worn out rake.' To the town, the sight of Henry Fielding installed as principal Westminster Magistrate was the best joke of the year."[346]

Despite this unpromising beginning, he made a good fist of his new appointment, the first magistrate to accept a stipend and eschew any profits of justice.

He came to be regarded as incorruptible, and did much to clean up crime gangs, then rampant in London. Together with his half-brother John, they formed the 'Bow Street Runners', a group of eight police enforcers who were the forerunners of the modern police force founded in 1829 by Sir Robert Peel.

When Henry retired, his brother John succeeded him at Bow Street. He was blind and was named 'the blind beak of Bow Street,' reputed to be able to recognise the voices of more than 3,000 criminals. He served from 1754 to 1780 and was knighted.

> "...he proved to be an outstanding magistrate, and turned his physical defect to his advantage by conveying the image of impartial 'justice' sitting blindfolded. He continued his brother's work in improving the efficiency and standing of his office and like him maintained a high level of integrity. His blindness did not stop him visiting the scene of a crime to carry out his own enquiries, and he was remarkably skilful in detecting criminals and in examining witnesses. His success in breaking up gangs of robbers led to a noticeable reduction in street robberies. [...] Fielding initiated a weekly bulletin giving descriptions of criminals who had departed London which was circulated to all parts of the country [...] it became the *Police Gazette*. In turn, justices in other areas sent to Bow Street particulars of those who had 'escaped justice' in their own counties, together with a warrant for their apprehension, which could then be forwarded to wherever it might be required. A kind of clearing house, in conjunction with the permanent criminal records, was therefore established at Bow Street for all criminal activity throughout England and Wales."[347]

Fielding had an assistant magistrate, Saunders Welch, formerly a High Constable and one of the Bow Street Runners, a man of outstanding ability and impeccable character.[348] Fielding and Welch together lobbied for salaries and were awarded £200 per annum. Fielding's salary increased to £400 in 1756.

---

[346] 'The Much Lamented Death of Madam Geneva,' pp.240-241.
[347] Skyrme, op cit, vol. 2, p. 146.
[348] Skyrme op cit, p. 145.

The Metropolitan Police Act of 1792 formally recognised the Bow Street arrangements, and extended them to all parts of metropolitan London except the city itself. The City of London remained under the control of the Mayor and Alderman because of their fierce opposition to the institution of stipendiary magistrates. The act created 7 new urban court districts, each to be staffed by three stipendiary magistrates on a salary of £400 each. Each of these courts was allotted six constables. Apart from the magistrates at Bow Street, the earlier stipendiaries were not highly regarded. The chief magistrate at Bow Street was always regarded as the chief stipendiary magistrate throughout England and Wales. Earlier magistrates included Sir Sampson Wright and Patrick Colquhoun, who was the author of *Treatise on the Police of the Metropolis*, which was the inspiration for the formation in 1829 of the London Metropolitan Police force.

The main differences between the emerging stipendiaries and the traditional justices of the peace were that the first were solely urban in origin, while the latter remained mainly rural; stipendiaries were full time, justices' courts were spasmodic; the only administrative work performed by stipendiaries, apart from licensing, related to the criminal law; the justices' courts dealt with a variety of other, mainly local government, matters.

In 1839, a new Metropolitan Police Courts Act consolidated the office of stipendiary magistrates and officially recognised the position of Chief Metropolitan Magistrate, annual salary £1,400. The salary for a stipendiary was then fixed at £1,200. Stipendiaries had to be barristers.

There was stiff opposition which prevented any great expansion of the office of stipendiary magistrates by justices of the peace who still had control of parliament. A few stipendiaries were appointed for the emerging industrial towns, but lay justices continued to deal with the bulk of minor crime in England. They still do. The two systems amalgamated in 1964.[349] Courts were for a time thereafter composed either of a stipendiary sitting alone, a stipendiary sitting with two justices of the peace, or two or three lay justices sitting together, with a legally qualified justices clerk advising them. The word 'police' was dropped from the name of the courts in the cities, which thereafter were known as Metropolitan Magistrates Courts, and the Stipendiaries became 'Metropolitan Magistrates.'

The institution of Stipendiary Magistrates disappeared altogether in Britain in the year 2000, when all remaining stipendiaries were renamed 'District Judges', and Petty Sessions were left to lay justices of the peace, advised by a solicitor. Paid magistrates, now simply called 'Magistrates' remain as something of an accident of history in Australia, dealing with the bulk of both criminal and civil law. These officials are all legally qualified and their salaries are now more than $300,000 per annum.

Game Laws

---

[349] The Administration of Justice Act.

We leave for the moment the peccadilloes of the city justice and return to the countryside.

The English gentry took their hunting very seriously. The Master of the Foxhounds was ranked second in a county after the Lord Lieutenant, and well ahead of bishops, members of parliament and magistrates.[350] (Oscar Wilde would probably have re-arranged the order of precedence. It was he who described foxhunting as: "the unspeakable in pursuit of the inedible").

> "A list of fines imposed at Quarter Sessions during the years 1825-1826 would almost lead one to think that the endeavours of the country gentry were simply aimed at preserving the interest of the landowners from the predatory habits of the starving poor.
>
> Their execution of the game laws aroused universal indignation."[351]

> "A typical episode is recounted by Sir Horace Walpole: 'In 1822, a farmer coursing hares on his own land, with the permission of his own landlord, was summoned by the keeper of the adjoining landowner for doing so. The adjoining landowner was the Duke of Buckingham, and the farmer was literally convicted by the Duke himself, in the Duke's private house, at the instance of one of the Duke's keepers, and on the evidence of another of his keepers.'"[352]

Trevelyan says:

> "The squires were jealous of the small freeholders as being politically and socially independent of their sway. The rage of game preserving characteristic of the epoch made them look askance at a fellow without a coat of arms who had the impudence to shoot partridges on his own patch of ground. Indeed, the squirearchal Parliaments of the later Stuarts had most tyrannically passed game laws which excluded all freeholders of under £100 [per annum income] from killing game even on their own land."[353]

In 1828, Lord Brougham told the House of Lords:

> "There is not a worse constituted tribunal on the face of the earth than that at which summary convictions on the game laws takes place (than) a bench or brace of sporting magistrates."

The game laws are a classic example of one law for the rich, an entirely different one for the poor. Who had the greater need to hunt and fish for game: the starving poor or the idle rich? It was the gentry which gave themselves and the nobility the exclusive right to take game. It was the gentry who used their influence in parliament to pass the repressive game laws, and then used those laws through

---

[350] Moir, op cit p. 157.
[351] Moir Op. cit p.126.
[352] Ibid. P. 127.
[353] Op cit at p. 525

their representatives, the justices of the peace, to enforce them in a ruthless manner.

Game laws had been in force from the Conquest in 1066. Hunting in the King's forests, then encompassing 17% of the area of England, was punishable by death, or at least a bit of limb-hacking. Henry II mitigated this a bit by a proclamation in 1225:

> No man from henceforth shall lose either life or limb for killing our deer.[354]

In 1389, the prohibition from hunting in the Royal Forests was extended to hunting for game anywhere by anyone, unless he was a gentleman, meaning thereby a person with an income from lands of at least 40 shillings per annum.[355] The property qualification was upped in 1671 to an income of £100 per annum. Thus hunting and fishing became the exclusive right of the nobility and gentry. The qualification to become a justice of the peace was upped in 1732 to the same amount (£100 per annum). Every justice of the peace was thereafter, if not before, eligible to hunt game. This furnishes some explanation as to why the justices were so hard on poachers.

Upwards of 100 amendments were made to the game laws from 1671 to 1831, mostly tinkering with the penalties for taking different sorts of game in different circumstances. During the economic downturn following the South Sea Bubble in 1721, gangs of poachers organised themselves and raided various forests, killing deer, and on one occasion, a gamekeeper's son. In order to do this and to avoid recognition, they blackened their faces. 'The Black Act'[356] was passed by parliament. This introduced the death penalty for 50 separate offences to do with gaming. These include going armed and disguised at night.

On one occasion, justices of the peace erected barriers in Hertfordshire to prevent poachers getting at game. A number of poachers assembled to tear down the barricades. A gang of magistrates set upon them and arrested many. They were hanged. One of the hanged, Reynolds, was placed in a coffin. The lid was in the process of being nailed down, when Reynolds took exception to the process and climbed out of the coffin. He was carted off in triumph by the mob to the nearest ale-house and propped against the wall. He was half-way through his first beer when he expired.[357]

---

[354] Skyrme, op cit vol. 2, p.118
[355] 13 Rich. II, st. 1, c.13
[356] 1723, 9 Geo.I, c.22.
[357] Reynolds was not the only person to perform this trick. In 1705, 'Half-hanged' Smith revived 15 minutes after being removed from the gibbet. He was tried twice more on capital offences. The first time, he was acquitted on a point of law. On the second occasion, the victim died the day before he was due to give evidence. Captain Kidd was not so lucky: the rope broke during his hanging, and he fell to earth alive, but they got a new rope and this time hanged him unto death.

Other acts of parliament specified penalties of imprisonment or fines for taking game. Some have argued that justices of the peace were quite fair in administering the game laws, because sometimes they only fined for breaches, when they could have imposed much harsher penalties.[358] The point is, justices of the peace ought not to have had anything to do with the administration of the game laws, a matter where they were so obviously biased, and protective of their own interests. Any monetary penalty imposed on the poor and desperate necessarily meant a gaol sentence. In those days if a court imposed a fine, the person fined was immediately imprisoned until the fine was paid.

It has been estimated that one-quarter of the prisoners in gaol in England in the 18th century were there for various breaches of the game laws. Other penalties that might be imposed were transportation (to the Americas, or later, Australia), and of course, the death penalties prescribed by the Black Act. It would seem that corruption in the magistracy was not confined to the 'trading justices' of London.

Move for Reform in Criminal Law and Sentencing; Alleviating the Lot of the Poor; Free Speech

The Anglican Church was moribund and seemed to have no time for the poor.

> "The churches were not meeting social problems in pre-industrial England and the poor often shirked churchgoing. Contemporary literature shows the churches as preserves of the upper and middle classes."[359]

A member of parliament, John Bright, addressed the House of Commons about the fact that there were still 243 capital offences in existence at the end of George III's reign:[360]

> "Our government at that time had become barbarous, and I am not aware that one of the 20 bishops and 20,000 ministers of the Church of England raised a voice about this infamy."

Schama said:

> "Many of the evangelists who burned to correct the evils of their age believed that the established church had become too rich, too complacent, too aristocratic, to fulfil its Christian pastoral mission, and was part of the problem rather than an instrument of solving it."[361]

Bright must have discounted John Wesley, ordained an Anglican priest in 1728: the Anglican Church itself disowned Wesley, the founder of the Methodist

---

[358] For example, Skyrme, op.cit, vol. 2, pp.124-126 and PB Munshe: *Gentlemen and Poachers. The English Game Laws 1671-1831*, CUP, 1981.
[359] EB, 15th Edition, Vol. 29, p.79
[360] Cited by Hamilton Fyfe in Peoples of All Nations, volume 3, p. 1762, Educational Book Company.
[361] *A History of Britain, volume 3, 1776-2000, The Fate of Empire.* pp.33-34.

Church. He began preaching to the masses, and soon built a huge following. The reaction of the Anglicans was to close their churches to him. He began to preach to large congregations in the open air. His converts were miners, foundrymen, weavers and day-labourers.[362] Wesley and his followers were mainly concerned with the spiritual and temporal welfare of the poor, but were unable to stand as a bulwark against the enforcement of unjust laws. However, they influenced many who were in such a position: Wilberforce, Eden, Blackstone, Bentham, Fielding, Paul, Howard, Paine and Wollstonecraft to name a few.

But it took an Italian, the Marchese di Beccaria, to set the ball rolling on serious reform. His treatise on 'Crimes and Punishments' was published in 1764. He made many points, but the three that attracted lasting attention were:

- Relativities in sentencing: It was wrong in principle to impose an identical penalty for crimes of differing seriousness. In England, for example, the penalty for theft of goods worth one shilling or more was death, the same penalty as for a mass murder. Felonies were all treated the same, though they differed greatly in culpability.

- The certainty of punishment is a more effective deterrent than rigour or cruelty.[363]

- Justice, in order to be effective, must be prompt; Justice delayed is justice denied.[364]

The first English translation of Beccaria's work contained an apologetic note from the sycophantic translator:

> "It may be objected that a treatise of this kind is useless in England, where from the excellence of our law and government, no examples of cruelty and oppression are to be found."[365]

Fortunately, some of the contemporary English commentators did not agree with the translator. In 1771, in his *Principles of Penal Law*, William Eden attacked the still current practice of peine forte et jure,[366] whipping, the impossibility of a fair

---

[362] Chambers Biographical Dictionary, edit M. Magnusson.

[363] Madan's: *'Thoughts on Executive Justice'* illustrates Beccaria's point with the final speech of the old lag about to be executed: "There are so many chances for us, and so few against us, that I never thought of coming to this. First, there are so many chances against being discovered. So many more that we are not taken; and if taken, not convicted; and if convicted, not hanged, that I thought myself very safe with at least a twenty to one in my favour."

[364] Whilst dot point 1 seems to have been belatedly addressed, dot points two and three are to this day alarmingly under-addressed, particularly the delays between apprehension and finalisation of trial and sentence, which can amount to years.

[365] Surely this bullshit needs no further comment.

[366] See p. 104.

trial[367], benefit of clergy,[368] hearsay evidence, sheriff's jury rigging, and so on. He concluded at p. 177:

> "Thus, ignorant of the form and language of the whole process, unassisted by counsel, unsupported by witnesses, discountenanced by the court, and baited by Crown lawyers, the poor bewildered prisoner found an eligible refuge in the dreadful moment of conviction"

Eden suggested alternatives for capital punishment for various felonies, and the replacement of the death penalty by imprisonment with hard labour.

In 1773, John Howard published his *State of the Prisons*, drawing attention to the deplorable state of England's prisons.

Jeremy Bentham set about designing a model prison, which he called a 'panopticon.' It was to be a circular building where all the prisoners could be kept in solitary confinement and be watched continuously from a central control tower by a series of mirrors. His exact design was never built, but Pentonville prison, built in 1842, was similar. In Australia, the penitentiary built in Tasmania at Port Arthur, and Pentridge gaol in Melbourne, had similar features.

These and similar agitations and demonstrations against the evils of English society in general, and the narrow eligibility for voting in elections and becoming a member of parliament were about the time of the French Revolution, and any criticism of the system was quite dangerous.

> "Through the spring of 1794 the British government had been bringing prosecutions against those whom it deemed to be the writers, publishers and purveyors of seditious literature. Its object was to employ the usefully vague medieval charge of 'compassing the death of the King' to make into an act of outright treason publications and discussions on the concept of a republic or even on manhood suffrage..."[369]

The Riot Act of 1715 was in place, discouraging gatherings of 12 or more people.[370] This was reinforced by the Seditious Assemblies Act of 1795.[371] To remain more than one hour after being directed to disperse was a felony, punishable by death, without benefit of clergy. The Combination Acts of 1799 and 1800 made any assembly of workmen with a view to discussing a wage increase an offence punishable by 3 months' imprisonment. There could be no

---

[367] See pp. 69-70.
[368] See p. 21, fn 43, 100, fn 294, 107-108.
[369] Schama, op. cit, p.66.
[370] It was a capital offence to remain part of a crowd more than one hour after the Riot Act was read. The one hour's grace was not always honoured. See also pp. 71, 77-78. The possibility of the reading of the Riot Act must have made some of John Wesley's gatherings fun.
[371] 36 Geo. III, c.8

meeting without the permission of 3 magistrates, a permission that was rarely forthcoming. Spies and informers were encouraged. Free speech had been a problem for many years.[372] The problem reached its peak at the time of the French Revolution and the Napoleonic Wars. William Cobbett became the champion of the poor, arguing their cause in his newspaper, the *Political Register*. For this, he was sentenced to two years' imprisonment in 1809, and when he resumed his activities, he had to flee the country to avoid arrest. On his return in 1819, he was again arrested for sedition, but acquitted.

> "The combination of propaganda, gang intimidation, genuinely patriotic volunteer militias, censorship, political spying and summary arrests succeeded in stopping the momentum of democratic agitation."[373]

Imprisonment: The Beginning of the Modern Era[374]

Howard, Eden and Blackstone drafted and succeeded in having passed through parliament the Penitentiary Act in 1779, on the understanding that imprisonment would be used mainly as a substitute for transportation, rather than a substitution for the death penalty, that is to say if and when the act was ever activated. In fact, it was not activated until 1816, after the end of the Napoleonic War. That was the year England's first penitentiary was closed for business,[375] the Millbank penitentiary. It cost £500,000 to build, said to be the costliest building in England.

Modern imprisonment is covered more fully in the next chapter, but it is worth setting out some of the aims and provisions of the Penitentiary Act here. While the idea was to substitute imprisonment for transportation, it was never universally practised. Transportation of prisoners continued to Australia until 1868. The act made provision for 'penitentiary houses,' for solitary confinement of prisoners accompanied by well-regulated labour and religious instruction. The objects of the act were:

> "The deterring of others, reforming the individuals and inuring them to habits of industry."

Working hours were to be regulated at 10 hours per day, 6 days per week. The length of a term of imprisonment was supposed to be about one half of the term which would have been fixed for transportation. Sentences of transportation were fixed at 7 or 14 years, or life. It is unlikely that a sentence of imprisonment would be fixed in substitution for a sentence of transportation for life, but common sentences later to be imposed were 3 years' imprisonment vice 7 years' transportation and 7 years for 14. Until penitentiaries could be constructed, prisoners still kept on the hulks were to be employed raising sand, soil and gravel from and cleaning of the River Thames.

---

[372] See, for example, the Trial of William Penn, at page 98.
[373] Scharma, op cit, p. 69.
[374] Earlier imprisonment has been considered at pp. 72-77.
[375] The author is unsure whether one opens or closes a gaol for business.

The use of the sentence of imprisonment had increased considerably in Britain over the last century, but only for minor offences, mainly for poaching[376] and vagrancy, but not at all for felonies, which still required the death penalty or transportation, which was not available as a sentence for 15 years after the outbreak of the American War of Independence. It resumed in 1787, with transportation to Australia.

Meanwhile, in America, the Quakers, who were opposed to the death penalty, opened, or rather closed the Walnut Street penitentiary in Philadelphia in 1792. In so doing, they were inspired by the English Penitentiary Act, and the works of Blackstone, Eden, Howard and Bentham. They adopted the 'Separate System'. Prisoners were confined to their cells and never allowed to see another prisoner. They were subjected to scripture readings and contemplation of their lot. Rehabilitation was the main aim (by contrast with the English Penitentiary Act, where deterrence was the main aim).

In the 1820s, the 'Silent System' was invented at the Auburn Prison in New York. Again, the main aim was rehabilitation. The prisoners were not isolated, but forced to work, for example, sewing mailbags, in total silence.

Back in England, not all reformers sat on their hands waiting for the end of the war with the French. One of them, Sir George Onesiphorus Paul, a very wealthy member of the landed gentry, justice of the peace, and High Sheriff of Gloucester, had studied the works of the English theoretical reformers and Beccaria. He understood that the old gaols were unsuitable for present purposes and achieved none of the aims of punishment. He set about constructing a new one, and spent the rest of his life trying to influence others to follow his example. To keep the prisoners busy, he had a treadmill installed in his prison. Eventually the regulations he drafted for prisons in Gloucestershire were adopted as the regulations for control of prisons throughout the country.

For the further development of prisons and the sentence of imprisonment as a substitute for some felonies, see next chapter at pages 147-151.

The Industrial Revolution; the Agricultural Revolution; Further Enclosures; Factory 'Apprentices'

"The law locks up the man or woman

Who steals the goose from off the common,

But lets the greater felon loose

Who steals the common from off the goose."[377]

The next round of enclosures that accompanied the Agricultural Revolution[378] was the reverse of the previous round of enclosures. This time fields were

---

[376] Many of the breaches of the game laws still attracted the death penalty. Minor breaches resulted in a sentence of imprisonment.

[377] By that prolific author, anon. From http://en.wikipedia.org(wiki)enclosure.

enclosed for crops, not sheep. Sheep had peaked in value by the mid-17th century. Wool was overtaken by other cloth made from cotton, flax or hemp, particularly cotton. The problem for landholders was that much of the land which they held still had medieval characteristics: strips of land separated by some distance from each other. This tranche of enclosures involved negotiations amongst the landowners of various areas, land swapping and consolidation of scattered plots into contiguous fields. Any remaining lands still shared in common with others were snatched up and consolidated into agricultural fields and then enclosed. By the early 19th century, the only common land left was of the occasional village green nature, where there was any village left.

These enclosures were authorised and recorded by private acts of parliament, thousands of them. These acts sometimes made provision for compensation of dispossessed owners, but not tenants, in the form of inferior land. Parliament usually sought consensus among the land owners, or four-fifths of them, before agreeing to pass these acts, but did not take into account the wishes of the dispossessed tenants.

Some authorities, such as the *Encyclopaedia Britannica*, maintain that these enclosures did not depopulate the countryside: agricultural labour was still required, and the excess ejected merely moved to the cities to become factory fodder for the contemporaneous Industrial Revolution.

> "The social effects of enclosure have been debated vigorously and emotionally. Recent studies show that enclosure did not depopulate rural districts. The need for agricultural labour did not decline. The citywide migration was that of the rural surplus."[379]

On the other hand:

> "England resolved its land problems by the enclosure movement, which drove the small peasants into the towns."[380]

The point can be argued either way. Most of the texts favour the depopulation theory. That theory helps explain the phenomenon of 'rotten boroughs', nearly empty villages still sending two members off to parliament. This was an 18th and early 19th century matter which created much ammunition for the 'radicals.'

In 1802, the practice of each village re-distributing its land by individual acts of parliament gave way to the redistribution taking place under the general Enclosure Act. By that time, there was very little land left to enclose. Ownership of rural land was in the hands of large landowners, the gentry, with a few smallholders.

> "The post-1815 agricultural depression hurt the small landholders severely."[381]

---

[378] 1760-1820 approx. Earlier enclosures are dealt with at pp. 18-19, 40, 64-66, 68, 71-72, 82-83, 95-96, 117-118, 134-136, 139.
[379] EB, 15th edition, Volume 29, pp. 77, 78.
[380] EB, 15th edition, Volume 22, p. 61.

Arthur Young was an agricultural scientist, first secretary to the Board of Agriculture, and a proponent of enclosures. Nevertheless, he said:

> "By 19 out of 20 Enclosure Acts, the poor are injured, and most grossly."[382]

Carter and Mears add:

> "There was no greater change in English history than this: that the mass of the population was driven from the countryside, so that England, which in 1759, had been largely rural, was by 1850 largely urban. It was in many respects a change for the worse."[383]

This tranche of enclosures had ramifications for the country-based justices of the peace. In the first place, they were the representatives of the landed gentry which profited most from it. Secondly, they still dominated parliament, which passed the thousands of enclosure Acts. Thirdly, by significantly lowering the rural population, they themselves were relieved to some extent from punishing the population vanishing in the general direction of the industrial towns, for their often corrupt city brethren to punish for being vagrants.

Much of a sentimental nature has been written of the rapidly disappearing English rural way of life. For example, Oliver Goldsmith wrote *The Deserted Village*. Of these laments, Schama had this to say:

> "The complaints and laments were, of course, unrealistically nostalgic for a bucolic utopia of caring parsons, avuncular squires and humane magistrates that had never existed except as an imaginary counter-example to the iron laws of country property."

The more or less simultaneous Industrial Revolution centred on, but was not confined to, the cotton industry. Machines streamlined production. The iron industry also expanded to make the necessary machines. Inland transport was revolutionised by canals and the invention of the railway. Many more people were needed to deal with the machines, the iron ore, the coke, the coal, the mines, the raw materials and the resulting manufactured goods, and the transport of these goods. 'The rural excess' is a partial explanation of the rapidly increasing labour forces in the new industrial towns.

According to Dowdell[384] much of the workforce came from the orphanages and Bridewells of Britain, particularly from London, by the cartloads. Three things to note: firstly, the orphans from the age of four years and up, were placed in the factories as apprentices; secondly, they had to be placed in an apprenticeship by justices of the peace, and enter into indentures, which required a payment to the justice, out of parish funds; thirdly, apprentices were unpaid. To a point, the fate

---

[381] EB. Volume 29, p.78.
[382] Cited by Carter and Mears: *'A History of Britain'*, section 5, 1688-1958, OUP, p. 662.
[383] Ibid.
[384] Dowdell, EG 'A Hundred Years of Quarter Sessions,' 1932, p.57.

of apprentices has been dealt with at pp. 75, 92. Hamilton Fyfe[385] describes the fate of the factory children thus:

> "Slavery cloaked as apprenticeship
>
> It was while they found it difficult to get 'hands' enough to man their machines that the manufacturers put into practice the apprenticeship plan. They arranged with the parish authorities in many parts of the country to let them have pauper children. These wretched little creatures were supposed to be 'apprenticed' to factory labour. They were, in truth, no better off than slaves. There was a regular slave trade carried on for the benefit of manufacturers and of the scoundrels who took children from workhouses and made a handsome profit by selling them, or leasing their labour. It would be an exaggeration to say that all such 'apprentices' were ill-treated, but there is no doubt that many of them suffered abominable torture. They were poorly fed, housed in miserable conditions, badly clothed. Their hours of work were very long, from 12-16 hours. They were beaten and tormented and brutal masters even riveted chains on their tender limbs if they tried to run away."

Magistrates and society under the Hanovers to 1815

It was during this period that the country squire lost his monopoly on the magistracy, and wealthy mine owners, traders and industrialists, as well as the 'trading justices' joined the ranks of justices of the peace. There is little evidence that this new blood improved the performance of the magistracy, and considerable evidence that things worsened. One of their worst efforts came in the fixing of wages.

So far as the field workers (agricultural labourers) were concerned, shepherds were paid £3.15.0 per annum; young maids £1.6.8 per annum; day labourer, 10 pence per day; women, same work, 6 pence per day; and for a ploughright, carpenter or mason, one shilling and four pence per day.[386] These were starvation wages. If the worker tried to pull the plug on that employment, he was liable to be branded (literally) as a slave.[387]

As to the factory workers, they were no better off.

> "The laws of the market-place determined the times of operating machines. Workers had no preparation for the new industrial discipline. In addition to physical adjustment, they had to make,

---

[385] 'Peoples of all Nations', volume 3, p. 1774.
[386] Rates fixed by the Oxfordshire Quarter Sessions in 1687, and adopted elsewhere, quoted in Skyrme, op cit, volume 1, p.245.
[387] See 'Vagrants', p. 72.

within two generations, a radical mental and moral adjustment to a new way of life."[388]

Justices of the peace had no power to fix wages for factory workers- this was left to the tender mercies of the factory owners. They certainly didn't pay their apprentices much.

So, what sort of society did all this produce?

The geography of England was changing. Forests were disappearing into housing in the newly emerging industrial towns and the ships for the navy and commerce. Country lands were being enclosed for crops as part of the agricultural revolution. Rural labour was disappearing into the towns. Rural villages were disappearing. Land was being acquired with new money by tradesmen, bankers, mine owners and industrialists.

> "Fielding in *Tom Jones* has drawn a picture of the coarser minded country squire, which has often been taken as typical of the 18th century. But its hunting squire, who was drunk every night of the week, was after all but one of a type, though a common one. There were also a good many country gentlemen who passed their time in cultured pursuits, and spent their money collecting books, pictures and furniture. This type...had sufficient wealth to indulge its tastes for the finer things of life."[389]

In either case, squires drunken or sober, they had three things in common: they were wealthy enough to indulge their whim; they did no productive work, and they did not share their wealth. Justices of the peace are representative of both these classes of wealth. British apologists emphasise the other side of the coin, that this indulgence lead to advances in the fields of literature, art, architecture, pottery, landscaping and other pursuits to enable the idle rich to pass the time.

Unless you were wealthy like the gentry described above, life was pretty grim.

> "It is not too much to say that large sections of the people were living in conditions of such hardship, such danger and discomfort, and even of such absolute bestiality as cannot now be easily conceived. The Cornish tinners, worked underground 'with hardly any room to turn their bodies, wet to the skin [...] by the glimmering of a small candle, whose scattered rays will scarcely penetrate the thick darkness of the place' (citing Clarke *Tour Through South England, 1791*). A doctor who worked among these miners saw his patient conveyed to a hut 'full of naked children [...] destitute of all conveniences, and of almost all necessities. The whole indeed is a scene of such complicated wretchedness and

---

[388] EB. Op cit 15th edition, volume 29, p.79.
[389] Carter and Mears, '*A History of Britain*', section 5, 1688-1958, OUP.

distress as words have no power to describe' (citing Pryce *Mineralogia Cornubiensis* 1778)."[390]

Life in the cities and newly emerging industrial complexes was no better. Life had to be endured in soul-destroying, dismally gloomy, jerry-built housing and factories. In country villages, the remnants of the population (those who had not escaped to the industrial towns or America) slowly starved following enclosures.

It was these poor people who came before the magistrates hoping for justice, but receiving instead sentences of death, whipping or transportation into slavery.

The visits of the poor to the law courts were probably the only intermingling of the two Englands. Disraeli referred to two nations who barely knew each other.

> [Of Wales]: "The island people, like the shepherds of the Meirionnydd Hills, were primitives, often dwelling in windowless hovels and surviving on oatmeal, milk and a little fish. Tens of thousands of them had been forced off their farms in the 1760s and 1770s to make way for profitable herds of blackface and cheviot sheep. In desperation, many had made the Atlantic crossing as emigrants to the new world.[391]

> Old British virtues had surrendered to modern British vices. Liberty had been perverted by patronage; justice blinded by the unforgiving glare of money.

> When he got sick and old (he) was turned away from one parish after another, as each attempted to off-load its responsibility for poor relief.

> Bewick's country people break rocks by the side of the road, slurp gruel in a wretched garret; or hang themselves by the wayside.

> [Of Scotland]: When, for example, (Bewick) walked through the highlands, unlike more sentimental tourists, he saw immediately that the sweeping vistas and empty uplands that so delighted romantic ramblers were actually the result of mass clearance of crofters: the conversion of a country which had once supported families to a country supporting sheep.

> In 1769, Philip Thicknesse wrote a horrifying account, accompanied with an equally horrifying print of 'Four Persons Found Starved to Death at Datchworth.'

> But there were probably as many wretched people like the Datchworth victims in the south (especially the impoverished south west of England) than in Bewick's Northumbria. For it was in southern England that the social results of 'rural

---

[390] Carter and Mears Ibid, pp.653,654.
[391] Schama, op. cit. These and the following paragraphs are extracted from pp.14-33

improvement'...were most dramatically apparent...when a succession of wheat harvest failures sent prices soaring and unleashed food riots in the towns and cities all the way from London to Derbyshire. [Citing Oliver Goldsmith's *The Traveller*:]

Each wanton judge new penal statutes draw.

Laws grind the poor and rich men rule the law.

The country came out of the fiery years of food riots, troop mobilisations and hangings with its institutions intact but with its faith in the paternalism and even the moral legitimacy of the aristocracy, the judiciary shaken.

...particular evils, invariably and significantly described as 'unnatural': prison sentences for unmarried mothers (often made pregnant by debauched young and not-so-young gentlemen); the state of the prisons to which they, as well as debtors and common criminals, were sent; the indiscriminate application of the death penalty for trivial felonies. The plight of children..."

The Gordon Riots of 1780

The Gordon riots of 1780 are important to the history of the magistracy because they demonstrated the inability or unwillingness of justices of the peace to quell large scale disturbances.

The occasion was a series of riots sparked by Lord George Gordon, a fanatical protestant. He acted in protest at the passing in parliament of the Catholic Relief Act,[392] and the fear that a similar Act might apply to Scotland. The Act was to relieve Catholics from previous acts disqualifying them from holding office. At the time, Catholics were desperately needed to fill gaps in the ranks of officers in the army during the War of Independence.

The riots resulted in attacks on Catholic Churches, Catholic houses and Catholics themselves. (There were still such things as Catholic Churches, attached to foreign embassies). Parliament itself was attacked, including the Prime Minister, Lord North. The military had to be called in, and shot and killed upwards of 300 rioters.

Until then, justices of the peace had responsibility to quell riots, by gathering constables and militia. On this occasion, the riots were too big and too out of control for the magistrates to handle. The then Chief Metropolitan Magistrate, Sir John Fielding was on his death bed. The *Catholic Encyclopaedia* thought that other magistrates were "too infatuated with the protestant association" to intervene, and still other justices were "cowards."[393]

As a direct result of the riots, the government introduced to parliament a bill entitled London and Westminster Police Bill, seeking to introduce a system of

---

[392] 1778, 18 Geo III, c. 60.
[393] http://www.newadvent.org/cathen/00669c.htm.

paid magistrates and a professional police force under the control of 3 commissioners. Justices of the peace opposed the bill and it was not passed.

The French Revolution and the Napoleonic Wars

Once the heads of the French nobility began to roll into the baskets, the English nobility got off their collective dates and began to attend magistrates' sessions and take an interest in preserving the status quo, and their own heads. Hitherto they had shown little interest in the goings-on of the justices of the peace.

The poor became more than factory fodder – they were now a convenient source of cannon-fodder. A sentence of death, commuted by service in the forces, became a common sentence. So, during the Napoleonic Wars two new sentences became available to justices: Service in the army or navy, and transportation to Australia. The latter was the preferred sentence for Irish political agitators, since it was thought they might not exhibit the required enthusiasm in fighting for England.

Subsidising Bread

Farm labourers subsisted on very low wages, their wages being controlled by the magistrates, who were the owners of the farms where they worked. The magistrates had control of rural wages since the Statute of Labourers in 1349. The labourers were able to subsist until the industrial revolution because of the income earned by their wives and children in cottage industries, particularly by the manufacture of clothes.

The Industrial Revolution, together with the enclosures of rural land and the Agricultural Revolution, brought about a crisis in rural living. Once the cottage industries essential to the subsistence of the rural poor had ceased to be competitive, because of the more efficient factories in the industrial revolution, families could not subsist on the farm labourers' wages alone. They began to starve, or they moved to towns to seek work in the factories. This last situation alarmed the gentry, who realised that, unless something was done, there would be no labour to run their farms for them, and as a consequence, some of their wealth might evaporate. Another cause for worry was that the rural poor might riot and it was necessary to avoid that threat.

The most obvious solution was for the magistrates to raise the wages above starvation levels, but, as the owners of land, and therefore the persons who would be expected to pay the increase, the magistrates baulked at this.

And so it came to pass that the magistrates of Berkshire in 1795, sitting at the Pelican Inn in the village of Speen, probably with the aid of the consumption of bulk English ale, came up with the Speenhamland system. That system was to subsidise wages based upon the price of bread and somebody else other than the gentry paying the subsidy. Once again, they cast that privilege upon the long-suffering parish. Parish rates were payable by the occupiers of land, not by the owners (the gentry), but by their tenants.

"One of the effects of the Speenhamland system was that ratepayers often found themselves subsidising the owners of large estates who paid poor wages."[394]

Trevelyan's comments on the system are as follows op. cit. at page 612:

"The condition of the agricultural labourer, deprived of the industries previously conducted by his wife and children, was, indeed most unhappy [...] The landlord class, represented by the justice of the peace, decided not to compel the farmers to pay a living wage. They adopted instead a policy elaborated upon by the Berkshire magistrates at Speenhamland in 1795 namely, to give rates in aid of insufficient wages. To keep the poor alive, it was decided to tax the ratepayers, instead of forcing the farmers and employers of labour to shoulder their proper burden. It was a fatal policy, for it encouraged farmers to keep down wages. The system, which lasted until the new poor law of 1834, made the rural labourer a pauper, and discouraged his thrift and self-respect. It paid better to cringe to the authorities for the dole, than to attempt any form of self-help."[395]

Skyrme cites Malthus, writing in 1800 defending the Speenhamland justices, with approval: "What else could have been done?" The obvious answer would have been to insist that the employers of farm labourers, the very wealthy gentry and justices of the peace, pay a fair wage instead of a starvation wage.

---

[394] Dr. Marjie Bloy: http://www.victorianweb.org/history/poorlaw/speen.html.
[395] Op. cit p. 612.

Chapter 6

Justices of the Peace 1815-To Date

The euphoria that greeted Waterloo, the end of the 20 something year war, a war that beggared the British and buggered the French, ought to have been followed by poor relief for the starving. Instead, the opposite happened. Two measures were taken by the government almost immediately. The first was the Corn Laws of 1815; the second, the abolition of income tax in 1816. The landed gentry certainly knew how to look after their own interests.

Corn Laws

The poor and the starving had the right to hope that, with peace and the lifting of naval blockades, importation into Britain of cheap grain would quickly follow. The landed gentry, who still controlled parliament, lobbied hard and successfully for new Corn Laws, which had the effect of taxing imported grain, and kept the price of local grain artificially high and the price of bread beyond reach for all except the rich. The poor were again reduced to starvation.

> "The one ray of light amidst the gathering economic gloom ought to have been lower food prices, now that the blockade and artificially high demand of the war had gone. But in response to complaints from landowners that their incomes would collapse, a Corn Law had been passed, letting in foreign grain only when home prices hit a designated ceiling. The effect, as intended, was to keep British farmers' profits artificially high. So bread remained punishingly dear at a time when the Quality looked as though it were embarking on an orgy of house building, each construction more extravagant than the last [...] at the same time as paupers, many of them bearing scars from the battlefields of India, America and Europe, were hammering on the doors of the Spitalfields poorhouse."[396]

Income Tax

Tax on the income of those who could afford it, the nobility and gentry, was imposed in 1798, to finance the Napoleonic War. It would have been a simple matter to have retained the tax for a few years, or indeed, permanently. This would have given the poor a fighting chance to recover. Instead, it was swiftly abolished, and revenue-raising reverted to taxation on goods and imports, and of

---

[396]   Schama op cit p.92

course, at a local level, on the parish rates. The abolition of the income tax had the effect that the poor remained poor, and the rich became richer. One hundred years later, over the same argument of whether or not there be an income tax, Lord Curzon addressed a political meeting:

> "The superior class by blood and tradition had inherited the right to rule over our children."

In a next-door constituency, Winston Churchill retorted:

> "What did the noble Lord say? That 'all great civilisations had been the work of aristocracies?' Why, it would be much more true to say that the upkeep of the aristocracy had been the hard work of all civilisations."[397]

The Corn Laws and the abolition of income tax caused a savage reaction against the landowning class, which coincided with an equally savage reaction against the justices of the peace, they being wealthy landowners, and because of their activities with the game laws, poor laws and as trading justices.

Reform Movement and Peterloo

Free speech was still a long way off. However, the growing tide of discontent could not be forever gagged. A report published in 1803 estimated that there were more than one million paupers in England and Wales, all on poor relief.[398] After 1815, with the men of the army and navy thrown upon the scrapheap, vying with each other and the poor for work, relief or food, the middle classes rose up to say 'enough!' Petitions with many hundreds of thousands of signatures were dumped on the floor of parliament. They were ignored. The only response was to hang three radicals who merely organised a strike of knitters and weavers in 1817 in Nottinghamshire.[399]

A crowd of 50,000-60,000 at St. Peter's Fields on the outskirts of Manchester, carrying banners calling for universal suffrage and singing hymns, were set upon by the local militia on the orders of six local magistrates, who included three Anglican priests. A little girl was trampled by their horses and killed. The magistrates then sent in regular troops, cavalry, to rescue the militia. They chopped and sliced their way through the crowd with their sabres, leaving eleven dead and 421 seriously injured.[400]

The execution of the Nottingham radicals and the massacre orchestrated by the justices of the peace at Manchester sparked an overwhelming protest from the people of Britain. They had had enough.

Independent of the moves for political reform, the Luddites had swung into action in the industrial towns, smashing machines that had replaced human labour.

---

[397] Schama op cit p.322.
[398] Ibid, p.97.
[399] Ibid, p.100.
[400] Ibid, p.101.

Justices of the peace were unable to control the unrest. Their home-grown, unpaid constables of watch and ward and their militia were unwilling to be employed against their friends and neighbours who were often involved in the targeted unrest. The professional army had to be employed. They camped around the various industrial towns and London ready to spring into action.

Ultimately, the government was forced to water down the Corn Laws in 1828.[401] A degree of Catholic emancipation was legislated. The death penalty for more than 100 offences was abolished in 1823.[402] Benefit of Clergy was abolished in 1827. Progressively from 1823 to 1860, the death penalty was abolished for all offences except murder, piracy, treason and arson in naval dockyards. The death penalty was finally revoked in 1965.

After extraordinary moves between the cabinet, the House of Commons, the House of Lords and the new King, William IV, some limited reform was made of eligibility to vote and to stand for election to parliament in 1832. This also involved the elimination of some rotten boroughs, and granting representation to some large industrial towns for the first time. However, the upshot of this reform merely increased those enfranchised by some 217,000 votes, and still left the lower middle classes and the poor without any representation at all. Parliament was still confined to property owners, but the reforms were a small, grudging step in the right direction.[403]

Police

Justices of the peace remained in charge of the unpaid police through the archaic system of watch and ward set up by the Statute of Winchester in 1285.[404] In the large cities such as London, it was apparent from the late 18th century that the system was inadequate, hence the creation of the Bow Street Runners.[405] These persons were rewarded with a percentage of fines collected or rewards offered. They were officially recognised in 1792 by the Metropolitan Police Act which created seven new stipendiary magistrates court districts within London, to each of which were allotted six constables.

Patrick Colquhoun was appointed a justice of the peace in 1785, and a stipendiary magistrate in 1792 under the Metropolitan Police Act of the same year. He persuaded the West Indies Planters Committee to fund the creation of a particular paid police force in 1798, not long after the publication of his *Treatise on the Police of the Metropolis* in 1796. This treatise went to seven editions. The West Indies planters were concerned at the great quantity of cargo stolen from the Pool

---

[401] The Corn Laws were only modified a bit in 1828; it took until 1846 for them to be repealed.
[402] JL Lyman: 'The Metropolitan Police Act of 1829,' (1964) 55 *Journal of Criminal Law and Criminology*, p.149.
[403] EB, op. cit. p.83. Skyrme op. cit. puts the figures at 250,000 new votes, bringing the total number of voters to a mere 700,000 out of a total population of about 15,000,000. Hardly startling reform!
[404] 13 Edw I, c. 6: see chart, pp. 27-36.
[405] See p. 126.

of London by dock workers. The answer was Colquhoun's police force, initially on a one year trial basis, the 'Thames River Police,' of 50 constables. They differed from the Bow Street Runners in that they received a salary, and were prohibited from taking private fees. They were so successful, they were made permanent, and absorbed into the London Metropolitan police force when it was finally established in 1829.

Colquhoun lobbied for an expansion of his police force.[406] No doubt the spectre of costs weighed on the mind of the government, and there was fierce opposition to the creation of anything resembling a professional paid police force, based on continental models. When he lobbied, Britain was still in the middle of the Napoleonic War. The fear, existing mainly with the gentry and middle classes, was not so much fear of the creation of a police state. That already existed. The objection was that somebody other than themselves might be in charge of it. The same people opposed the expansion of the system of stipendiary magistrates, for the same reason. The opposition won for the time being. The government had previously tried to pass the London and Westminster Police Bill following the Gordon riots in 1780, and it was voted down.

By 1829, the government really had no option but to try again to create a professional police force. Things had been out of control for so long, and to such an extent, there was no alternative. Even the reactionaries had to consent to its enactment. The Metropolitan Police Act was passed in 1829, and set up a full-time paid police force in London under the command of two justices of the peace, Richard Mayne and Colonel James Rowan, who were relieved of any bench duties.

A measure of the success of the new London police can be gauged from the howl of outrage from a non-London justice of the peace, Thomas Marriott:

> "The increased vigilance of the police in the cities and large towns
> has driven a great number of sturdy beggars, rogues and vagabonds
> to infest small towns, villages and retired houses."

Successive Acts gave counties, if they thought fit, the right to introduce a full time professional police force in the county, paid for out of county funds, and under the control of a Chief Constable and the county Quarter Sessions. This power was taken up by just over half of the counties.

As far as the county boroughs were concerned, police forces, if established, were to be under committees. Justices of the peace were not automatically to be included in the committee.

Another Act of 1856[407] made it compulsory for all counties to create professional police forces along the lines of the earlier acts. In 1868, responsibility for the operation of all county police forces was vested in a standing joint committee

---

[406] As well as being a stipendiary magistrate, he was also appointed superintendent of his river police.
[407] 19 and 29 Vic. c. 69.

with an equal number of members from the county council and the local magistrates' bench. Responsibility for the day-to-day running of each new police force created was vested in its Chief Constable.

Thus it came about that the justices of the peace lost their function of policing.

Modern Imprisonment[408]

An annexure to the Walnut Street Gaol[409] in Philadelphia, USA in 1790 was inspired by the British Penitentiary Act of 1779, and the writings of Bentham, Howard, Blackstone and Eden. The movers and shakers (Quakers) added their twist to the British theorists, and made rehabilitation of the prisoners the main aim of their penitentiary. Whilst one of the aims of the British Penitentiary Act was rehabilitation, its main aim was "the deterring of others."

The annexure to the Walnut Street gaol adopted a regime called 'the separate system.' Each prisoner was allotted a cell and kept separate from his fellow inmates. No work regime was installed, and the prisoner was left to contemplate his lot. He was occasionally subjected to readings from the scriptures.

The idea of long-term solitary confinement has long since been accepted as counter-productive, and the Philadelphia (separate) system was later abandoned. It failed to reform. A new penitentiary was established in 1814 in Auburn New York. This gaol did not isolate its prisoners, but forced them to work 10 hours per day, six days per week, as suggested by the (British) Penitentiary Act. The work, for example, sewing mail bags, was to be done communally, but in silence. If a prisoner so much as lifted his head from his work, he was flogged.

These prison systems, the separate and the silent, set the bar for prison brutality, not only in the USA, but back in England when they eventually got round to establishing their penitentiaries. The first of these, the grossly expensive (£500,000) Millbank Prison in London, closed for business in 1816.

One of the problems with a gaol system that includes rehabilitation as one of its primary aims, is that it still must also be seen as a deterrent. It has to appear to the general population that it is better to be out of gaol than in the gaol. Early gaols didn't appear too bad. A mayoral proclamation of 1617 lamented:

> "...outrages committed by the prisoners within the gaol of Newgate [...] drunk and disordered [...] wine, tobacco, excessive strong drink and resort to women of lewd behaviour, by reason of which [...] persons intent to commit felonies upon the hope of lewd company and such lewd comforts as they find in gaols."

(Let me in! Where do I sign?)

---

[408] The development of imprisonment as a punishment up to the 19th century has been considered earlier, see pages 72-77, 133-134.

[409] The British spelling is retained, rather than the American 'jail.'

By contrast, in the mid-18th century, Henry Fielding[410] described life outside gaol for the poor, being the majority of the population of Britain:

> "Some families only had a single loaf of bread as their entire food for a week, and if any of these creatures falls sick (and it is almost a miracle that stench, vermin and want should ever suffer them to be well) they are turned out into the street by their merciless host or hostess, where, unless some parish officer of extraordinary charity relieves them, they are miserably sure to perish, with the addition of cold and hunger to their disease."

The people of whom Fielding was talking would have been better off in the Newgate gaol. The conditions described by Fielding became worse over the next 100 years, with the plight of the poor becoming more and more desperate. The challenge for the authorities, bent upon an increasing use of imprisonment as a punishment for crime and a substitution for the death penalty and transportation, became a challenge to make life in the new penitentiaries worse than life outside, even for the desperate poor. The authorities believed they had to make the penitentiaries so unattractive to the desperadoes outside that they would not commit crimes to get in. The penitentiaries had to pass the 'terror test.' The British authorities rose magnificently to this challenge.

The result of making terror or deterrence the main aim of the new penitentiaries was that they could kiss goodbye to any hope of rehabilitation of its prisoners. If there is one lesson to be learned from the 200 year experiment with modern prisons, it is that they rarely reform the inmates.

Millbank Penitentiary, the first penitentiary constructed in England in 1816, was the culmination of nearly 50 years' planning. It became the national penitentiary for the whole of England, and it never worked. For a time, it was used as the staging post for all prisoners about to be transported to Tasmania in Australia, each transportee being incarcerated in Millbank for 3 months before transhipment. The gaol had to be emptied in 1818 because of rioting. In 1823, it had to be emptied again because of disease, and it was to all intents and purposes abandoned in 1843 in favour of a newer panopticon model gaol at Pentonville.[411] It was demolished in 1891. The Tate gallery is now erected on the site.

Pentonville prison was run on both the separate and silent systems of imprisonment devised by the Americans. A prisoner was not allowed to see another prisoner. Even in chapel each prisoner was locked in a cubicle and all he could see was the preacher. Silence was enforced. The guards wore soundless slippers. The prisoners went mad and committed suicide in droves. There were 120 cases of insanity from Pentonville prison alone each year.[412]

Each prison in Britain was under the control of its own board of management, usually made up of justices of the peace from the local Quarter Sessions. It was

---

[410] See p. 125-126.
[411] See page 132 for an explanation of a panopticon.
[412] S and B Webb: 'English Prisons under Local Government.'

up to the board whether or not to enforce work in their gaol. They all did eventually.

The original prison labour was picking oakum and sewing. Oakum was tar-soaked old rope, stiff as a board, and the prisoners were required to unpick it and pull it apart until it was as fine as silk. Picking oakum was both arduous and tedious. Many found it impossible to fulfil their required quota, which was 3 pounds' weight (about 1.36 kg) per day. You had to fulfil the quota to get fed. The resulting threads were used for caulking ships or remaking rope. In some gaols, breaking rocks for making roads or buildings was another labour. Sir George Onesiphorus Paul had a treadwheel installed in Gloucester Prison in 1811. In 1818, Sir William Cubbitt invented a cheaper and more efficient treadwheel, or treadmill, for prisoners to tread, initially to be used for grinding corn. This was quickly adopted by the British penitentiaries, and became the cornerstone of hard labour, punishment and imprisonment over the next century.

The wheel consisted of a circle of stairs. The convict was required to grip a handrail and walk all day up the stairs, thus turning the wheel, which revolved on an axle. At first, the object was to grind corn or pump water, but eventually it became policy for the wheel to turn nothing but the axle and a meter which recorded the number of revolutions of the wheel. The daily requirement for the number of revolutions varied at first from gaol to gaol, but was later fixed by regulation at the equivalent of a daily ascent of the Matterhorn, 12,000 feet or approximately 4,000 metres. The wheel was a dreadful punishment.

> "'Manchester Merchant' pitied the treadwheel men as 'they went out to their labour, and noticed the sweat running down their faces on their return. After a spell on it, it was not unknown for big strong fellows to be led away crying."[413]

In competition for useless prison labour was 'Appold's ''ard labour machine'; the crank. This was a wheel set against cogs turned by a machine weighted at will (of the guards, not the prisoners) to fix the amount of exertion required to make a revolution. In order to get fed, the prisoner had to turn the wheel a required number of revolutions. In a fiendish refinement, at Coldbath Fields prison, a group of prisoners on the treadmill was set against a group of prisoners on the crank. The motion of one worked against the motion of the other.[414] The final piece of useless labour concocted by the fertile imagination of 19th century penologists was shot drill. This required lifting cannon balls from a pyramidical pile, one by one and carrying them 3 metres, placing them on the ground and forming another pyramid. When that was finished, the prisoner began all over again.

Probation and Parole

---

[413] Priestley: *Victorian Prison Lives*, p.128.
[414] Those interested in the alleged recent invention of repetitive strain injury (RSI) or occupational overuse syndrome may be interested in references to 'crank oedema' in the surgeon's journal referred to in the 1854 Leicester Inquiry: Priestley, op. cit, p.130.

In 1837, Alexander Maconochie, then in Van Diemen's Land (Tasmania) formulated a plan for reform of prisoners based on a system of 'marks.' Under his plan the length of a sentence of imprisonment was no longer to be determined as a fixed time based upon his felony. It was to be determined by the length of time it took a prisoner to earn a pre-determined number of marks calculated by the amount of work performed by the prisoner, with marks deducted for bad behaviour. Maconochie submitted his plan to the House of Commons Transportation Committee in 1837, 1838. At that time, the committee was disturbed by reports of brutality dished out to prisoners on Norfolk Island. While the committee did not give unqualified assent to Maconochie's plan, it appointed him Commandant of Norfolk Island in 1840 to give his system a try.[415]

> "I found the Island a turbulent, brutal hell, and I left it a peaceful, well-ordered community. Almost the first words of Sir George Gipps[416] report on it (in spite of some strong previous impressions in his mind against my plans) are: 'Notwithstanding that my arrival was altogether unexpected, I found good order everywhere to prevail, and the demeanour of the prisoners to be respectful and quiet.'"[417]

Maconochie was the commandant of the Norfolk Island penal colony from 1840 to 1844, and then dismissed. Norfolk Island was the penal settlement for the prisoners in New South Wales and Tasmania who had offended again – the very naughty boys. Maconochie achieved outstanding results in reforming prisoners. He was given the worst of the worst, and yet, of the 920 allegedly hopeless cases discharged under his marks scheme, only 20 of them were ever re-convicted. Why then was he dismissed? The answer is that his system failed the 'terror test.' Norfolk Island no longer had the reputation for the brutalising treatment of prisoners that it had previously earned. It was no longer a deterrent for the prisoners on the mainland minded to re-offend. Nevertheless, out of his marks system emerged two enduring penal icons: time off for good behaviour and parole.

The publication in 1847 no doubt helped Maconochie to obtain new employment from the justices of the peace who formed the Board of Governors at the newly constructed Birmingham Gaol in 1849.

According to Skyrme, Maconochie:

> "...spent so much time theorising and ventilating his views that he had little time to spend on supervising the actual administration of the prison. The justices therefore appointed a deputy governor, a Lieutenant Austin, who ran the prison with great severity.

---

[415] *Norfolk Island* by Captain A. Maconochie, first published in 1847, reprinted in 1973, Sullivan's Cove Publisher, p.8.
[416] Governor of New South Wales.
[417] Maconochie op. cit. p. 17.

> Becoming aware of this, Maconochie asked the justices to dismiss Austin."[418]

Instead, the board dismissed Maconochie. Austin was promoted to Governor. Austin inflicted such cruelty that one too many inmates committed suicide. The justices launched an enquiry, which whitewashed themselves, Austin and the other prison officers, but a Royal Commission in 1854 uncovered the truth and tipped a bucket over the justices.

Centralisation of Control of British Prisons

Until 1877, it was the various boards of the individual gaols which set the degree of sadism to be practised within their gaol. In 1877, all British prisons were put under one central control of a Comptroller-General. The first one was Sir Edmund du Cane (sometimes du Quesne). He was of Huguenot descent and joined the army. He was dispatched to the colony on the Swan River (later Western Australia) with their first batch of adult convicts in 1850 as a lieutenant. There he was appointed a magistrate. He was recalled to England in 1856. He was appointed to the board of military prisons in 1863. He became chairman of the board of convict prisons in 1869. He was appointed the first Comptroller-General of prisons in 1877 and remained in that post until 1895. His regime was noted for its savagery. He is said to have obtained the post of Comptroller-General by submitting "a fraudulent or deceitful prospectus," and was described as "belligerent, obsessive and avaricious."[419]

This was the end of the responsibility of justices of the peace for prisons.

Poor Law Amendments 1834

The Poor Laws had been more or less untouched since their consolidation in 1601. They were changed in 1834. The new laws spelt the end of 'outdoor relief.' Outdoor relief had been provided for in the consolidation of the Poor Laws in 1601. Some of those entitled to relief by those laws, for example the blind and the decayed (meaning the elderly), could receive the 'pencion' while remaining in their homes. The new Poor Laws put a stop to that. If anyone were to apply to the parish for relief, they were to be imprisoned in the workhouse. The act removed responsibility for the implementation of the poor laws from the local justices of the peace, and vested it in a central commission.

> "The new Poor Law enacted by the Whig government in 1834 was designed expressly for those habitually slothful types, as they were perceived, from sponging off the rates by making the regime inside the workhouse so close to that of a prison that no one remotely capable of gaining any kind of legitimate work would submit themselves to it. Inmates of the 'Bastilles' (as they were popularly known) were brutally shorn, so that they were instantly

---

[418] Op.cit. volume 2, p. 192

[419] Roger Hood, Director for the Centre of Criminological Research, Oxford University, http://www.timeshighereducation.co.uk/story.asp.

recognisable on the 'outside', and dressed in uniform drab. Husbands were strictly separated from wives and both from their children – the most heart-breaking aspect of the institutions. In a society supposed to value the family as the school of social morality, it was the first casualty of misfortune. But of course, most of the Poor Law guardians solemnly believed that the misfortune had been earned through some sort of moral failing. Weakness of backbone, then, had landed the reprobate in the workhouse. It would do him or her no favour to make the place flow with the milk of human kindness."[420]

"But where the most conspicuous exercises in Benthamite social improvement were concerned – the new Poor Law of 1834 in particular- the pain seemed a lot more visible than the gain. Paradoxically, it took money to make the workhouses so horribly penal that even the desperate would not want to surrender themselves to them."[421]

"The new Poor Laws turned out to be an unpopular measure in the country and led to outbreaks of disturbances. Its basic principle- that outdoor relief should cease and that conditions in workhouses should be 'less eligible' than the worst conditions in the labour market outside- was attacked by writers like Thomas Carlisle and Charles Dickens as much as by workingmen themselves."[422]

"The new Poor Law of 1834 was a major source of grievance in the provinces..."[423]

But the new Poor Laws had the one good outcome: justices of the peace were no longer responsible for administering them.

Local Government and Health

Beginning with the Municipal Corporations Act of 1835, and culminating in the Local Government Act of 1888, borough councils, until now self-perpetuating oligarchies, were forced to face annual elections, and justices of the peace were relieved of their local government responsibilities.

A Royal Commission in 1835 into local government had concluded there was widespread:

"...mistrust of the municipal magistracy, tainting with suspicion the local administration of justice, and often accompanied with contempt of the persons by whom the law is administered."

---

[420] Schama, op. cit. p. 134.
[421] Ibid, p. 203.
[422] EB Vol. 29, 15th edit. P.83
[423] Ibid, p. 84.

By 'municipal magistracy', the Royal Commissioners meant justices of the peace in towns with a Royal Charter for self-government. In those towns, the magistracy was appointed by the self-perpetuating town councils, and they had a very bad reputation. Within those towns, Quarter Sessions were conducted by a recorder, an experienced lawyer appointed by the Lord Chancellor. It was only at Petty Sessions that lay justices sat in chartered towns.

The Local Government Act of 1888 provided that all administrative matters within counties, but excluding chartered Burroughs, were to be determined by fully elected county councils. In practice, at least for some decades, these enactments made little difference at first, because it was the same landed gentry who were elected to the councils as were the justices of the peace. This was notwithstanding the granting of full adult male suffrage in 1884.

Responsibility for health matters was removed from the magistracy by the Public Health Act of 1848. That Act set up a General Board of Health under three members, and provided for the setting up of local boards of health. In towns under a Royal Charter, the now elected Town Council became the board; elsewhere local boards of health were to be elected by ratepayers.

Further Reform in the 19th, early 20th Centuries; Corn Laws; Factories; Transport; Religion; Civil Service; The Vote; Law Reform; Land Ownership; Labour Party; Old age Pension; Poor Laws.

- The Corn Laws were modified in 1828, but not abolished until 1846, largely due to the potato famine in Ireland.

- Britain lost its competitive edge in industry, mainly to the USA and the German States, mainly in textiles, iron and steel. Unions ceased to be banned and became legal in 1871. In 1875, by the Employers and Workmen Act, employers and workmen were placed on an equal footing with regard to breaches of contract. Bars to an employee suing an employer for damages for negligence were removed in 1880 by the Employers Liability Act. (Previously a worker could not sue for damages if the injury was caused by a fellow worker; if the worker was aware of a risk, but continued to work; or if he was guilty of even a miniscule bit of contributory negligence). A limited form of Workers Compensation was allowed in 1897 by the Workers Compensation Act, whereby the employer could insure against injury to the worker, and the worker could recover payment irrespective of who was to blame for the injury. The Factory Act of 1878 reduced working hours per week to a maximum of 56. Unions were allowed to picket and strike from 1875. A Working day was fixed at 8 hours for miners in 1908.

- Transport, in the form of train travel and motor cars, was undergoing a revolution.

- Disqualification of Catholics from office was removed in 1828.

- A Civil Service Commission was set up in 1854, and entrance to the civil service became by way of a competitive examination, rather than the previous system of advancement of chinless wonders and village idiots by well-connected parents.

- Eligibility to vote and stand for parliament was further enlarged in 1867 by the Reform Act. This increased the number of those entitled by about 1 million. There were thus about 2 million now entitled to vote out of a population of about 20 million. A further reform of 1884 gave full adult male franchise. Women did not get the vote until 1918.

- Law Reform. The Pillory was abolished in 1816. So were public whippings. Benefit of Clergy was abolished in 1827.[424] Prisoners on trial were allowed legal counsel in 1836 by the Prisoners Counsel Act.[425] A prisoner was finally allowed to give evidence at his or her own trial by the Criminal Evidence Act of 1898.[426] An appeal against conviction was finally allowed in 1907 by the creation of the Court of Criminal Appeal. The procedure at Petty Sessions and Committal hearings was streamlined by a series of acts; the Jervis Acts of 1848.[427] The Judicature Act of 1876 fused law and equity, which to then had been running in competition with each other.[428] In 1933, the institution of the 'Grand Jury' was abolished. Thereafter, it was left to the justices of the peace in Committal proceedings whether or not a person charged with felony be sent for trial to Quarter Sessions or the Assize Court.

- Due to increased competition from overseas, particularly Canada and Australia in the 1890s, land rents fell, and the landed gentry began to sell off their land to town dwellers, mainly to rich industrialists.

- The Labour Party was formed in 1893.

- Old age pensions were granted to those over 70 in 1908.

- The Poor Laws simply faded away. Some remnants remain, but the persecution of vagrants has long ceased. As pensions and unemployment benefits came on stream, the workhouses fell into disuse. Some became hospitals during World War II.

Magistrates Administrative Functions

By 1888, justices of the peace had lost control over police and the multiplicity of local government and other functions that they had enjoyed since about the year

---

[424] 7 and 8 Geo IV, c. 28.
[425] 6 and 7 Will. IV, c.114. See pp.69-70 for the previous laws.
[426] 61 and 62 Vic, c.36: see also pp. 69-70.
[427] The Indictable Offences Act 1848, 11 and 12 Vic, c. 42; Summary Jurisdiction Act 1848, 11 and 12 Vic, c.43; the Justices Protection Act 1848, 11 and 12 Vic, c. 44. Another act a year later, the Petty Sessions Act specified places where justices could and could not hold Petty Sessions. For example, no more Petty Sessions were to be held at the local pub.
[428] William Sheppard had advised such a reform was necessary as far back as 1656 in his book *England's Balme*.

1300. There was one exception: they still retained power over liquor licensing, despite the balls-up they had made of it over the years.[429] Liquor licensing was regarded as a semi-judicial function rather than an administrative matter.

Justices still retained their judicial functions sitting in Quarter and Petty Sessions, but for a while it was touch-and-go whether they retained them at all, or whether they were to be replaced by legally qualified stipendiary magistrates. In 1848, when introducing the Jervis Acts reforming summary jurisdiction, the Attorney-General, Sir John Jervis commented on "the divided opinions as to whether amateur justices should be entrusted with such extensive powers."[430]

Eligibility to be a Justice of the Peace: Late 19th, early 20th Centuries

The eligibility test for magistrates remained the same as it had been for centuries: owning land generating at least £100 per annum, notwithstanding that eligibility to vote had no such requirement after the Reform Act of 1884. This property qualification was removed in 1906,[431] and in theory at least, anyone could be appointed a justice of the peace, provided that he was a male.

Eligibility was one thing: getting appointed was an altogether different matter. All appointments were made by the Lord Chancellor, who consulted with the various Lords Lieutenant in the counties. He was also lobbied directly by the political parties. Appointments tended to be along political lines. This caused such a degree of controversy that a Royal Commission was set up specifically to examine the question of appointments of magistrates. The commission recommended that men of every social grade be appointed, and added:

> "It is in the public interest that working men with a first-hand knowledge of the conditions or life among their own class should be appointed to the county as well as the burrough benches."[432]

Skyrme was of the opinion that this recommendation was never implemented to any great extent.[433]

The Royal Commission recommended that nominations for justices of the peace continue to come from the Lords Lieutenant of the counties, and that they should establish within each county an advisory committee. The Justices (Supplemental List) Act of 1941 provided that all justices of the peace who attained the age of 75 years should be put on a supplemental list. This meant that justices who attained the age of 75 years could retain the title, but were barred from sitting at Quarter or Petty Sessions. The act also barred any below the age of 75 years who had lost the plot.

There are unsubstantiated rumours that from time to time over the centuries, some (very few) women were appointed as justices of the peace; it was generally

---

[429] See for example 'The Gin Craze' at pp 118-121.
[430] Skyrme, op. cit, volume 2, p. 176.
[431] By the Justices of the Peace Act, 1906.
[432] Cited by Skyrme op cit volume 2, p. 226.
[433] Ibid.

considered they were ineligible for appointment.[434] In 1907, the Qualification of Women (County and Burrough Councils) Act allowed women to serve on local government councils, notwithstanding the fact that they were ineligible to vote in a general election. Sometimes it transpired that women became chairman or mayor of the council, and that fact would normally mean they simultaneously became a justice of the peace. The act, however, provided that, if that eventuality occurred, they were still disqualified from being a justice of the peace. It was only in 1919, by the Justices of the Peace (Qualification of Women) Act that women could finally become magistrates. At that time, one woman, Mrs. Ada Summers, was mayor of Stalybridge in Cheshire. She therefore became the first official female justice of the peace. A committee was set up to make recommendations for women to be appointed. All the members of the committee were immediately appointed justices of the peace. They were: the Marchioness of Crewe; Beatrice Webb; Margaret Lloyd George; the Marchioness of Londonderry; Gertrude Tuckwell; and Mary Ward.[435] The committee drew up a list of 212 recommendations and, with the exception of a few who declined, all were appointed.

The first woman stipendiary magistrate (indeed, the first woman professional judge) was Sybil Campbell, appointed a stipendiary in 1945. She was one of the first woman barristers, called to the Inner Temple in 1922. She gained a reputation for being a bit hairy-chested when it came to sentencing. She gave a station porter 6 weeks' imprisonment for stealing 3 cakes of soap, provoking a protest by 5,000 factory workers. She retired in 1961. The next stipendiary was Miss Jean Graham Hall, appointed in 1965. She was later promoted to circuit judge.

The Magistrates Association of England and Wales was formed in 1921. Scotland formed its own association in 1923.

Increases in Jurisdiction of Quarter and Petty Sessions

As the number of capital offences were reduced during the 19th and 20th centuries,[436] matters which formerly were sent to the Assizes Courts were retained and dealt with by Quarter Sessions. The Administration of Justice (Miscellaneous Provisions) Act of 1938 said that a Quarter Sessions bench, provided that it was chaired by an experienced barrister, could try a specified number of offences which previously was beyond its jurisdiction. By 1951, all counties had such a chairman.

By the end of World War II, the work of Quarter Sessions was the trial of indictable offences,[437] plus appeals from Petty Sessions, including licensing appeals, and rating appeals from local government.

---

[434] Skyrme, op cit, volume 2, p.233.
[435] No relation.
[436] See page 145.
[437] Felonies, that is, serious offences.

An array of legislation over time gave Petty Sessions power to deal with more and more serious offences, and as time went by, there was a considerable increase in the volume of work due to population increases and traffic matters. The Criminal Justice Act of 1925, for example, gave them jurisdiction over a large number of offences previously only triable before judge and jury. However, the sentencing parameters of Petty Sessions were narrowed to a maximum of 6 months' imprisonment and a fine of £100. From this time on, 98% of all criminal matters were dealt with by Petty Sessions.

The magistracy in England and Wales 1950 to Date

There was another Royal Commission into the magistracy in 1946 following a series of scandals involving justices of the peace immediately post-war. The assumption underlying the Commission was that the existing system of unqualified justices of the peace should continue as in the immediate past. The Royal Commission was therefore toothless, and limited to tinkering around the edges of the magistracy with recommendations for appointments and dismissals.

The Association of Justices (The Royal Association of Justices from 1962) offered training for justices of the peace almost from its beginning in 1921, but few undertook their training.[438] The Royal Commission of 1946 recommended training, so the committees of the various justices' courts instituted schemes for the ongoing training of their magistrates. The Royal Association in conjunction with the Lord Chancellor introduced a correspondence course and prepared a booklet entitled *Notes for New Magistrates*.[439] In 1948, Sir Thomas Skyrme was appointed to the position of Secretary to the Commissions (of justices of the peace) for England and Wales, and served as coordinator of justices of the peace until 1977. He also became secretary of Commissions in Northern Ireland and Scotland, and vice-chairman of the advisory committee on the training of justices from 1974 to 1980. He was a founder of the Commonwealth Magistrates Association (later, the Commonwealth Magistrates and Judges Association), and a long-time magistrate himself. It is no coincidence that there has been a complete shake-up of the magistracy in the last 50 years, much of it due to the efforts of Sir Thomas Skyrme.

The four courts historically run by the justices of the peace (Quarter Sessions, County; Quarter Sessions, Burrough; Petty Sessions, County; and Petty Sessions, Burrough), were now run as follows. Quarter Sessions, County: Justices of the peace sitting with a legally qualified chairman; Quarter Sessions, Burrough: by a legally qualified Recorder, sitting without justices of the peace; Petty Sessions, both County and Burrough: by justices of the peace, but with a legally qualified clerk on hand to advise them.

In 1972, the Courts Act of 1971 abolished Quarter Sessions and Assizes courts, and replaced them with the new Crown Court. In theory, justices of the peace were permitted to be part of the Crown Court; however, the new court was to be

---

[438] Skyrme, op cit, volume 2, pp. 316, 317.
[439] Ibid.

presided over by a High Court or Circuit Court judge, or a Recorder. In trials, guilt or innocence was to be determined by a jury instructed by the judge or recorder, and the presence of justices of the peace on the bench was purely decorative. In 1988, this farce was terminated by direction of the Lord Chancellor, and thenceforth, justices of the peace were excluded from Crown Court trials. They continued to deal with appeals from Petty Sessions in the Crown Court.

Over the last half-century, Petty Sessions jurisdiction has been substantially increased by allowing an increasing number of indictable (serious) offences to be disposed of summarily by justices of the peace without jury. In addition, the justices have been given responsibility in a number of family related matters, child maintenance, domestic violence and the like.

Summary

The institution of the magistracy began out of an attempt to rein in a country spiralling out of control with violence. The attempt recruited the freeholders of land in England, a small proportion of the population consisting of the nobility and the gentry. Sheriffs had been previously tried and found wanting. The freeholders were tried because of the roles they had played since Roman times in the old Hundred and Shire courts. The nobility played little part in the institution. It was they who were largely responsible for the law-and-order crisis. When it came to bringing the nobility under some sort of control, the gentry/justices of the peace failed, and it was left to the court of Star Chamber headed by the ruthless Cardinal Wolsey to partially achieve this. The gentry, as justices of the peace, were reasonably successful in keeping the majority of the population, the poor, from joining in the disorder. They were ineffective against serious organised rebellions, such as the Peasants' Revolt, Kett's rebellion or the religious upheavals in Tudor times. They kept the bulk of the population in subjection. They took over responsibility for local government, without conspicuous success.

Often it appeared as if subjection of the poor was the main aim in life of justices of the peace. It was only after the voting reforms of the 19th century, which took until well into the 20th century to achieve much, that a change came over the institution. It was no longer the exclusive preserve of the landed gentry, but took on a more democratic hue. With policing and local government powers stripped away, they were able to concentrate on petty crime and liquor licensing. With compulsory training, they managed this to the apparent general satisfaction of the population.

As things now stand, the system is clumsy, with a typical court requiring the rousting out of 3 justices of the peace, and a legally qualified clerk to advise them, as well as the usual clerical support staff. They are only about one half as efficient as a legally qualified stipendiary.[440] Nevertheless, there is undoubtedly an attraction in a system whereby the people are judged by the people. Throughout their long history until recent times, this was not so. The poor were

---

[440] Skyrme, op cit, Volume 2, p. 418 said: 'Justices of the peace work more slowly than stipendiaries, and take longer to reach a decision...'

judged by an alien race: the rapacious landowners. But now a fairer and more acceptable, if inefficient, system seems to be in place.

Chapter 7

Court Short Down Under

It is not asserted that all these stories actually occurred: they are merely *said* to have occurred, usually by someone holding a glass of red wine in one hand.

***

Godfrey Foy Hall served as a magistrate in the southern half of the Northern Territory of Australia in the early 1970s. He succeeded James Esk Lemaire. Lemaire was scrupulously fair and proper, wearing a three-piece suit even in the Centralian mid-summer. It is said that he would cross the road if he saw a policeman on the same footpath, lest he be disqualified by bias for mere propinquity.

'Scrubby" Hall was different, in some respects more attuned to the rough and ready frontier town that was (and still is) Alice Springs. On occasion, he would give a glimmer of the way he was thinking in court when he began to whistle or sing, or turn his back upon a witness or a lawyer. Sometimes, in the middle of a plea *in misericordiam* ("My client was born at a very early age, dropped on his head when 4 years old, rogered by the scoutmaster at the age of seven…" – you know the type of plea), Scrubby would sit back in his chair and sing: "Tell us anotherie, do." He rarely gave reasons for any decision, civil or criminal. This did earn the wrath of the Supreme Court and may well have led to his retirement. Yet he was well regarded and usually right.

The only occasion I met Scrubby was at Tennant Creek, 500 km north of Alice Springs, a township of some 2,500 persons, and usually referred to as TFC. It is a rough and ready mining township, marginally surviving on the price of gold. Don't get me wrong – I love the place. It was in early 1975. I was on my way from Darwin to Adelaide after my house blew away in Cyclone Tracy. Scrubby was bringing law and/or order to TFC. We met in the evening at the pub and had a few convivial ales and a game of pool. At or about 10pm, the publican announced to the crowded bar: "Time, gentlemen, please." Scrubby leaped on to the top of the bar and addressed the audience: "MAY I HAVE YOUR ATTENTION! THE LICENSING COURT OF TENNANT CREEK IS NOW IN SESSION. I HAVE BEFORE ME AN APPLICATION FOR THE EXTENSION OF TRADING HOURS. IS THERE ANY OBJECTION? (Silence). THE APPLICATION IS GRANTED. (Loud cheers)." The conviviality continued.

Scrubby was a unique character.

***

Andy Hogg clerked for James Esk Lemaire (mentioned above), and it was always: "Good morning Mr Hogg," "Good morning Your Honour." After 10 years of this, Andy was summoned one evening into the magistrate's chambers in Alice Springs. "Mr Hogg, I have been giving this matter of appellation considerable thought, and I think that we may now address each other by our Christian names."

"Thank you James and goodnight."

"And goodnight to you too Andy."

The next morning, Andy received another summons into the chambers.

"I have been giving the matter further anxious consideration overnight, and I think we should revert to our earlier practice."

"Very well, Your Honour."

"Thank you Mr Hogg."

***

The question of appellation was a touchy one. The correct address for a magistrate is 'Your Worship', but the practice was always followed in South Australia of distinguishing legally qualified stipendiary magistrates from honorary justices by calling the stipendiaries 'Your Honour' and the honorary justices 'Your Worship.' The same practice was followed in the Northern Territory. Elsewhere in Australia the stipendiary magistrates were addressed 'Your Worship.' In the Australian Capital Territory magistrates were supposed to be honoured, but many of the lawyers came from New South Wales and invariably worshipped the stipendiaries. (Occasionally a very nervous litigant might elevate you to 'Your Majesty'). It is now universal practice for magistrates throughout Australia to be honoured.

L E Clarke ('Ellie') was appointed as a magistrate in South Australia in 1934. He was still on the bench when I commenced my articles of clerkship (in 1960). He had a bomber command moustache and a fierce demeanour. One day a lawyer who ought to have known better addressed Ellie as 'Your Worship'. "What do you mean?" thundered Ellie. "The proper title is 'Your Honour'". There was a pause while the lawyer produced half a dozen reference books from his bag, and arranged them on the bar table.

"'If Your Worship will permit me, I will endeavour to persuade you to the contrary." (Opens the first book and begins to read).

"Oh! Very well, call me what you please."

"If Your Honour pleases…" The lawyer capitulated.

***

Proceedings in court are now electronically recorded. Early transcriptions were not edited, and some remarks probably best not uttered sometimes appeared. Something like the following would occasionally turn up in the transcript.

Counsel: 'Objection!' HH: 'Objection overruled!! Counsel (resuming seat): 'If your honour pleases silly old bastard wouldn't know if his arse was on fire.'

Recordings and transcriptions thereof made magistrates and judges more careful in their choice of language. But they didn't deter Kevin Townley Dobson – 'Dobbo'. Dobbo was a colourful character who was a stipendiary in NSW before switching to the Australian Capital Territory. A stickler for punctuality he would march into court at the stipulated hour, court ready or not. In an address to the ACT legislative assembly on Dobbo's death, Big Bill Stefaniak said: "His bark was worse than his bite. He certainly terrified a lot of people, including junior practitioners, but you did get used to him." Well, Bill would know, because he suffered Kevin's wrath as much as anyone. Kevin used to have monumental dust-ups with John Gallop QC, later a Supreme Court judge. Dobbo would sit back in his chair and raise his arms to show he was not using them for any microphone switch-off trick. "Well, you know what you can do Gallop: you can @#$%&*." Gallop would immediately think he had Dobbo at last on appeal, but the offending words never appeared on transcript. It was not until after Dobbo retired that it was discovered that he had a foot switch for the microphone installed.

> Dobbo was greatly admired by all who knew him. He used to enjoy an ale or three, and a corner of the front bar at the Ainslie Hotel was named after him.

***

Derek Finlay Wilson, supervising stipendiary magistrate of the Adelaide Magistrates Court, was the founding father of the Australian Magistrates Association. If he was alive, he would be astonished to hear that assertion. It happened this way. There was no association of magistrates in South Australia prior to the mid-1970s. There was opposition to such a body. It might become (shudder!!) a trade union, demanding better pay and conditions. The eastern states had such associations and as far as one could tell from such a distance, they didn't go on strike or make much noise. One day, I got a call or a letter from someone in Sydney stating that they were contemplating forming an Australia-wide association. I don't now recall why but it appeared that in order for this to go ahead, they needed support from South Australia. It was necessary for us to form an association of SA magistrates first, and then cast our vote in favour of having an Australian association. I thought the idea was a sound one and circulated all the SA magistrates with a view to forming the association. Derek then circulated everyone to express his horror at the idea. "It would merely be an excuse," he said, "for dinners, alcohol and jollification." This was the clincher. All the previous doubters thought: What a good idea! Thus it came to be that not only was the South Australian Magistrates Association formed, but the Australian Stipendiary Magistrates Association (ASMA) as well. ASMA is now AAM (the Australian Association of Magistrates). Although Derek never joined either, it can be said that his words of inspiration were responsible for the founding of both.

It is ironic that Derek was the cause of the situation that led to the nearest thing the SA association came to industrial action. He had occasion to sentence a doctor for Medibank fraud, the sentence consisting of the equivalent of a tap on the wrist with a wet feather. The SA Attorney-General, Peter Duncan told a radio talkback audience that he regarded the sentence as unduly lenient. In a fit of pique Derek immediately disqualified himself from dealing with any state-initiated prosecution. He thought he would be able to occupy himself with Commonwealth government prosecutions. Instead, he was transferred to the civil jurisdiction. Derek regarded this as the equivalent of a transfer to the Oodnadatta court or the Elizabeth court or somewhere equally unpleasant. There was talk of strike action, which worried me a bit, since I was the association's president. I recall a night visit to see the Premier, Don Dunstan, and I recall he was not particularly sympathetic to Derek. Derek resigned not long after.

Derek had a keen intellect and wrote the occasional amusing judgement, but he held himself aloof from the legal profession and from the other magistrates.

Derek once had to deal with a *bete noire* of the magistracy, Mr K. K was a product of World War II Europe, and his experiences had unsettled him in the upstairs department. He would regularly disregard protocol in addressing the court (see above) by addressing the magistrate: "You pig dog Nazi bastard" or similar. One day his behaviour was much milder and he merely said to Derek: "You, you, you, you're treating me like a second class citizen."

> Derek replied (without looking at him – Derek never looked at anyone): "Mr K, you flatter yourself."

***

SA magistrates had been civil servants since 1874. The nomenclature was changed in 1936 to 'public servant'. We were attached to the Attorney General's Department. This meant we were employed by the same department as the prosecutors who prosecuted the more serious crimes. (The more routine matters were prosecuted by the police). In *Fingleton v. Christian Ivanoff* (1976) 14 SASR 53, the SA Supreme court held that a magistrate had properly disqualified himself for perceived bias, since the magistrate and the prosecutor were both employed by the same department. It was reasonably believed that the decision meant we would be taken out of the public service, but no. We were transferred to the Department of Tourism, Recreation and Sport. I never did find out to which of those categories we belonged.

***

I have served as a stipendiary in three different jurisdictions, the Australian Capital Territory, South Australia and the Northern Territory. As far as I know, the only other magistrate to have been so peripatetic is John Murphy (Murph). Murph was a great magistrate and well regarded in the NT and the ACT as well as Victoria, but he has another dubious claim to fame. He is the only magistrate to have survived having missiles thrown at him twice.

The first time was in Alice Springs in the south of the NT, when a disgruntled young counsel flung his pen at the wall in apparent disagreement on hearing one of Murph's decisions.

The other occasion, in the ACT, was more spectacular. David Harold Eastman was being held in custody on a charge of murdering the assistant Police Commissioner. Eastman had some mental issues, and was very difficult to deal with. Late one day Eastman was applying for bail and Murph was trying to tell him something. Eastman was trying to talk him down. Voices were raised. Eastman suddenly grabbed the heavy water jug from the bar table and threw it at Murph's head. Murph saw it coming and ducked, which was just as well, because it was a very accurate throw. The jug smashed on the wall just behind where the magistrate was sitting. Pausing only to say: "Bail denied," Murph made his way out the back door of the court on his hands and knees.

Another occasion of a direct physical attack on a judicial officer in the middle ages was reported in law French something along these lines. The defendant 'ject un brickbat a le dit justice que narrowly mist.'

The only other occasion of which I am aware was when Charles Kingsley Ward was the magistrate in the Darwin Court on 19/2/1942, and appearing before him was barrister Dick Ward, later Mr Justice Ward of the NT Supreme Court. The attack consisted of a swarm of Japanese bombers dropping bombs in the general direction of the court at 10.10 am, necessitating an early morning tea break.

***

In 1880, a Western Australian magistrate, George Leake, threw an inkpot at the barrister, Septimus Burt (son of the Chief Justice), but history does not record whether his aim was true.

***

In 1973, the South Australian Government formed a new court (SA Family Court, dealing with family and juvenile matters) consisting of two judges and a magistrate. The judges were John Marshall and Kemeri Murray. John had been a magistrate since 1959, but Kemeri then had no such experience so she sat with John for a while to see how he approached the job. The day came for her to fly solo, and she was dispatched to Port Adelaide with instructions that if anything went wrong, she was to adjourn the court and telephone John for instructions. She was given a telephone number.

In due course during a trial an objection to evidence was taken and Kemeri adjourned the court and dialled the number. A voice on the other end of the phone began intoning: "Our Father, which art in heaven…" Kemeri had been given the number of Dial-a-Prayer.

***

Reginald Badenoch was hearing a summary trial in one of Adelaide's suburban courts. He had a device inserted in his ear. It was assumed it was a hearing aid. In the middle of the afternoon, a witness was droning on, when suddenly Reg leaped to his feet and cried out: "He's out. He's out!!" Reg had been tuned into the cricket.

***

On the subject of hearing aids, I once had a lady appear before me in the ACT, charged with many street offences. I was obliged to read each charge out to her, but she was not obliged at that stage to plead to the charges. She elected to do so anyway, and we got into a sort of rhythm not unlike a saint's litany.

"You stand charged with disorderly behaviour."

"Not guilty."

"You stand charged with offensive language."

"Not guilty."

"You stand charged with resisting police."

"Not guilty."

"You stand charged with assaulting the police."

"Not guilty.

"You stand charged with anything else we can think of."

"Not guilty."

At the end of the charging and pleading, (there were many more charges than I have set out above, can't remember them all now), I thought it appropriate to neatly sum up the situation thus far: "So," I said, "You are pleading not guilty to everything are you?"

She replied: "TURN UP YOUR F@#$%G HEARING AID."

***

SA magistrate, Les Mclean Wright wore a hearing aid, but I think he switched it off when defence counsel spoke.

***

Les did a King Canute when he tried to stamp out drink-driving in the Elizabeth district. His ploy was simple. Everyone was sent to gaol, first offence or not. The Supreme Court brought this experiment to a merciful conclusion.

***

'Speed' Merity wasn't deaf, but he must have been myopic. He failed to see the wheelchair under barrister Paul Anderson, and ordered him to stand when he was addressing the court. Paul replied with some dignity: "I would if I could, Your Honour."

***

'Dobbo' (see above) used to delight in ordering a diminutive barrister to stand when he was addressing the court, which invariably provoked: "I am standing."

***

Cameron Stuart was an identity in the Adelaide Magistrates Courts for many years, and he roped me in to assist on a mission impossible training course for justices of the peace who were still used in those days for minor traffic matters. He had got word that they wanted to discuss why they were so often upset on appeal. To me this seemed pretty basic stuff: they were either not having sufficient regard for the maximum penalties set down by the legislation creating the offences, or they were ignoring sentencing guidelines laid down by the Supreme Court. Cameron agreed that he should address them on the need to have regard to what parliament dictated, and I would tell them about the Supreme Court processes. Knowing that politically the justices of the peace were a trifle, shall we say conservative, it was felt that both addresses should concede that, when it came to sentencing, neither parliament nor the Supreme Court would know if their backsides were aflame, but they still had to be obeyed. Unbeknown to me, Cameron had invited the news reporter, Jim Kernahan, to the meeting. Jim liked an occasional drink and the meeting was scheduled for the evening.

We delivered our addresses and settled in for tea and cakes when Jim finally arrived, in his cups. He fondly patted the backside of any female JsP, and freely spilt his tea around the floor. Cameron snatched the notes from my address and gave both my notes and his own to Jim, explaining that it was the only way of ensuring there was any accuracy in the reporting of the night's events. I later, but too late, discovered that Cameron had snatched his own notes back from Jim, claiming they needed to be revised (mine didn't?).

Next day, the banner headline in the news read: MAGISTRATE BLASTS JUDGES. I expected to be summoned to the Supreme Court, but nothing happened – they must have had a sense of humour.

***

Sometimes newspapers headlines can be very well crafted. There was a case in Darwin where a man was charged with rape and trespass. He had entered a house at night and snuck into the bedroom of a man and his wife. They were apparently very sound sleepers. The burglar was in the process of having his wicked way with the wife (who supposed it to be her husband) when the husband eventually awoke and brought the proceedings to a halt. After the case went to court, the *NT News* had the headlines, whether accurate or not I cannot say: 'MAN COMES BETWEEN HUSBAND AND WIFE'.

***

An off-duty wharfie, clad in blue singlet and shorts, and his wife were shopping in the Port Adelaide area. The wife wanted some clothes and realised her husband was reluctant to be seen in the vicinity of a dress shop, asked what he would do. He had never been inside a court in his life, and told her he would go and watch the proceedings. The presiding beak was Laurie Johnston. The improperly clad wharfie was in the court for some time when Laurie's eyeball fell upon him. Before he knew what was happening, the wharfie was in the cells for contempt of court, and his wife was wandering around outside wondering what had become of him.

***

When Les McLean Wright was trying to bring law and/or order to Elizabeth, he sometimes imposed a recognisance with wording out of tune for the customers, who, in that district, might occasionally be short in the grey matter department. One condition required a youth 'not to frequent' a particular bar. When apprehended in the forbidden bar and charged with breach of recognisance, he protested vigorously: "I didn't go there frequent. I only went there four times a week."

***

Clarrie Hermes had been a magistrate in SA, appointed in 1961. Later, he became the Chief Magistrate for the ACT. It is said that when he was in the army during World War II, he was stationed in Darwin when it was bombed by the Japanese (see above). Orders were given that the army should retreat and regroup down the Stuart Highway. Since the Stuart highway is 3,000 kilometres long and traverses Australia from north to south, some differing interpretations were given to the order, which was not very specific. Some retreated to the outskirts of Darwin, some to Katherine 300k south of Darwin, and some made it all the way to Adelaide. Clarrie was well on the way in his obedience to the orders, when he remembered he had left his watch behind. It had been a present from his mother for his 21st birthday, so he returned to his headquarters in town and found his commanding officer the only person left in the building. Clarrie was awarded a 'gong' and promotion for being the only other one not to flee.

***

When Clarrie retired as chief, one of the other magistrate's hopes to become the new chief were high. However, 'Champagne Charlie' got the job instead. 'Disappointed Expectations' refused to converse with Charlie during the entire time he was in the job, and notes had to be passed under the door. Even after Charlie left, mention of his name by any of the other magistrates involved forfeiture by them of a bottle of French champagne.

***

The conviviality surrounding magistrates' conferences can be amusing, but the papers and/or discussions do not often set the world on fire. At one Darwin conference, Loadman, Birch, Cavenagh and myself had strategically arranged ourselves at the back of the room, while some newish female magistrate from Western Australia was waxing enthusiastic about a new approach being taken by some other WA magistrate in a remote part of the state. It appeared that the magistrate would require all the offenders to remain behind until the court had finished. They were then required to form a circle, join hands and (she concluded breathlessly): engage in *Transcendental meditation*! Loadman awoke and bellowed: "WHAT A LOAD OF F@#$%G FROGSHIT!" The session could not continue.

***

Katherine was a small township of about 2,000 persons in the early 1970s. It was a centre of tourism even then, with proximity to Katherine Gorge, Edith falls and the Cutta Cutta caves.

In those days, there were two local lads who sometimes featured in the court lists. Their names were Electric Motor and his brother Diesel. There was also a lady who went by the single name of 'Mary.'

Practice required that if a defendant was not actually in the court room, the court crier was required to step out of the courtroom and call the name of the missing miscreant three times in a loud voice. Today the court crier is usually a person employed by the court, and has many other duties besides calling the names of latecomers in the court foyer. In the early 1970s, there was no foyer in the Katherine court, and the crier had to step out of the front door onto the footpath of one of the main streets in the town. We had to borrow a policeman to act as court crier for the day.

So what did the tourists make of it when a burley policeman appeared in their midst, and began bellowing; "ELECTRIC MOTOR, ELECTRIC MOTOR, ELECTRIC MOTOR; DIESEL MOTOR, DIESEL MOTOR, DIESEL MOTOR; MARY, MARY, MARY?"

***

Sometimes a court crier would improvise. You could hear them at work if they did their job properly ie in a loud voice. Once, the crier was heard: "ROMEO, ROMEO, WHEREFORE ART THOU ROMEO?"

***

Of course, mischievous court staff will sometimes 'set up' other court staff, particularly the new ones. We had a new girl starting work and on her very first day she was assigned the task of calling the names of the people in the list for the day. Somehow a fictitious name appeared in the list, which was something like 'Karnive Ophelia Dickie', and I'm told that when the 'name' was called several young male lawyers stepped forward.

***

Names can sometimes be difficult. Giovanni Cilli (pronounced 'Chillie') was convicted by a magistrate for wilful damage. The evidence suggested that, in a fit of rage, Giovanni drove his bulldozer up to a stationary, temporarily unoccupied police vehicle, and proceed to smash the bucket of the 'dozer on the top of the vehicle many times, compacting the police car to less than half its normal height. He was convicted. He appealed to the Supreme Court. He lost. He appealed to the full court of the Federal Court, which then heard appeals from the Supreme Court in the NT. Giovanni was not legally represented at the appeal, which is the legal equivalent of endeavouring to urinate into a fairly stiff hurricane. Things were not made any easier for the appellant with the senior judge of the tribunal addressing him throughout as 'Mr Silly.'

***

I admit that at times I might have been a bit harsh on the subject of honorary justices, but I want to pay tribute to two of them here: Ken (Slippery) Slide and Ian McGregor. They often helped out with our lists in Darwin NT when we were busy and undermanned. Slippery ran a gift shop and Ian was a real estate agent. The two of them gave great service and were rarely appealed, because they gave everyone a fair hearing. Slippery was so well regarded that he was made a special magistrate and put on the payroll for a time. Last I heard of him he had migrated to the Philippines and opened a bar called 'The Koala Club.'

***

On a visit to Nhulunbuy, I found the police tracker, Muguli, charged with being a habitual drunk. The prosecuting police sergeant delivered a thundering denunciation of Muguli's drunken habits and demanded a sentence of imprisonment to allow him to 'dry out.' He then marched to the witness box, swore himself in, and gave an impassioned plea for mercy on Muguli's behalf, pointing out what a good tracker he was and how difficult it would be to replace someone with his skills. The sergeant's performance was a wonderful example of impartial policing, but left me a bit perplexed as to precisely what he was getting at.

Resuming at the bar table, the Sergeant reminded me that police regulations were such that if Muguli's sentence was more than seven days, the sentence would have to be served in Darwin and he would then surely be dismissed from the police force, but that if it was any less than seven days, he would surely die.

There are times when I'm a bit slow on the uptake, but it didn't take me long to sentence Muguli: seven days in the local lock-up, which was attached to the police station.

That night a group of us went fishing on a prawn trawler. We returned to the vicinity of the police station at about midnight. A monumental booze-up was in session. The police inspector was being farewelled and the local police certainly knew how to let their hair down. I sought out the police sergeant who had put on the performance that morning, mainly because I was worried about the possibility that Muguli might consider it a trifle unfair that he was serving seven days for behaviour not unlike that on display in his vicinity. 'Oh, don't worry about him. He's being looked after.' And he was – they had been passing beers to him through the bars of the cell all night.

***

Roger Steele was a minister in the CLP government in the NT when it introduced mandatory sentencing for crimes of theft, the theory being that thieves would be deterred if they knew that a sentence of imprisonment was inevitable. As far as I recall, a first offender got 14 days' gaol, a second offender 3 months and a third or subsequent offender 12 months minimum. The policy had no effect on the crime rate but it severely affected the quality of justice.

Roger was at some function when he saw an Aboriginal standing on his own. He went over to introduce himself, extended his hand to shake the hand of the person, and said: "Roger Steele."

The Aboriginal replied: "Nothing much and they gave me 3 months for it."

***

Exits from and entries to courts should be reasonably dignified. I have already mentioned Murph's hands and knees exit from court, and the somewhat hasty adjournment of the Darwin court when it was bombed in 1942.

There are occasional mistakes made as to which court one is occupying. It can be a bit unnerving if you are in the middle of a plea, and there is a roar of 'Silence! All stand!' and you look up, and there is another magistrate hovering above you not quite sure what to do, since the seat he coveted is already occupied.

One incident in Alice Springs makes me check the furniture each time before court began. I was required to go into court for what was said to be a very brief adjournment application only to find that someone had removed the magistrate's chair. I thought (since it was promised to be only a very short session) that I could bluff my way out, so I pretended to sit down. I was able to maintain a pretend sitting posture by grabbing hold of the bench. Just try a half squat posture, and see the tremendous strain it puts upon the calf muscles. Counsel began delivering a lengthy speech as to why an adjournment was necessary. My calf muscles were in spasm. The pain was excruciating. I interrupted: "Yes, adjournment granted. Court adjourns"

***

There was a certain police prosecutor in Adelaide who timed his entrance from the back of the court to perfection. He would arrive before the magistrate, but when the court was full of lawyers and their clients, and roar: "SILENCE! ALL STAND!" everyone stood, and he would make his way to the bar table in silence and take up the prosecutor's chair before he said: "Thank you everyone, you may be seated."

***

In the Alice Springs Court, a session was commenced by the magistrate's clerk banging thrice on the door to which was attached a serious brass door knocker. One of my fellow magistrates had some children running loose about the courthouse. One of them swung lustily on the knocker, while the court was in session, causing everyone (except me) to rise, like Pavlov's dogs. I was very angry, temporarily forgot where I was and called to my clerk, Helena: "Go and tell Freddie to f@#k off." All cases depending upon the intemperate use of the word 'f@#k' were withdrawn, for that day at least.

***

This has nothing to do with the magistracy, but I'm telling it anyway. A court orderly in Darwin fell asleep during a jury trial. The judge's associate realised what had happened, and aimed a well stretched rubber band at the slumbering figure. It hit him on the face, and he immediately leaped to his feet and bellowed: "SILENCE! ALL STAND!" Everyone obeyed, including the judge and jury. Everyone paused, wondering what to do next. It slowly dawned on the orderly that he might have made a mistake. Again he bellowed: "SILENCE! ALL SIT!" And they did. And the trial continued.

***

John Waters, a Darwin barrister, was sometimes late for court, not a recommended practice if the court was constituted by Mr Justice Gallop. One day, John skidded into court, late, wig on sideways, and said: "I'm terribly sorry I'm late, Your Honour, but I lost my watch and had to borrow my daughter's Mickey Mouse watch and it wasn't…"

Gallop J: "I don't give a Donald Duck about your Mickey Mouse watch – you're late."

***

Travelling to and from court normally presents no more problems than travelling to any place of regular employment. However, circuits can be different.

Katherine is 330 km south of Darwin and it was normal to catch the 'milk run' flight from Darwin when I was doing the circuit in 1974. That was all very well for most of the year, but the airline schedules were fixed in accordance with the time in the south-eastern states. In summer, with the introduction there of daylight saving, combined with the fact that the NT did not have daylight saving, the plane to Katherine used to leave at 6.00 am. This meant being picked up by the Commonwealth car driver at 5.00am, which meant getting up at 4.00am… That occurred every Monday. Of course, court had to finish early, because the plane returned an hour early during summer and we had to be at the airport at 2.30pm to get back to Darwin. Court therefore had to begin at 8.00am.

Not many of our customers were early risers, and it's all very well starting court early, but you can't get much work done if there is no one there. Katherine was the court for places as far away as Hooker Creek (now Lajamanu) some 400km from Katherine. Often the police from Hooker Creek were a bit late bringing up their customers – they were sometimes held up by the wet season, and it was often a squeeze to get the court finished in time.

My first trip to Maningrida on the Arnhem Land coast was also my first trip on an old war-time DC3. I was surprised how smooth the old plane was in the take-off. During the flight, I was intrigued by a small trickle of oil running back from one of the engines and when it turned to smoke and then flames, I thought it proper to make enquiries. "Is that normal?" I asked the hostess. She never replied. She took one look at it and bolted for the cockpit. The plane executed a very smart U-turn and made it safely back to Darwin and as we landed there were two fire engines racing alongside the plane, which pulled up at once. We had to wait for a bus to drive us back to the terminal.

***

One circuit I enjoyed was to the Gove peninsula, on the top left hand corner of the Gulf of Carpentaria, and then on to Groote Eylandt. David McCann was our chief magistrate, and a very good magistrate and chief he was. At Groote Eylandt, the airport was situated ten km from the courthouse, and the police used to fetch us from the airport and escort us to the court. David was worried about this, with good reason. It was not a good look to be taken to court by the police. One of the functions of a court is to act as a bulwark between the police and the defendants, and to be transported by the police could be construed as bias. At the time it was bias by necessity, because no one else was picking us up.

David managed to hire a car on Groote by remote control (i.e., sight unseen, the transaction being concluded by phone).

I was the first person to benefit by this arrangement. Sure enough, when I arrived at Groote International Airport, there was a clapped out old Ford waiting for me, with keys in the ignition, and a dead Wedge-tailed eagle stuck irretrievably in the front grille. I drove the offending vehicle along the dead straight road from the airport to the court (which was attached to the police station). The usual knot of police and clients were gathered in the front of the court waiting for proceedings to commence. I took my foot off the accelerator and put it on the brake. My foot went straight to the floor, there was no foot brake. It took me about one km to pull the vehicle up and execute a U-turn to get back to the court.

***

A group of us, court staff and lawyers were stranded in Nhulunbuy thanks to a combination of the airline overbooking, and the fact we were the last to the airport (For an explanation of why we were the last at the airport, see the 'Muguli' story, above). Rather than spend another night there, the lawyers arranged to hire a plane and invited us to share it with them. We were airborne when my clerk, 'Bod', enquired as to the whereabouts of the toilet. There was what you might call a pregnant pause before the pilot informed that small aircraft such as his did not boast such a luxury. This caused some consternation. It was to be a two-and-a-half-hour flight. A solution was found when someone produced a bottle of red wine (Penfolds Bin 28, a very fine drop). A corkscrew was located and the bottle passed from hand to hand, or mouth to mouth until emptied. Bod then promptly filled it, which fixed his problem, but I think it created a similar problem amongst the rest of us. When the plane pulled up at Darwin in front of the hanger, we all got jammed in the door in the rush to disembark and just made it to the hanger's facilities.

***

Another stranding in Nhulunbuy. This time the airline's pilots had gone on strike. Another plane was hired, smaller than the one in the previous story, but only myself and Bod to fly. Or so we thought. Once airborne, the pilot asked us if we would mind if he put down at a place called Smith's landing on the northern tip of the Coburg Peninsular to pick up more passengers. It was said in such a way that we knew we did not really have any choice. It turned out that there was no landing field or airport at Smith's Landing and we put down on the beach, which was a first (and last) for me.

Two very burley characters staggered out of the head-high spear grass, heavily laden with baggage. Bod and I had to alight while the pilot stowed the luggage. The pilot and all the other passengers clambered in, and I was the last to get in. As I sat back, (I'm fairly large) the front of the plane slowly rose in the air until we were all pointing at the sky, the rear of the plane wedged on the ground, and the front of the plane pointing straight up. Everybody out. Re-load, re-embark, this time the plane was barely horizontal, but we managed to get off, just. I remember almost running out of beach before the plane managed to lift.

***

Travelling to remote areas by road took longer, but was (usually) safer. However, on our way to Kalkaringi (near Wave Hill) in the wet season, we were running late and still had about 160 km to go when we came to a swollen creek near Top Springs. There wasn't time to send anyone to cross the swollen river, and in any event none of the women would volunteer to remove their clothing and cross the river to see if I could drive the car over. So we broke one of the first rules of outback driving and set out to cross anyway. Half way across, the water came mid-way up the door, but we made it over (just), and arrived only one hour late to start court.

***

Ma Hawkes owned the isolated Top Springs pub for many years. She rarely went to the nearest town, Katherine, 300 km away. When she died, a policeman declared that he had found 'x' thousands of dollars hidden under her bed, and forwarded this sum to the Public Trustee. Some weeks later, when the original policeman was on leave, a relief policeman saw the police station dog digging furiously in the back yard of the police station. Suddenly, bank notes began to fly in the air, and it became apparent that the original police officer had appropriated unto himself, and buried in the back yard of the police station, 'y' thousands of dollars belonging to Ma Hawke's estate. He was charged and sentenced to a substantial term of imprisonment.

***

Not long before I made the mistake of turning 65, thus becoming statutorily senile, my wife and I were occupying a motel room in Alice Springs. I was due to drive to Ti Tree the next morning and hold the first court session there. When I awoke in the morning, it took some time before I realised that something was different, and the difference was that we had been burgled during the night. My car keys, wallet, money, Johnny Walker and car had vanished. I was obliged to borrow another car to get to Ti Tree. My car was located at the casino about a week later, and the thief apprehended. Eric was brought before the court. Unfortunately, I was the only magistrate in town, and I had the dubious pleasure of reading the charge alleging that Eric had stolen my keys, my money, my wallet, my whisky and the government car. (If there was to have been an application for bail, I had a magistrate on standby in Darwin to handle the matter by video link. Eric, however was on parole with five years remaining on his sentence, and his lawyer did not apply for bail. Eric subsequently pleaded guilty and admitted the breach of parole and was sentenced in the Supreme Court).

***

Cathy Deland was the second woman to be appointed a magistrate in South Australia. Jay Sanders was the first. (One could mount an argument that Kemiri Murray was the first, but she was appointed simultaneously as a judge of the SA Family Court, and it was never intended she work as a stipendiary, but rather family and juvenile court type matters. Within a comparatively short time, she was absorbed into the Federal Family Court). After some years, Cathy resigned and became the second woman appointed to the magistracy in the Northern Territory. (Sally Thomas was the first: she later became the first woman to be appointed chief magistrate and the first woman to be appointed a judge of the Supreme Court in the NT, and the first woman to be appointed as Administrator of the NT). Cathy was, however, the first woman to be the second woman appointed to the magistracy twice.

Cathy and I worked for two or three years together in Alice Springs. She was (and still is) a great magistrate with a quirky sense of humour. (Sometimes when counsel was pressing that his or her client had finally seen the light, she would hold up a hastily drawn depiction of pigs flying). We were concerned with a phenomenon which occurred on circuit – the lunch-time drift. Customers would front up for court in the morning at some remote settlement, but when the court had adjourned for lunch, they either thought it had finished for the day, or they just got tired of waiting. So they would drift away and not come back.

Some of these courts were really busy – I remember one trip to Yuendumu where there were 135 matters in the list, including a number of trials listed for contested hearings. Cathy suggested that the court put on a barbecue for lunch and feed the remaining customers, thus keeping them interested until the court resumed. So the court sausage sizzle came into being, and it worked! Not only did it persuade our customers to remain, but it tended to break down barriers that sometimes existed between sentencer and sentencee. I mean, you can't be shovelling food into some poor old down-on-his-luck bastard one minute, and savagely sentencing him the next. One tends to look at life through the other person's perspective after feeding him.

After a while, however, I personally tired of the diet of sausages at lunchtime Mondays, and spent Sundays marinating rump steak in my secret marinade (olive oil, garlic, lemon juice, soy sauce and sweet chilli sauce), cutting meat, bacon and capsicum, and threading the result on to skewers. The first time I thought I had enough for the staff and myself, but still had the sausages for the masses. Don't let anyone tell you the Aboriginal people aren't gourmands. I remember offering a sausage to the head of the queue, but he impatiently waved it away, pointing insistently at one of the shashliks. The same thing happened all the way down the queue, and guess who ate the sausages?

The court barbecue became quite a social event and it wasn't confined to the court attendees. At one barbecue, (I think at Kintore, near the Western Australian border), the entire township turned up, and I was forced to purchase more sausages from the store and get the police to raid their fridges.

***

I got tired of the camp dogs. At remote courts, held wherever was available, sometimes in reasonably primitive buildings, the dogs would inevitably creep in, and form a huddle somewhere in the room. I would be distracted, watching and waiting for the inevitable, when I could see one dog's tail heading into another dog's mouth. CHOMP! CHAOS! BARKING! Resignation: "Adjourn the court- get rid of those @#$% dogs."

***

Many years ago, people were coy about referring directly to certain acts, usually of a sexual nature. This applied equally to preparation of an information, the document which initiates a charge against an alleged offender. Let me give you an example or three.

R v. Rowed (1842)114 ER 476: the information alleged that the two defendants

> Being persons of nasty, wicked, filthy, lewd, beastly and unnatural dispositions, and wholly lost to all sense of decency and good manners… did meet together for the purpose and with the intent of committing and perpetrating with each other, openly lewdly and indecently in the said public place (Kensington Gardens) divers nasty, wicked, filthy, lewd, beastly, unnatural and sodomitical practices…

The information continues in this vein for quite some time, but the draftsman omitted, in his adjectival zeal, to say precisely what it was that the defendants were alleged to have done. He was too coy to say simply that they had buggered each other in Kensington Park in the presence of others who were not buggering each other in Kensington Park.

Of the Female Factory in Sydney set up for the female convicts, built not so much to keep the ladies in, but the men out, the surgeon on a boat which had delivered a fresh batch of females from England went to see how they were faring. He found them surrounded by hordes of idle fellows plied with spirits, and "subjected to excesses which decency forbids to mention."

Coleman Phillipson in *Three Criminal Law Reformers* at page 32 refers to the mix in prison, with guilty thrown in with innocent, debtors mixed with cut-throats, men mixed in with women, with results "better not to describe."

Stephen, *History of the English Criminal Law* refers to an "unnatural offence."

Pollock and Maitland, *History of English Law* at page 556 refers to "the crime against nature."

From Hughes *"The Fatal Shore"* at page 530, referring to a letter from Tasmania by Bishop Nixon to his home office: "I cannot depict the horrors committed here daily...the most disgusting crimes that ever stained the character of men...hitherto unheard of in a Christian country." (Unheard of, perhaps, because no one ever stops beating about the bush, and says what they were doing.)

In his *Commentaries*, Blackstone feels compelled to describe these matters in a foreign language: "Inter Christianos non nominandum."

In the late 1960s, Sir Richard Blackburn, Supreme Court judge in the Northern Territory, was astonished to hear his associate arraign an accused thus:

> "You stand charged with the abominable crime not fit to be mentioned amongst Christians."

A quick adjournment revealed that the information had been drafted from an elderly copy of Archbold on *Criminal Law and Procedure*, the sole legal text in the building. The resulting fuss is said to have brought about the present day rather well equipped Supreme Court library in Darwin.

The Northern Territory to this day has a section in its Summary Offences Act, Section 50, which makes it an offence "against decency by the exposure of his person in any [...] public place." A defendant before me once argued that he did not expose his person, he exposed his penis. The question became: is a person a penis? (Is a penis a person? Can a woman be guilty of an offence under this section?)

This topic can be rounded off with a reference to the case of *L v. Commonwealth of Australia* (1976) 10 ALR 269, where the plaintiff, a prisoner on remand in the Fanny Bay gaol, succeeded in a claim for damages for the negligence of the gaol guards for failing to prevent the perpetration upon *L* of various lewd, abominable, unmentionable, deplorable, unheard of, disgusting, dreadful, unnatural, gross, debauched, unchristian practices which decency forbids me to mention.

***

I was once conducting a committal hearing in Canberra in the Australian Capital Territory. The case was a bit unusual in that it alleged an Aboriginal male had raped an Aboriginal female. The defendant was represented by Aboriginal Legal aid, and an unnecessarily aggressive and pushy counsel he was. He cross-examined the victim in such a manner that he was in breach of the Evidence Act, and I was obliged to intervene. His cross-examination of the investigating detective went something like this:

> Q. You don't care about Aboriginal people, do you?
>
> A. Well I ...

Q. You don't even know any Aboriginal people, do you?

A. Well as a matter of fact, I ...

Q. You can't speak any Aboriginal languages, can you?

A. Yes I can. I can speak fluent Pitjantjara, can you?

Moral: Always know the answer before you ask the question. But what were the poor bastard's chances of getting the only policeman in Australia who could speak Pitjantjara?

***

Aboriginal offenders rarely bore a grudge. I encountered one while walking along a street in Alice Springs. He was pushing a pram and was surrounded by wife and children. He stopped me: "Mikel, this is my wife, these are my children." He turned proudly to his wife and said: "This is Mikel. He is my magistrate. He gave me six months." His wife looked suitably impressed.

***

I was pushing a trolley down an aisle in a supermarket in Alice Springs when a middle-aged Aboriginal woman pushing her trolley in the opposite direction put up her hand for a 'high five'. I obliged. I still don't know what that was about.

***

A middle aged Aboriginal man approached me outside the post office. He looked a bit nervous. He said: "Hey Mikel, I bin coming to court next Tuesday. You look after me, eh? Might give me fine or community work order?"

How could you take offence at this? I simply made sure he was not in my list next Tuesday.

***

On an Aboriginal land claim, one of the lawyers wanted to know the location of a place that had been mentioned in earlier evidence. He phrased his question in some sort of rough pidgin:

"Hey Tommie, that place you bin talkin' about, where bin that place? Sun come up way? Sun go down way? Which way?"

The witness:

"The place to which you refer, sir, is approximately 73 kilometres' south-south-west from here."

***

On another land claim, the applicants, believing that a previous claimant had died, applied to take over the claim. (As I understand it, if a group dies out, Aboriginal law permits the neighbouring group to take over the land). These particular applicants were extremely embarrassed when the supposedly deceased claimant turned up at the hearing, very much alive. An explanation from the applicants was called for, and part of the explanation involved precisely when they had come to (mistakenly) believe that the traditional owner had died.

> Q. How long did you think that Tommy bin dead? Short time? Long time? Which one?

> (Long pause)

> A. We bin think he bin dead for <u>all</u> time.

***

There was a Commonwealth Magistrates and Judges conference in Sydney. Magistrates and judges were there from all over the world. I attended a dinner for the conference at the Opera House with JD from Canberra. We may or may not have had a few heart-starters before attending. The next scheduled such conference was three years hence in Harare, Zimbabwe. JD latched on to the Chief Justice of Zimbabwe, who had obviously been educated at Oxford or Cambridge, but JD still insisted on speaking to him in pidgin: "You got home in Harare? Nice home? Big home?" The Chief Justice sportingly pleaded guilty to all three charges. JD: "We all come stay with you!"

Two days later, it was announced that the venue for the next conference had been changed from Harare to Victoria Falls.

***

Three young boys whose ages totalled 18 years managed to steal a car and drive it 200km. The one steering was so small, he had to stand on the front seat to see to steer, while the other two boys crouched on the floor and operated the foot pedals.

***

Cathy Deland had two Aboriginal ladies before her charged with bad driving. They were intercepted by the police driving from an outlying settlement in towards Alice Springs. The lady behind the steering wheel was totally blind, and the lady in the passenger seat calling the shots (turn left, turn right, slow down, speed up) was blind drunk.

***

A man driving a car was stopped by plain clothes detectives for bad driving. He attacked the police and had to be handcuffed before he could be removed to the police station. Both detectives gave evidence that the driver was obviously drunk. One of them said: "At this stage, I noticed a foul odour emanating from the defendant. I said to him: 'You appear to have messed your pants. What is your reason for this?' He said: 'You. You give me the shits.'"

***

In 1974 there were only three dentists in Darwin. I convicted all three of them for shooting protected birds. Apart from them, the nearest dentist was 1,500km away. I have brushed my teeth carefully ever since.

***

A lady was charged with keeping a brothel in Darwin in 1974. Her defence was that, while men visited the premises to arrange sex, the sex took place elsewhere. The prosecutor cross-examined: "Oh, come on Mrs X, men go to the premises, pay their money, and sex takes place on those premises". The madame coyly replied: "Well, Mr Y, you should know. You've been there."

***

There was a firm of solicitors which consisted of a husband and wife team of European extraction, the wife being of volatile temperament. They had represented a man claiming damages for injuries sustained in a car accident. Before the claim was finalised, there was a parting of the ways between solicitor and client. The solicitors sent the client a bill of costs for the work done by them so far. The client refused to pay. In order to sue, the bill of costs must be in taxable form, i.e. in a form that conforms to guidelines contained in court rules. The solicitors sued and at trial represented themselves. ('Confucius say: Lawyer who represents himself in court has fool for client.') Their former client represented himself in court. The male part of the partnership acted the part of counsel for the plaintiff. He called their first and only witness, his wife. The entire transcript of the evidence went something like this.

Q. Did you act for the defendant? A. Yes

Q. Did you cease acting for the defendant? A. Yes

Q. Did you render to him a bill of costs? A. Yes

His Honour: Q. Was it in taxable form?

The witness, totally ignoring his honour, leaps to feet, faces plaintiff's counsel, and bellows: A. I tell you he ask me this, you bastard!! She exits the court.

The plaintiff was non-suited.

***

Australian courts are not bound by decisions of the English courts, but regard them as highly persuasive. This is particularly so if a magistrate's court in Australia is asked to follow the English Court of Appeal. I had a case where the defendant was charged with possession of cannabis for the purpose of supply. He admitted possession, but denied that his purpose was to supply. He said that he was merely looking after it for a third person who had supplied it to him, with a view to returning it to that person. I was referred to a decision of the English Court of Appeal: *Maginnis* (1986) Crim.LR 237, which held that those circumstances do not amount to possession for the purpose of supply. On the 26/2/1987, I said the Court of Appeal was wrong, refused to follow that decision, and convicted the defendant. Exactly one week later, the House of Lords overruled the Court of Appeal's decision: *Maginnis* (1987) 2 WLR 765, delivered on the 5/3/87.

***

Cases involving animals attract undue publicity. One case I was involved in had national publicity. The defendant was charged with unlawfully and maliciously killing a dog. The publicity sparked much correspondence and some poetry.

In my reasons I said:

> "Ringo, a small dog of mixed heritage, hereinafter referred to as "the deceased", became enamoured of the defendant's pedigreed Doberman Pincer bitch. The culmination of these carnal canine desires occurred on the 10th January 1977 when he was discovered by the defendant mounting the object of his affection. (Ringo's actions) were natural, foreseeable and probably licit. That is, there was no evidence that the Doberman was underage, or that she withheld the necessary consent, or that the deceased had other than reasonable grounds for believing that she consented to his advances."

I went on to find that the defendant armed himself with a .303 rifle, and shot Ringo who was by that time retreating, sated. I found the defendant guilty.

The poetry came from Brendan Burley.

> The magistrate's name was Ward
>
> Tried a case 'tween a bitch and a dawg.
>
> The bitch's condition
>
> Brought the dog his perdition,
>
> When he jumped, then he humped, but he scored.

***

Two officers from the Alice Springs branch of Community Corrections went to check up on some parolees thought to be working at a table grape farm in the geographical centre of Australia. As they drove up to the farm, they estimated there were about 40 workers in the field. When they pulled up, about half of the workers ran away to all points of the compass and hid in the surrounding bush. The two officers approached the remaining workers and said: "What was that all about?" The workers explained.

"They think you are from the department if Immigration."

"Oh no," the visitors replied. "We aren't from the Immigration Department; we are from Community Corrections." Whereupon the remaining workers took to their heels and disappeared into the bush.

***

Dean Mildren, in his book *Big Boss Fella All Same Judge* at page 41 sets out an affirmation devised by a special magistrate Joseph Wesley Nicholls for Aboriginal witnesses, as follows.

"Jacky, you bin see that big boss fella, all same judge, bin sit longa there? (pointing to judge).

Jacky: You-eye (meaning 'yes').

Now you bin tellum all-same judge fella all about that trouble bin come up longa Yuendumu. You bin tellum all same true fella what you bin see longa your own eye, not what some fella bin tellum longa your ear. No more gammon, no more humbug

Jacky: You-eye.

Now you bin tellum all same judge, big loud voice, all same corroboree.

Jack: You-eye"

A judge decided to cut this short:

"Jacky, what happens if you tell the court lies?

(Long pause)

Jacky: Might be I go to hell?

Very good Jacky. And what happens if you tell the truth?

Jacky: Oh, I'll go straight to Fanny Bay gaol."

***

The brothers E got the first licence to run a crocodile farm in the Northern Territory. One of the brothers was a hard living fellow who liked a drink or three, and had earned himself a bit of a reputation along those lines. The other was a reformed character who no longer drank: he was the public face of the business. The NT Conservation Commission helped them to start the farm by agreeing to give them 200 crocodile hatchlings. The hard-doer was dispatched to pick up the hatchlings from the Commission headquarters in Darwin. The Commission had painted neat little individual numbers on the back of each little baby in indelible blue paint, so that each crocodile was individually numbered from 1 to 200. E put them all in the boot of his car and drove off. Unfortunately, the road back to the crocodile farm went past the Noonamah Hotel, and E pulled up for just one drink.

Many hours later, he emerged and continued his way home with the car weaving a bit. E got out of the car and remembered that he had 200 babies in the boot of his car. He was too shickered to cart them all the way to the crocodile enclosure, so he put them in the family swimming pool.

Next morning it was discovered that the pool was empty. The little creatures had climbed out of the pool overnight and scattered over 360 degrees into the bush. The brothers E were in deep trouble, because the farm was to be held accountable for each of the little fellows. This was the first such venture that the Conservation Commission had allowed after many years of crocodile conservation.

A few days later, the Conservation Commission came out to the farm to see how their little babies were getting on. They counted, and sure enough, there were 200 little crocs in the enclosure and two nervous and exhausted brothers. A closer inspection revealed the crocs were of varying size, the paint on their backs did not quite match the paint put on them by the Commission. There were three number sevens and two number thirteens and so on. A quick interrogation and a few admissions later, it became apparent that one or more of the brothers had disappeared into the bush, rounded up what hatchlings he or they could. Some were escaped hatchlings; some were taken from the wild. The brothers were charged accordingly. The brother who liked a drink went first, represented by a senior counsel. He pleaded guilty and the magistrate said in sentencing (and this was reported in the press) that he would be lenient, because the defendant was a man of 'impeccable character.' This had many people looking in the dictionary for the new meaning of the word 'impeccable.'

***

It was one o'clock in the morning. I dreamed that I was duty magistrate. The phone rang and some police officer from Darwin introduced himself, said he had a person with him who wanted to apply for bail. He had been found in possession of a commercial quantity of illegal hard drugs. He had been interviewed, and the interview was televised. During the interview he had made full admissions as to his guilt. "Better put him on the phone," I said. He came on the phone and I dreamed I said: "Why should I give you bail?"

He said: "Because I am innocent."

I dreamed I said: "Oh, f@#k off." And I hung up the phone.

The next morning, I related my dream to my son.

"Dad," he said: "That was no dream. I heard it and here is the warrant for you to sign and fax back to the police."'

> I suspect the tape recording of that phone call is still played at the annual police Christmas party.

***

After I had passed the 30-years-on-the-bench mark, perhaps unwisely, I let it be known that there would be a discount on sentence for any defendant to make submissions on sentencing that I had not heard before. Stewie O' Connell, a very bright young lawyer from the Central Australian Aboriginal Legal Service, represented an Aboriginal male charged with carrying and offensive weapon in Todd Mall, the main pedestrian thoroughfare in Alice Springs. The facts were that the defendant was seen striding purposefully along the Mall with a large and vicious looking knife in his hand and murder in his eyes. The submissions went something like this.

"My client is something of an inventor."

"Yes?"

"And he has just successfully invented an ingenious trap for catching kangaroos."

"Yeees?"

"And word had just got through to him that a trap he had set up had just caught a kangaroo."

"Yeeeeesss?"

"And he was on his way to dispatch the unfortunate kangaroo when he was apprehended by the police."

The Bench: "Is your client prepared to divulge the secret of his invention?"

"May I obtain instructions, Your Honour?"

[Instructions, instructions, instructions]

"My client instructs me he is not prepared to divulge his secret until the patent is granted."

The Bench: "You win. He gets a discount in sentence."

***

Larapinta Drive is one of the loveliest drives in the world. It leads due west out of Alice Springs, and passes such beauty spots as Simpson's Gap, Standley Chasm, Serpentine Gorge, Ormiston Gorge and finally Glen Helen Gorge before the bitumen runs out some 120 km from the Alice. On a visit to Glen Helen, I accidentally locked my car keys in the boot of the vehicle. The quickest way out of this fix was to ring the Automobile Association of the Northern Territory (AANT). There is only one public phone located in the middle of the lounge bar. The lounge bar was full of tourists. They became very interested in the phone call as it progressed. Naturally, I was trying at first to whisper, lest they all figure out what a goose I was for getting in this predicament. The phone number I had to ring was connected to an answering service somewhere in India.

"Hello, how can I be helping you?"

(Whisper) "I've locked my car keys in the car and I need someone to come out from Alice Springs to unlock the car."

"You will have to speak up, please. I cannot be hearing you."

(Raised Voice) "I said, I've locked my car keys in the car, and need someone to unlock it."

"I am still having trouble hearing you."

(Shout) "I said I've locked my bloody keys in the bloody car."

(A hush and big smiles have fallen upon the audience).

"Whereabouts are you?"

"Glen Helen."

"Where is Glen Helen being, Sir?"

"Its 120 kilometres from Alice Springs."

"And where is Alice Springs, Sir?"

"In the Northern Territory of Australia."

"And what is the address, Sir?"

"What do you mean, 'address': it's a single building 120 kms due west from Alice Springs."

"Oh, I must be having an address, Sir. What street is it in?"

"Lara-bloody-Pinta Drive."

"How do you be spelling that Sir?"

"L-A-R-A-P-I-N-T-A D-R-I-V-E"

"What number in the street, Sir?"

"LOOK, MATE. JUST TELL THE BLOODY AANT MAN IN THE ALICE THAT I'M STUCK AT BLOODY GEN BLOODY HELEN AND THAT'S ALL HE NEEDS TO KNOW."

Miraculously, the AANT man did turn up two hours later and did unlock the car and retrieve my keys.

***

On one occasion, I had ensconced myself on the veranda of the police station at Kalkarinji in the NT, informally dressed for the climate (45 degrees Celsius, 90% humidity). It was late in the afternoon and I was reading through the court list for tomorrow's court and simultaneously sucking on a beer. A police sergeant materialised. He was not currently employed at that police station, but had been some months previously. He had returned for a case in which he was required to be a witness the following day. I had never met him before.

"What's that you're reading?" he asked. I told him. He snatched the list and went through it with helpful comments such as, 'This one's not a bad bloke. This one's an oxygen thief. This one's a waste of space' and so on, right through the list.

He concluded his commentary: "Anyway, I hear were getting some smartarse magistrate from Alice Springs for the court tomorrow." At this stage, I deemed if prudent to introduce myself. "Oh shit," he cried, jumped off the veranda, climbed in his car and drove around the block. He climbed back up onto the veranda and said; "Can we start that again?"

***

A Glaswegian thief was apprehended in the act by a policeman in Sauchiehall Street. The policeman put him in a headlock and dragged him by the head 150 metres along the street and then around the corner into Bath Street. It was only then that he formally arrested him. "Whit yae dae that for, ya bastard?" asked the mystified crook.

"Because I cannae spell Sauchiehall, ya thieving c#@t."

***

Bazza was an inexperienced lawyer. At the conclusion of his client's trial, the magistrate delivered his verdict of 'guilty.' He proceeded to give reasons for his verdict. At the conclusion, Bazza leaped to his feet and said: "Can we appeal that decision?"

"Certainly," said the magistrate, "you have the right to appeal."

"We appeal," said Bazza.

"Appeal dismissed," said the magistrate.

***

Bibliography

Ackroyd, P. *The History of England.* Pan Books.

Babington. *The English Bastille.*

Baker, J. H. (2007). *An Introduction to English Legal History.* 4th ed. Oxford University Press.

Beccaria, Marchesa De. (1764). *Of Crimes and Punishments.*

Blackstone. (1765-1769). *Commentaries on the Laws of England.*

Bland, Brown and Tawney. (1949). *English Economic History.* Bell.

Bloy, M. http://www.victorianweb.org/history/poorlaw/speen.html.

Blum, Morgan, Rose, Schlesinger, Stamp and Van Woodward. *The National Experience: A History of the United States.* 5th ed.

Bohun, E. *The Justice of the Peace: His Calling and Qualifications.*
Burn. *Justices of the Peace and Ecclesiastical Law*

Carter and Mears. (1688-1958). *A History of Britain.* Oxford UP.

Catholic Encyclopaedia. http://www.newadvent.org.cathen/00669c.htm.

Chambers Biographical Dictionary, editor Magnussen M.

Davenant, C. *Essay on Ways and Means of Supplying the War.*

Defoe, D. *Augusta Triumphans.*

Dillon, P. (2002). *The Much Lamented Death of Madame Geneva.* Review.

Dowdell, E. G. *A Hundred Years of Quarter Sessions: the Government of Middlesex 1660-176.'* Cambridge UP.

Eden, W. *Principles of Penal Law.*

Encyclopaedia Britannica, 15th ed. volume 29.

Fielding, H. *Covent Garden Journal.*

Fisher, H. A. L. (1911). *The Shallows and Silences of Real Life.* Cambridge University Press.

Fyfe, H. *People of All Nations.* Volume 3. the Educational Book Company.

Gilligan, J., and Earle, P. *The Middle Ages.*

Hargeaves and Helmore. (1963). *Land Law of New South Wales.* LBC.

Harrison, W. (1577). *Description of Britain.*

Heaton, H. (1948). *Economic History of Europe.*

Holdsworth W S. *History of English Law.*

Hood, R. http://www.timeshighereducation.co.uk/story.asp.

Howard, J. (1773). *State of the Prisons.*

Joliffe, J. E. A. *The Constitutional History of Medieval England.* 3rd ed.

Langbein. *The Origins of Adversary Criminal Trial.*

Linklater, A. (2002). *Measuring America.* Harper Collins.

Lyman, J. H. (1964). The Metropolitan Police Act 55. *Journal of Crim Law and Criminology.*

Maconochie, A. (1847). Norfolk Island. Suillivan's Cove Publishers.

Madan. *Thoughts on Executive Justice.*

Matthews, N. (1984). *William Sheppard: Cromwell's Law Reformer.* Cambridge UP.

Moir, E. (1969). *The Justice of the Peace.* Penguin.

Moore, T. *Utopia.*

Munshe, P. B. (1981). *Gentlemen and Poachers: The English Game Laws 1671-1831.* Cambridge UP.

Parry, Judge. *Vagabonds All.* Cassell & Co.

Phillipson, C. *Three Criminal Law Reformers.*
Plunknett, T. F. T. (1956). *Concise History of the English Common Law.* 5th ed.

Price. (1778). *Mineralogia Cornubiensis.*

Priestly. *Victorian Prison Lives.*

Rous, J. (15th Century). *Historia Regum Angliae.*

Rymer, O. *Select Charters.*

Schama. *A History of Britain 1776-2000; The Fate of Empire.*

Sheppard, W. (1656). *England's Balme.*

Shoemaker, R. *The London Mob.* Bloomsbury.

Shoemaker, R. Reforming the City: the Reformation of Manners Campaign in London. In: Davison, Hitchcock, Kiern and Shoemaker, ed., *Stilling the Grumbling Hive.*

Skyrme Sir, T. *History of Justices of the Peace.* Barry Rose Publishers.

Stephen. *History of English Criminal Law.*

Stubbes. *The Constitutional History of England.*

Thomas. *Prisons and Prisoners in England, 1500-1800.*

Trevelyan. *History of England.* 3rd ed. Longmans.

Webb, S. & B. (1906). *English Local Government: the Parish and the County.* Longmans.

Webb, S. & B. *English Prisons under Local Government.* Longmans.

Yass, M. *The English Aristocracy.* Wayland Publishers.